Children's informal ideas in science

The ideas that children have about science concepts have for the past decade been the subject of a wealth of international research. But while the area has been strong in data, it has suffered from a lack of theory. *Children's Informal Ideas in Science* addresses the question of whether children's ideas about science can be explained in a single theoretical framework. Starting from an overview of the literature, the contributors explore between them a variety of theoretical perspectives and illustrate the possible approaches by some analyses of data collected from children and families. Theoretical perspectives come from a variety of sources, including Piagetian developmental psychology and the theories of Gordon Pask. The book concludes with a discussion of how a theory can be built up, along with suggestions for ways ahead in the research. It will be particularly valuable for higher degree students, educational researchers and curriculum developers.

P. J. Black is a Professor of Science Education at the Centre for Educational Studies, King's College London. A former co-ordinator of the Nuffield A-level course in physics, Paul Black is well known for his publications on assessment in science. He has consulted for both the OECD and the US National Science Foundation. **A. M. Lucas** is Principal and Professor of Science Curriculum Studies at King's College London. He came to the University of London with wide experience as a researcher and lecturer in the USA and in his native Australia. As well as publishing in many areas of science education, Arthur Lucas has consulted extensively in Spain.

Children's informal ideas in science

Edited by PJ Black and AM Lucas

ROUTLEDGE

London and New York

First published in 1993
by Routledge
11 New Fetter Lane, London EC4P 4EE

Simultaneously published in the USA and Canada
by Routledge
29 West 35th Street, New York, NY 10001

Typeset in 10 on 12 point Garamond by LaserScript Limited, Mitcham, Surrey
Printed and bound in Great Britain by
Biddles Ltd, Guildford and King's Lynn

British Library Cataloguing in Publication Data
A catalogue record for this book is available from the British Library.

Library of Congress Cataloging in Publication Data
Children's informal ideas in science/edited by P. J. Black and A. M. Lucas.
    p. cm.
Includes bibliographical references and index.
ISBN 0-415-00539-6
1. Science – Study and teaching. 2. Science – Study and teaching
(Elementary) 3. Educational psychology. I. Black, P. J.
(Paul Joseph), 1930–   . II. Lucas, A. M. (Arthur Maurice), 1941–
Q181.C4657   1993
370.15'65 – dc20   92-41878
                                                                  CIP

ISBN 0-415-00539-6

Contents

Figures

Tables

Contributors

All the contributors to the book have been associated at some time with the Centre for Educational Studies, King's College London, University of London, or with its predecessor, the Centre for Science and Mathematics Education, of the former Chelsea College, University of London. Each has been a research student, research fellow, member of staff or visiting scholar, and some have fitted more than one of those categories at different times. The list below gives each author's institutional affiliation at the time of publication.

Paul Black is Professor of Science Education, Centre for Educational Studies, King's College London.

Joan Bliss is Reader in Education, Centre for Educational Studies, King's College London.

Guy Claxton is Senior Lecturer in Education, Centre for Educational Studies, King's College London.

Wynne Harlen is Director of the Scottish Council for Research in Education, Edinburgh.

Arthur Lucas is Principal and Professor of Science Curriculum Studies at King's College London.

Jon Ogborn is Professor of Science Education, University of London Institute of Education.

Jayashree Ramadas is a researcher at the Homi Bhabha Centre for Science Education, Tata Institute of Fundamental Research, Bombay.

Terry Russell is Director of the Centre for Research in Primary Science and Technology, Department of Education, University of Liverpool.

Neil Ryder is Senior Lecturer in Communication Studies, Centre for Educational Studies, King's College London.

Michael Shayer is an ESRC Senior Research Fellow, Centre for Educational Studies, King's College London.

Joan Solomon is Lecturer in Education, Department of Educational Studies, University of Oxford.

Introduction

Investigations of the ideas that children have about science concepts are a very widespread part of the world-wide research effort, and have been so for the past decade. The early work of Driver and Viennot is well known, and they, their collaborators and others have shown a diversity of ideas held by children in an increasing range of science topics. These children's ideas have been variously described as 'misconceptions,' 'preconceptions,' 'alternative frameworks', as well as by other labels. Whatever the label, aspects of the research movement are finding their way into science curriculum development, into teacher training, and into broader aspects of schooling such as anti-sexist and anti-racist education.

There are, however, serious questions to be asked about this research movement. Does the label used to describe the work determine the ways different groups approach the problem, so that it colours the way they talk to, and about, each other? Are the accumulated data a set of observations in search of a theory? Are the theoretical positions so diverse and diffuse that the protagonists cannot properly debate the differences in the positions they may take? Has the approach that has labelled ideas that depart from orthodox science as 'children's alternative conceptions' merely re-labelled 'wrong' ideas, or has it taken excessively seriously a relativist position that accepts as 'appropriate' the most bizarre and idiosyncratic accounts of natural phenomena? Has it confused respect for the child's ideas with respect for truth?

Above all, is there any great value in more researchers collecting more data about more phenomena from more groups of children in more countries? Is it now more profitable to devote effort trying to fit the existing work into a theoretical framework? But is that last question naive: is there any reason to suppose there is one theoretical position that is best? Might there not be a number of theoretical orientations that can be illuminating for different purposes? It seems fruitful now to attempt to use the existing data in a number of ways: for pedagogy; for curriculum decision making; to illuminate aspects of cognitive and/or social psychology.

It was with questions like these in mind that the contributors to this volume took part in a series of seminars to explore the basis of this dominant research movement in science education. We were a diverse group, with interests in psychology, curriculum, sociology, communication, and some who were conducting research broadly within the framework of exploring children's ideas of science topics. We were by no means committed to any particular methodology, interpretative framework, or theoretical position. We were seeking to explore, from deliberately critical standpoints, a movement that seemed to have taken on a life of its own as *the* approach to understanding children learning science. We invited speakers from outside; we produced critical working papers, and learned from each other as we debated, argued and disagreed.

The chapters in this book are a result of that informal seminar series. The debate has not produced a clear consensus among us, although we all agree the ideas must be taken seriously and that it is important to examine the basis on which we might act if we are to use these ideas in pedagogy or curriculum development. The chapters are a contribution to the professional debate, not a resolution to it. All participants retain their own position, their favourite metaphor, their guesses at what will be important in the long term and what will prove to be a stage in the emergence of understanding.

As editors we did not force our contributors to use a uniform terminology. To do so would have prejudged some of the issues of the debate. We did, however, have to decide on a title for the collection. After some, only partly tongue in cheek, suggestions from the group that we use titles like *Alternative Misconceptions of Children's Scientific Ideas* we settled on the suggestion of *Children's Informal Ideas in Science* as a relatively neutral expression: it conveys a concern with ideas that children hold that are not the same as the formal expositions of scientific concepts; it reflects the concern about the possible origins of the ideas outside the formal classroom setting; and it suggests a way of thought that may be common to all of us in our less formal interactions within society.

In editing the collection we have retained differences in viewpoint. In arranging the chapters to give structure to the book, we started with a brief introduction to the field by Joan Solomon. She provides a classification of the research not by its content, but by its methodological and ideological orientations.

Then follows a group of chapters, written from different perspectives, that provide possible interpretations of the research. Joan Bliss points out that Piaget's work is not, as is sometimes thought, antithetical to the broad constructivist views of the development of knowledge that are common in the literature of this field. Guy Claxton offers an alternative to the 'alternative framework' explanations of the phenomena, seeing 'minitheories' as providing a better account. Terry Russell classifies the sources from which children may obtain information that they use to produce ideas about the world, and shows that different research orientations have been concerned with different sources of knowledge. Joan Solomon presents an interpretation of the origins of children's ideas from the perspective of the social construction of knowledge theorists, illustrating the approach with some of her own work on 'energy'. Jon Ogborn stands aside from the immediate debate and looks critically at the problems associated with assessing what it means to understand someones ideas, a vital step in interpreting what it is that children know and believe.

Jon Ogborn and Joan Bliss explore children's ideas of motion, in the first of four chapters that present some original data. Their chapter is not a complete analysis, but serves to illustrate a technique for exploring children's ideas. Arthur Lucas points out that it is possible to collect unobtrusive data while people are interacting with museum exhibits, a possible source of some informally acquired ideas, and Neil Ryder presents an account of a family reacting to a crisis and uses it as a basis for exploring ideas about the nature of scientific knowledge used in a 'vernacular' way. Jayashree Ramadas and Michael Shayer, using some data concerning phenomena related to light, show that it is possible to analyse the children's reactions to test items to reveal hierarchical relationships in their responses.

The final contributions are concerned with the translation of the research into practice. Guy Claxton presents some issues derived from the general psychological literature that need to be borne in mind when deciding upon the purposes of teaching science, and Paul Black and Wynne Harlen look carefully at the problems inherent in using the data from research into children's ideas when choosing the content of a primary science curriculum.

In our editors' postscript we reflect upon the debate included in the chapters, and draw together some issues that need to be considered by the researchers in the field, and by those who use the results.

Chapter 1

Four frames for a field

Joan Solomon

There have been several excellent reviews of the literature concerning children's out-of-school notions about scientific matters: Driver and Easley (1978), Sutton (1980), West *et al.* (1983), Driver and Erickson (1983), Gilbert and Watts (1983) and Driver (1991). Each of these provides, in its own way, both a guide to the field of research and a survey of published work in it. Pfundt and Duit (1991) provide a comprehensive bibliography.

There is no need to apologize for adding yet another introduction to this field for it grows most vigorously, not just by expansion but also in a more exciting way by diversifying its philosophy, its evaluative stance, its methodology and its inter-disciplinary boundaries. This arises because the subject is intriguing enough to have attracted scholars of several different research complexions. This chapter will show that the variety of work is not random but interestingly framed by the perspectives of the researchers and, inextricably mixed with this, their aim.

Driver and Easley subdivided the field into the *ideographic* and the *nomothetic*; West *et al.* used the *revolutionary* and *evolutionary* approaches to the growth of knowledge; Gilbert and Watts adopted the sociological perspectives of the *eklaren* and *verstehen* schools. In this chapter, four, rather than two, approaches will be specified, and I shall show that they may be complementary rather than mutually exclusive. At first, in order to point out the proper differences, it may seem that the boundaries between the four research programmes are rather sharply inflicted upon the work. Only by recognizing the complete frame of each can their contributions to the total field be understood and assessed.

THE ETHNOGRAPHIC APPROACH

The guiding plan for research in this tradition is to ask children to explain their ideas and then to listen carefully to their words in the *verstehen* tradition. It aims to be entirely value-free, as an anthropologist might try to be while examining the culture of an alien tribe. Probably the early work of

Jean Piaget (1929), where he records young children's ideas about an animistic nature and a curiously moving 'watching' moon, first inspired this sort of exploration. Such an inquiry, however, does not easily survive a more theory-driven aim where either cognitive structure or school learning is the mainspring of the work. These reasons, and the more recent liberation of the social sciences (Armistead 1972), may explain why it was a comparatively rare mode of educational research until it surfaced in the early work of Driver (1973). Here she recorded the informal classroom comments of some high school science students. In an even purer form it is to be found in the interviews of individual French children about their notion of light by Guesne (1978), and about heat by Tiberghien and Delacote (1978).

These early works inspired many more, so that any examples given must be chosen essentially at random. By the early 1980s the topics covered included biological concepts (Deadman 1976), heat (Erickson 1979) and simple mechanics (Watts and Zylbersztajn 1981). This last topic has proved an exceptionally interesting and popular one for research.

The methodology employed was remarkably uniform: 'In a face to face interview the skilled interviewer is apt to ask relevant questions, he is understood by the interviewee and allowed to penetrate the child's thinking without influencing the answers too much' (Leboutet-Barrell 1976).

Despite the anthropological influence it has been extremely rare for natural groups of children to be interviewed, or for them to be recorded talking together. Probably Barnes and Todd (1977) is one of the few published examples of the latter type and even here the emphasis was more upon social turn-taking than on the substance of children's ideas. Thus the interviewing of children, on their own and often by an unfamiliar adult, became almost the exclusive research implement, even though it had some obvious practical disadvantages. The whole operation was unfamiliar to the child and often so daunting that free and un-prompted flow of speech was hard to achieve.

It was in answer to this problem that Osborne and Gilbert (1979) developed the technique of *Interviews About Instances* using simple line drawings on card as either a prompt or a prop for the interviewee. Others asked the students to use apparatus to demonstrate their ideas in an experimental situation, a method sometimes called *Interviews About Events*. Engel (1982) used syringes, plastic and metal spoons in hot water and other simple objects to elicit explanations. McCloskey (1983) got his subjects to aim an already moving puck so that it crossed a table and entered a designated gate. The use of children's comics by Bliss and Ogborn (this volume, Chapter 7) is a highly original answer to this methodological problem.

There was no question of giving clues or judging the notions: that would have run entirely contrary to the neutral observer's stance. Yet, quite early in this research programme, it became clear that many observers were developing a strong theoretical position. The lone-child-and-the-neutral-inquirer mode may itself have engendered the belief that the ideas being described were a coherent system which had been personally constructed by each individual child. George Kelly's Personal Construct Theory (1955) and its more recent exposition in an educational context by Salmon and Bannister (1974) was explicitly adopted by several researchers, such as Pope and Keen (1981). 'Each man contemplates in his own personal way the stream of events upon which he finds himself so swiftly borne,' (Kelly 1955).

The point of view which held the children's notions to be coherent, personally constructed pictures of the world, albeit on a small scale, is also reflected in the choices of terminology which this group of researchers commonly used – *alternative frameworks* by Driver, and *children's science* by Osborne and his New Zealand school of research. Kelly's picture of *Man-the-Scientist* continually constructing hypotheses and confirming or disconfirming them through daily experiences of the world seemed to many to be a particularly happy and value-free description of what children might be doing outside the school science laboratory. It was also sometimes claimed that this gave it a strong affinity with science itself, especially as interpreted by Feyerabend's anarchist philosophy (1975). Thus it was that this group came to reject so emphatically the phrase 'children's *mis-conceptions*', with its in-built assumption of the superiority of scientifically accepted concepts.

Strong theories tend to prove hard masters. There were signs that this notion of a child's explanatory framework could itself drive a research project. Engel (1982), for example, disallowed any evidence which suggested that two different *alternative frameworks* could be held by the same child. Other researchers who turned up inconsistent or even contradictory views from one and the same child had difficulty in reconciling this with the original quasi-scientific constructivist position.

The other difficulty was in accommodating to a teaching process. If children's 'science' had been tested and tried by them in much the same way as science was, it certainly explained why they held to it so strongly but raised a difficult question about how these pupils might be weaned from it. Although this research was never closely related to school science, some of its practitioners did recognize its importance and so were forced to tackle the dilemma. Perhaps an enormous mental conversion process might be needed, not dissimilar, as was often remarked, to the paradigm shift required in Kuhn's picture of revolutionary science?

This problem of 'conceptual change' became the subject of several major theoretical articles (e.g. Hewson 1981, Posner *et al.* 1982). By slow degrees what had begun as a value-free exploration of prior notions approached the door of the classroom. Was there any practical advice that could be culled from the corpus of results? For some the task remained in the hands of the teachers, and instructions were given about the kind of programme of experiences which might produce the discomfort of 'cognitive dissonance'

(Festinger 1962) and hence lead to a conversion. Others (e.g. Cosgrove and Osborne 1983) hoped to keep the reins firmly in the pupils' hands, as indeed they had been during all their research interviews. They argued that only through negotiation and argument could the children decide collectively upon the correct theory. Others argued that the process itself might instruct children about scientific method: 'Alternative frameworks suggested by pupils offer teachers readily available opportunities to illustrate characteristics of the scientific pursuit through appraisal of competing interpretations . . . ' (Driver 1983).

Empirical results were not always kind to such analogies. Children's notions did not seem to be consistently applied, as scientific explanation is supposed to be. Contradictory explanations were given for similar events occurring in very similar contexts (Engel and Driver 1982; Gunstone 1980). 'The students . . . never notice that a proposition they have used to explain one of the situations is directly contradicted by the proposition they use to explain the motion in another situation' (Champagne and Klopfer 1982).

Worse still, some pupils gave garbled accounts which appeared to be midway between their own ideas and taught scientific ones. Still, the original belief in children's 'science' was heroically maintained:

> Such views of the world and meanings for words held by children . . . are part of conceptual structures which provide sensible and coherent understanding of the world . . . There is growing evidence that the learned amalgam of children's science and teachers' science can co-exist.
>
> (Gilbert *et al.* 1982)

Exhortations to change methods of teaching had invited action research. This was forthcoming (e.g. Hewson and Hewson 1983; Smith and Lott 1983), but the results remain hard to interpret. They did produce some successes, although a few of the children's prior conceptions always proved remarkably resistant to experimental or argumentative refutation. What seemed successful on short term post-test reverted to the original pre-conceptions after a longer period (Shipstone and Gunstone 1984). The most substantial piece of action research to be based on this notion of conceptual change brought about through a 'conflict situation', cognitive dissonance by another name, is the Children's Learning in Science Project, CLISP (Driver and Oldham 1986).

The ethnographic line of research began with a simple descriptive objective in the *verstehen* tradition, 'with no overt intention of determining future action' (Gilbert and Watts 1983). It does not easily generate a guide to the daily practice of teaching.

MISCONCEPTIONS

In this frame the research is more of a commentary upon the learning of school science than an ethnographic study. It concentrates on the difficulties pupils have with particular topics, catalogues their mistakes, and may suggest remedial action. Mere statistics of success and failure cannot claim a place in its ranks: for inclusion, we need to find both an examination of the mistakes, and of the children's explanations for them. Although their starting point is different, these 'misconceptions' researchers often make use of some of the methods of the first research group, because they need to know how the children are reasoning if they are to understand their school mistakes. It is a pragmatic endeavour, often atheoretical, and sometimes methodologically inventive and subtle. Unlike the previous frame of research it is unashamedly value-laden: its objective is sound correct learning and so there are no qualms about labelling student responses either 'right' or 'wrong' according to the dictates of textbook science.

The boundary between work which merely categorizes common errors, and that which seeks out the genesis of mistakes within the children's own notions, is not always sharp. It would seem, for example, that research like that of Archenhold (1975), which tabulates the different levels of under-standing of the concept of potential energy, is probably just outside the area, while that of Helm (1981), which examines common misunderstandings about concepts among South African students by identifying some of the key words that reveal these problems, might be included. The criterion is deliberately exploration of the students' misconceptions, and not just an analysis of incorrect performance.

The connection between school and research is more or less close and of particular interest in this frame. Once again the examples of research illustrating the field have been chosen more to illustrate the teaching–research relation than to cover the complete range of topics.

One of the most influential of these studies was on spontaneous methods of reasoning in mechanics by Viennot (1979a). The cohorts of subjects used were physics undergraduates and advanced school students in France, Belgium and Britain. This meant that some assumptions could be made about their previous and present teaching, and that the main research questions could be formulated in familiar ways – the oscillations of a spring or the path of a simple projectile. That constituted the full extent of the formal learning connection, and yet the first part of her introduction to the work left the reader in no doubt as to its purpose:

> The work described here has its origins in practical teaching problems, and its ultimate aim is to contribute to the improvement of teaching . . . We shall show that such spontaneous reasoning constitutes not just a few mistakes made by some students, but a way of thinking found in everyday conversation and in much that one reads.
>
> (Viennot 1979a)

Viennot's results displayed the common school mistakes, such as identifying force with the direction and magnitude of the velocity of an object. To substantiate her assertion, above, about the origin of these ideas she not only asked the students for their own reasons, she also examined newspaper articles and common figures of speech (Viennot 1979b). This interesting extension of educational research into the everyday culture will be the nub of the research frame to be explored in the next section.

Others who found themselves at some remove from the actual teaching of science tried to mend the defect by contriving a programme of individualized teaching to correct the misconceptions they had observed in the investigative phase of research. The thesis of Pines (1978) is an interesting case. He explored primary school children's use of a variety of notions, e.g. 'alive', 'energy', 'seeds', 'electricity', by recorded interview before A/T (audio tutorial) instruction, and then followed this by more interviews. The inclusion of Pines' work in this research frame is put in no doubt both by comments such as 'a concept of energy riddled with *misconceptions*', and also by his findings about the concepts themselves. His evidence suggested that the children's notions 'change over time, are complex, multifaceted . . . highly situational and contextually dependent'. His failure to contrive an adequate categorical system drove him to write 'it is true that specific responses can be categorized but almost any child interviewed will exhibit responses characteristic of many categories, irrespective of the category system used'.

In this research frame there will, of course, be no attribution of a quasi-scientific structure to the children's ideas. If a researcher combines this activity with teaching, the evaluation of children's notions as wrong and therefore 'misconceptions' might appear inevitable. Minstrell (1982), for example, describes the difficulty his students have in understanding the forces acting on an object which is at rest on a table. The succession of teaching ruses he employs, to challenge their assumptions and to change them, makes good and realistic reading. He relies upon verbal responses in brief classroom discussion to estimate the proportion of his class that adheres to one idea or another. The inventive pragmatic approach is valuable, but his assumption that the notions are 'well formulated', or 'have served well over the years', marries ill with the findings of other researchers and seems to have been imported from theory to support the ethnographic research perspective.

One of the most complete and impressive research projects to be couched in terms of the misconceptions frame concerns concepts of respiration and photosynthesis (Arnold and Simpson 1980). One of the authors is a science teacher and the other is a research psychologist, which may account for both the variety of research modes and the closeness to school science. It includes an exploration of Scottish students' mistakes, interviews with the students and with their teachers, the design and trial of new materials which are based both upon the researchers' knowledge of students' difficulties and on a careful selection and use of educational theory.

Arnold and Simpson, in common with other school-based researchers, found the 'meaningful learning' theory of Ausubel (1963) to be nearest to their purpose. Many have used the slogan 'start where the student is'; rather fewer have searched the theory more closely: 'the interaction of new learning tasks with existing cognitive structure is the distinctive feature of meaningful learning' (Ausubel 1963). Arnold and Simpson acted upon this advice and carefully reconstructed the biology course in order to ensure that suitable advance organizers were placed within the students' cognitive structures before each new piece of learning.

One way to assess the impact of a school science course on children's existing ideas is by some form of longitudinal study. This has been done by Nussbaum (1979) on the concept of terrestrial gravity and by Duit (1981) on energy.

It would give quite the wrong impression to suggest that the listing of misconceptions followed by the design of new school courses is the aim of most research projects. Close and inventive analysis of mistakes in school courses has yielded a harvest of results which expands our understanding of the misconceptions of science. Wells (1984) and Karrqvist (1984) have both examined the naive 'models' for electricity first discovered and named by Osborne (1981), and found them to be used almost, but not quite, indiscriminately. Others, such as Joshua (1984) and Caillot (1984), have shown that a simple circuit diagram is difficult for even advanced physics students to transform topologically. Viennot (1983) has examined in detail the different notions and strategies used by students in kinematics problems, and Closset (1983) has traced the continual resurgence of the 'sequential' misconception as new instruction was received in electricity. Several pieces of research (e.g. Gunstone and White 1980, Strauss 1983, and Faucher 1983) have indicated that students who can successfully solve numerical problems often fail when the same kind of problem is set in a non-quantitative verbal context. Gott (1984) used Assessment of Performance Unit results to assert that students who have little or no correct conceptual understanding of electric current can sometimes cope very well with practical work.

A breathless catalogue of 'misconceptions' results seems at first sight both amorphous and without direct predictive value for school science. What must certainly be admitted is that, so far, it is without an overall explanatory theory. Each topic, each approach, and even each kind of problem that the students encounter, seems to bring its own kind of trap for the unwary. If, however, the fourth frame of research in this field, the one that aims to explore mental representations, is to succeed then it will need to both measure itself against this kind of evidence and also explain it.

CULTURAL EFFECTS

Workers in this frame are concerned with the children's ideas about science as reflections of the social influences and informal instruction which are at large within the community. The extent to which a child picks up one strand rather than another, or constructs out of the available knowledge some individualistic philosophy, is not the main issue. In this way it differs markedly from research carried out in the first mode. Few of the studies in the *cultural-effects* frame refer to the interaction between cultural learning and school learning (as was the case with Viennot 1979a) for reasons which may become apparent later.

Cross-cultural studies of pre-school scientific notions go back several years. Their importance lies in the support they give to the argument of cultural relativism in relation to children's ideas and their learning successes. Mori *et al.* (1976) studied the concept of speed in Japanese and Thai children, finding that the Japanese, who have the same word for 'early' and 'speed', did noticeably worse than Thai children who had different words for the two concepts. In 1980 Ross completed a comparative study of pupils' use and understanding of words like 'evaporate', 'light', 'energy' and 'electricity' among different groups of children in Nigeria. His results showed an interesting dependence not on the language of instruction, but on the mother tongue of the pupils, suggesting again that the influence was cultural rather than related to the school instruction. The growing body of literature from the developing countries, for example, Mohapatra (1991) and Jegede and Okebukola (1991), demonstrates the deep cultural significance of their students' prior conceptions. These authors have no doubt that such deep-seated affective responses produce procedural as well as cognitive effects.

There has been a considerable amount of research on children's cosmologies, on their understanding of the earth's position, shape, and gravity. Nussbaum and Novak (1976) and Mali and Howe (1979) studied children from various countries, found differences, but had some difficulty correcting for differences of school instruction. Sneider and Pulos (1983) found that they could identify differences as 'cultural' not only between countries, but also between communities that were either rural or urban within the same country.

In the context of this kind of research, culture tends to be, in the words of Wittgenstein, 'a language game'. The implications of this are strong for an exploration of concept dependence on word use. The work of Duit (1981) spans this area with a study which looks at the differences in the use of both 'force' and 'energy' among German students before and after instruction, German-speaking Swiss students, and Filipino students, all under the same school conditions.

The problem with examining word use is that meanings are never unique for a word in everyday use, as they are for scientifically defined words. Duit gives pie-charts to display the frequency with which a word is used by students to apply to different areas of thought or activity. His raw data are often whole sentences, as are the data used by Solomon (1983c) in the context of energy. More structured work on students' and adults' word associations for terms in mechanics carried out by Preece (1976) enabled him to devise inter-conceptual maps. This endeavour, which tries to probe the students' mental representations, will be discussed further in the next section.

The strong form of linguistic relativism is enshrined in the Saphir–Whorf hypothesis (Whorf 1956) that no two observers can have the same picture of the universe unless they share the same linguistic culture. Halliday (1978) modified the hypothesis to a form which has more value for the present work: cultures have 'different patterns of meaning which are significant not in the sense that they determine ways in which members of the community *perceive* the world around them, but in the sense that they determine what they *attend* to'.

Cultural, linguistic effects cannot be extinguished by school learning: if they could the result would be a damaging alienation from the everyday world. To this extent cultural explanations for children's prior notions make perfectly clear why everyday concepts are so resistant to change. A phenomenological approach has been used by both Solomon (1983a) and Redeker (1980) to make this point, and to redescribe the school learning of science as a secondary process of socialization, different in many substantial respects from the earlier socialization into knowledge of the life-world. Schutz and Luckmann (1973) compare the movement from one system of thought to another to the shock of wakening from a dream. Solomon (1983b, 1984) used classroom research to illustrate this discontinuity in several different ways. Her way of connecting this research with school learning was to concentrate on those strategies which gave children greater help in the difficult transition from life-world thinking to scientific thinking.

The difference between the two domains of knowledge can also be shown by a sociological comparison (Lin 1983). This approach stresses the contrast between a coherent logical system in which sharp polarized argument is the norm, and a system based on social interactions in which the aim is consensus. (See also Solomon in this volume Chapter 5.)

Various notions which appear to be explicitly about science are also available within almost all cultures. In primitive tribes much scientific knowledge is valuable in what Bourdieu (1977) has called the 'habitus': it exists there, within the culture, but at a remove from the formal codified knowledge, which may be confined to an élite. It is beginning to become clear that a very similar situation exists within our own scientific and technological society. Ravetz (1971), in a book about the social and historical problems of science, defined *folk science* as 'a part of a general world-view, or ideology, which is given special articulation so that it may provide comfort and reassurance in the face of the crucial uncertainties of the world of experience'. Some evidence for this curious sub-science culture is apparent from the interviews with adults recorded in Solomon (1983b) and it is to be hoped that the work on scientific literacy (e.g. Layton *et al.* 1986, Solomon 1992, Wynne 1992, Ziman 1991) will help to clarify our view of this insidious 'general knowledge'.

The negative effects of folk science, not mentioned in the comforting words of Ravetz, has been a little more researched. There has been some work on pupils' reactions to radiation and nuclear energy in the face of carefully prepared modules of teaching on the relevant scientific concepts (Fleming 1984) and on pupils' perceptions of the energy crisis (Solomon 1985). The STIR (Science Teachers in Research) group has explored the fearful notions about electricity common among young school students (Solomon *et al.* 1985). What appears in these studies is always the 'blind strength' of such folk reactions. Dreyfus and Jungwirth (1980) found in a biological context, as Fleming had done in a physical one, that such emotional reactions tended to submerge scientific thinking, especially among less able pupils – another example perhaps of the difficult transition between life-world and scientific thinking.

Western cultures also include informal ways of learning parts of more orthodox science: these include impromptu conversations with experts (Lucas 1981), television, newspapers (Wellington 1991) and visits to museums or botanical gardens (Lucas 1983). The effects of some science programmes on television has been examined by Ryder (1982) by means of recorded discussion with a small group of children. Solomon (1983c) has tried to analyse the effects of unspecified television viewing on school pupils' ideas about the energy crisis. Both have observed a filtering action by which viewers select portions which they find interesting, memorable, or with which they agree. This 'perceptual interaction' (McQuail 1972), which is also to be observed in the empirical work in museums (Lucas, this volume, Chapter 8), thus introduces yet more noise into science instruction.

There seems to be no way in which scientific knowledge can be absorbed into the cultural consciousness without also acquiring those social traits which militate against the kind of impersonal abstract thinking for which science has traditionally been valued. This takes us far beyond the initial assertion that children have personal ideas of their own about scientific matters. They are assaulted by information from all kinds of sources, and it seems that what is sensational, or comfortably agreeable, survives at the expense of accuracy. That makes such socially derived knowledge even more persistent.

MENTAL REPRESENTATION

The subject of research in this frame is still children's notions, but now the focus of interest has moved from the substance of these notions to the way in which they operate within the child's mind. At first sight this may seem almost a metaphysical quest, but it can be argued that quite the opposite is true. 'Introspection is not a direct route to understanding the mind' (Johnson-Laird 1983). In this frame, as in the others, we shall need to rely heavily upon empirical methods to explore, or possibly to simulate, the mental representations and structures of the thinking, learning child.

Joan Bliss (this volume, Chapter 2) argues that Piaget's work is as constructivist as it is structural. This is the synthesis which makes his work the starting point for this section. His earliest explorations have been mentioned before for their seminal influence on the ethnographic approach to children's ideas. In later work, after the structure of Genetic Epistemology had been articulated, Piaget reflected upon two kinds of knowledge – 'knowing how' which is contextually-bound pre-operational thought, and 'knowing that', which is propositional, formal thought. He stressed the radically different learning movements required by the two systems, one moving from the context of action to that of thought; the other going from thought towards action: 'the co-ordination of the action in terms of its own schemata, and the conceptual, logico-mathematical or causal co-ordination in which thought . . . culminates' (Piaget 1978).

The notion of two different domains of knowledge has arisen before, in the section on culturally derived effects, as life-world and symbolic knowledge. It is not hard to see that we may now be considering something essentially similar but observed from quite a different perspective. Where the Two Domain model sprang from contrasting processes of socialisation, Piaget is here referring to different schemata, to the ordering mental structures themselves.

Because Piaget's work was essentially one of cognitive development it can be used in a normative way to criticize and adjust the cognitive requirements of the school science syllabus. This was the work of Shayer and Adey (1981). It is not at all clear, however, if the more theoretical aspects of Piaget's insights can be applied to the process of learning.

Preece (1976) used word association tests to display children's 'burrs' of ideas. This has no obvious significance for mental organization. For a higher order construct to grow out of such loose associations some careful structuring, in what Preece (1978) was later to call 'semantic space', will need to be done. Kempa and Hodgeson (1976) and Schaefer (1979) attempted to probe the organizational principles that pupils used as their knowledge became more comprehensive and, possibly, their science lessons helped them to develop new cognitive models. Was concept building a matter of listing, of common descriptive features, of a common operational function, or of application of scientific definitions? Only the third would allow children to extract from their own context-dependent notions a concrete operational concept.

Concept mapping is a term used to refer to more complex hierarchical genealogies drawn out to show how an individual relates the meaning of one concept to that of another. It was employed by Pines and Leigh (1981) to display the notions of students that have been given a structured interview, and by Preece (1978) to measure the semantic distance between pupils' concepts. It was developed by Novak and Gowin (1984) as a teaching device which involved the students in understanding their own cognitive progress, and also as a research tool for probing and assessing their knowledge structures. Champagne *et al.* (1980) used a similar method for displaying the interconnections between scientific concepts given by novices and experts. It is not clear whether these researchers believed that concept maps actually mirror mental organization or merely record how students have used concepts during some problem-solving activity.

Cognitive psychology should be able to provide valuable insights into how the prior notions of children interact with new knowledge in this research perspective. Traditionally it has been more concerned with small skills than with whole mental structures and this has already given a little insight into the memory problem. Tulving (1976) showed by controlled experiment that this vital retrieval process was strongly influenced by the input learning conditions, whereas recognition and decisions were not. These kinds of experiments, with rather trivial lists of items, discourage their large-scale importation into the complex situation of scientific notions. Nevertheless it might possibly shed a little light on the way items learnt through experience or social interaction are more easily recalled than those learnt at school.

At MIT, diSessa (1980) has both used a computer, 'the dynaturtle', to explore students' misconceptions about vectors, and used the computer perspective to draw out a protocol of how a student recalled and gave priority to 'phenomenological primitives' (naive notions) when dealing with problems in physics. Students' protocols were then compared with the explanations used by an expert physicist. Larkin *et al.* (1980) carried this work further, observing how 'recognition of a pattern often evokes from memory stored information about actions and strategies which may be appropriate in contexts in which the pattern is present'. The novices, it seemed, had no such entire procedural schemata stored in the memory and had to cast around for intermediate goals. The way in which the computer simulation acquired and reinforced these schemata was a slow recursive bootstrap affair by which it learnt by its own successes. Solved examples were then added to the procedural pattern, which was stored away for matching to future problem situations.

Rumelhart and Norman (1981) have suggested that our knowledge might be categorized as either *declarative* and unstructured, or *procedural* and hence structured. The human knowledge representation system thus offers both 'knowledge that' which is accessible but atomistic, and 'knowledge how' which is often tacit and always context-dependent. This is strikingly similar not only to Piaget's dichotomy of knowledge, but also to the children's prior notions about events in the everyday world as compared with taught science knowledge.

Johnson-Laird (1983), in his striking book about mental models, uses the computer analogy to explain that a procedural programme would need parallel computation to give it speed and flexibility, but this would make it almost impenetrable to analysis. Hence such knowledge might well be tacit or unarticulated, and only available in the right context or as an analogy.

Rumelhart and Norman (1981) also argue that new schemata can only be built up by using whole programs of procedural knowledge transferred by analogy from another context. This process, they argue, is then followed by a 'tuning' procedure which trims and alters the procedural knowledge so that it now fits the new situation. Here, it seems, the new liaison between science education and cognitive psychology is about to yield advice for school teachers. Unfortunately the authors' own teaching experiments had not been very successful.

The idea of teaching through analogical transfer is also the subject of work by Gentner and Gentner (1983). In their experiments they tried to identify the spontaneous analogy which novice physics students brought to the study of electric circuits and the success it achieved for them. In another experiment (Tenney and Gentner 1984) groups of similar students were taught about water circuits before electrical circuits and it was shown that very few could spontaneously form the expected analogy. Only when they were explicitly told to make this analogy did the learning of this group show marked improvement over that of the control group.

CONCLUSION, DENOUEMENT, OR MORAL?

A chapter like this one cannot have a conclusion, nor indeed should it have any unexpected denouement, although there may perhaps be a certain gathering of momentum within the research story. It does seem just possible that some kind of moral can be drawn from it.

In 1978 Driver and Easley argued that the field was still preparadigmatic; no doubt many would still see it so today. However, I believe that the outline of a resolution may just be beginning to appear. It seems clear that none of the four frames on their own can produce complete understanding. Indeed while the first two or three were alone in the field there was a tendency for ideological differences between them to sharpen into disputations about terminology – 'conceptions', 'preconceptions' or 'misconceptions' – rather than to integrate the different perspectives. Only a few, such as Arca et al. (1983), were prepared to contemplate schemes of knowledge where different kinds, from different sources, could be combined.

Runciman (1983) has suggested that any inquiry in social science requires at least four different perspectives: insider description, reportage of data, theoretical explanation, and evaluation (from the stance of the researcher). Apart from two – insider description and theoretical explanation – they do not have a one-to-one correspondence with the frames used in this review. Nevertheless, elements of all these complementary categories are present in the research. What may be missing is an acknowledgement of the multiple nature of children's learning about science.

An attempt to understand how the different inputs merge, integrate, or construct knowledge in the head of the learner might be either theoretical or empirical, but it is more likely to be the former than the latter. This is a natural subject for philosophical reflection. Thus Osborne and Wittrock (1985) described in detail a 'generative model' of learning in which the learner's existing ideas might influence either one or all of the following: the use of the senses, attention to sensory inputs, the generation of links to items stored in the memory and hence the construction of personal meaning. Now a wider, more philosophical sense of constructivism, to cover the teaching as well as the learning of science concepts, has superseded its original Kellian meaning within science education. Several in this field, notably von Glasersfeld (e.g. 1986) have debated and extended the discussion of 'radical constructivism', and yet still fail to integrate the four obstinately separate frames.

The cognitive complex stands in urgent need of some empirical exploration which it is, perhaps, less likely to receive in the modern climate, of action research and very loosely grounded theory, than might have been the case in an earlier period of psychological dependency. Some aspects of this exploration are to be found in an analysis of how pupils' life-world knowledge of dissolving impinged on their science learning (Longden et al. 1991). A study of cognitive structure showing how school knowledge of energy could be either added to the stock of socially derived life-world knowledge, or used to construct a formal system, is described in Solomon (1992).

Value-free ethnography, as an end in itself, can have no long-standing place in educational research. The misconception frame struggles to teach better and may need help from some distanced explanatory theory. The cultural school of research has observed and understood the difficulty of moving from the social to the school domain, but needs to explore the cognitive tension between individual learning and cultural knowledge in a way that helps the school endeavour. Traditional psychology used to study isolated skills in somewhat artificial contexts. Now that mental and cognitive structure has become a field of research, this last frame, that of the new cognitive psychology, takes us into the very heartland of the research problem. Armed with the powerful computer analogy, it has just met up with the new educational research. At least one interesting research group (Strauss 1986) has been deliberately organized to exploit such collaboration. There are signs, however faint, that a union of our four frames might yet produce the necessary synthesis.

REFERENCES

Arca, M., Guidoni, P. and Mazzoli, P. 1983. 'Structures of understanding at the root of science education. Part 1. Experience, language and knowledge.' *European Journal of Science Education*, 5: 367–75.

Archenhold, W. F. 1975. 'A study of the understanding by sixth form students of the concept of potential in physics.' MPhil. thesis, University of Leeds.

Armistead, N. (ed.) 1972. *Reconstructing social psychology*. Penguin, Harmondsworth.

Arnold, B. and Simpson, M. 1980. *An investigation of the concept of photosynthesis in students entering SCE 0-grade*. Aberdeen College of Education, Aberdeen.

Ausubel, D. 1963. *The psychology of meaningful verbal learning*. Greene & Stratton, New York.

Barnes, D. and Todd, F. 1977. *Communication in small groups*. Routledge & Kegan Paul, London.

Bourdieu, P. 1977. *Outline of a theory of practice*. Cambridge University Press, Cambridge.

Caillot, M. 1984. 'Problem representation and problem solving procedures in electricity.' In Duit, R., Jung, W. and Rhoneck, C. (eds) *Aspects of understanding electricity*. IPN, Kiel, pp. 139–52.

Champagne, A., Klopfer, L., Solomon, C. and Kahn, A. 1980. *Interaction of students' knowledge with their comprehension and design of science experiments*. Learning Research and Development Center, University of Pittsburgh.

Champagne, A. and Klopfer, L. 1982. 'Cognitive research and the design of science instruction.' *Educational Psychology*, 17: 31–53.

Closset, J. 1983. 'Le raisonnement sequential en elector-synaptic.' PhD thesis, Université Paris VII.

Cosgrove, M. and Osborne, R. 1983. *The electric current. Developing the concept. Teachers' guide to electric circuits*. Science Education Research Unit, University of Waikato and Hamilton Teachers College, New Zealand.

Deadman, J. 1976. 'The structure and development of concepts associated with the topic of evolution in secondary school boys.' PhD thesis, Chelsea College, University of London.

diSessa, A. 1980. 'Momentum flow as an alternative perspective in elementary mechanics.' DSRE working paper, Massachusetts Institute of Technology, Cambridge, Mass.

Dreyfus, A. and Jungwirth, E. 1980. 'A comparison of the prompting effect of out of school with that of in school contexts on certain aspects of critical thinking.' *European Journal of Science Education*, 2: 301–10.

Driver, R. 1973. 'The representation of conceptual frameworks in young adolescent science students.' PhD thesis, University of Illinois, Urbana, Illinois.

Driver, R. 1983. *The pupil as scientist?* Open University Press, Milton Keynes.

Driver, R. 1991. 'Students' conceptions and the learning of science.' *International Journal of Science Education*, 11: 481–90.

Driver, R. and Easley, J. 1978. 'Pupils and paradigms: a review of literature related to concept development in adolescent science students.' *Studies in Science Education*, 5: 61–84.

Driver, R. and Erickson, G. 1983. 'Theories-in-action: some theoretical and empirical issues in the study of students' conceptual frameworks.' *Studies in Science Education*, 10: 37–60.

Driver, R. and Oldham, V. 1986. 'A constructivist approach to curriculum development in science.' *Studies in Science Education*, 13: 105–22.

Duit, R. 1981. 'Students' notions about the energy concept before and after physics instruction.' In Jung, W., Pfundt, H. and Rhöneck, C. von (eds) *Proceedings of the International Workshop on 'Problems concerning Students' Representations of Physics and Chemistry Knowledge'*. Ludwigsburg Pädagogische Hochschule, Ludwigsburg, West Germany.

Engel, E. 1982. 'An exploration of pupils' understanding of heat, pressure and evolution.' PhD thesis, University of Leeds.

Engel, E. and Driver, R. 1982. 'Investigating children's scientific ideas.' Paper given at a conference at Leicester University.

Erickson, G. 1979. 'Children's conceptions of heat and temperature.' *Science Education*, 63: 221–30.

Faucher, G. 1983. 'Advanced physics courses do not provide students with conceptual change.' In Helm, H. and Novak, J. (eds) *Proceedings of the international seminar on misconceptions in science and mathematics.* Cornell University, Ithaca, NY, pp. 322–6.

Festinger, L. 1962. 'Cognitive dissonance.' *Scientific American*, October.

Feyerabend, P. 1978. *Against method*. Verso, London.

Fleming, R. 1984. *Scenarios for teaching about a nuclear power plant and about genetic engineering*. University of Saskatchewan, Regina.

Gentner, D. and Gentner, D. R. 1983. 'Flowing waters of teeming crowds: mental models of electricity.' In Gentner, D. and Stevens, A. (eds) *Mental models*. Lawrence Erlbaum Associates, Hillsdale, NJ, pp. 99–131.

Gilbert, J., Osborne, R. and Fensham, P. 1982. 'Children's science and its consequences for teaching.' *Science Education*, 66: 623–33.

Gilbert, J. and Watts, M. 1983. 'Concepts, misconceptions and alternative conceptions: changing perspectives in science education.' *Studies in Science Education*, 10: 61–98.

Glasersfeld, E. von. 1986. 'Steps in the construction of "others" and "reality".' In R. Trappl (ed.) *Power, autonomy, utopias: New approaches toward complex systems*. Plenum Press, London, pp. 107–16.

Gott, R. 1984. 'The place of electricity in the assessment of performance in science.' In Duit, R., Jung, W. and von Rhöneck, C. (eds) *Aspects of understanding electricity*. IPN, Kiel, pp. 49–61.

Guesne, E. 1978. Lumière et vision des objets: un exemple de représentation des phénomènes physiques pré-existant à l'enseignment.' In Delacote, G. (ed.) *Physics teaching in schools*. Taylor and Francis, London, pp 265–73.

Gunstone, R. 1980. 'Word association and the description of cognitive structure.' *Research in Science Education*, 10: 45–53.

Gunstone, R. and White, R. 1980. 'A matter of gravity.' *Research in Science Education*, 10: 35–44.

Halliday, M. 1978. *Language as social semiotic*. Edward Arnold, London.

Helm, H. 1981. 'Conceptual misunderstandings in physics.' *Perspectives 3. The teaching of physics*. School of Education, University of Exeter.

Hewson, P. 1981. 'A conceptual change approach to learning science.' *European Journal of Science Education*, 3: 383–96.

Hewson, M. and Hewson, P. 1983. 'Effects of instruction using students' prior knowledge and conceptual change strategies on science learning.' *Journal of Research in Science Teaching*, 20(8): 731–43.

Jegede, O. and Okebukola, P. 1991. 'The relationship between African traditional cosmology and students' acquisition of a science process skill.' *International Journal of Science Education*, 13: 37–48.

Johnson-Laird, P. 1983. *Mental models*. Cambridge University Press, Cambridge.

Joshua, S. 1984. 'Students' interpretations of simple electrical circuit diagrams.'

European Journal of Science Education, 6: 271–5.

Karrqvist, C. 1984. 'The development of concepts by means of dialogues centred on experiments.' In Duit, R., Jung, W. and Rhöneck, C. (eds) *Aspects of understanding electricity.* IPN, Kiel, pp. 215–26.

Kelly, G. 1955. *The psychology of personal constructs.* W. W. Norton, New York.

Kempa, R. and Hodgeson, G. 1976. 'Levels of concept acquisition and concept development in students of chemistry.' *British Journal of Educational Psychology,* 46: 253–60.

Larkin, J., McDermott, J., Simon, D. and Simon, H. 1980. 'Expert and novice performance in solving physics problems.' *Science,* 208: 1335–42.

Layton, D., Davey, A. and Jenkins, E. 1986. 'Science for specific purposes.' *Studies in Science Education,* 13: 27–52.

Leboutet-Barrell, L. 1976. 'Concepts of mechanics among young people.' *Physics Education,* 11: 462–5.

Lin, H. 1983. 'A cultural look at physics students and physics classrooms: an example of anthropological work in science education.' In Helm, N. and Novak, J. (eds) *Proceedings of the international seminar on misconceptions in science and mathematics.* Cornell University, Ithaca, NY.

Longden, K., Black, P. and Solomon, J. 1991. 'Children's interpretation of dissolving.' *International Journal of Science Education,* 3: 59–68.

Lucas, A. M. 1981. 'The informal and the eclectic.' Inaugural lecture. Chelsea College, University of London.

Lucas, A. M. 1983. 'Scientific literacy and informal learning.' *Studies in Science Education,* 10: 1–36.

McCloskey, M. 1983. 'Intuitive physics.' *Scientific American,* 248(4): 114–22.

McQuail, D. 1972. 'The television audience: a revised perspective.' In McQuail, D. (ed.) *Sociology of mass communications.* Penguin, Harmondsworth, pp. 135–65.

Mali, G. B. and Howe, A. 1979. 'Development of earth and gravity concepts among Nepali children.' *Science Education,* 63: 685–91.

Minstrell, J. 1982. 'Explaining the "at rest" condition of an object.' *The Physics Teacher,* 20: 12–14.

Mohapatra, J. 1991. 'The interaction of cultural rituals and the concepts of science in student learning: a case study on solar eclipse.' *International Journal of Science Education,* 13: 431–7.

Mori, I., Koyima, M. and Tadaing, K. 1976. 'The effect of language on a child's conceptions of speed: a comparative study on Japanese and Thai children.' *Science Education,* 60: 531–4.

Novak, J. and Gowin, D. 1984. *Learning how to learn.* Cambridge University Press, Cambridge.

Nussbaum, J. 1979. 'Children's conception of the earth as a cosmic body: a cross-age study.' *Science Education,* 63: 83–93.

Nussbaum, J. and Novak, J. D. 1976. 'An assessment of children's concepts of the earth utilising structured interviews.' *Science Education,* 60: 535–50.

Osborne, R. 1981. 'Children's ideas about electric current.' *New Zealand Science Teacher,* 29: 12–19.

Osborne, R. and Gilbert, J. 1979. *An approach to student understanding of basic concepts in science.* Occasional paper. University of Surrey, Guildford.

Osborne, R. and Wittrock, M. 1985. 'The generative learning model of learning and its implications for science education.' *Studies in Science Education,* 12: 59–87.

Pfundt, H. & Duit, R. 1991. *Bibliography: Students' alternative frameworks and science education,* 3rd edition. IPN, Kiel.

Piaget, J. 1929. *The child's conception of the world.* Paladin Press, London.

Piaget, J. 1978. *Success and understanding*. Routledge & Kegan Paul, London.

Pines, L. 1978. 'Scientific concept learning in children.' PhD thesis, Cornell University, Ithaca, NY.

Pines, L. and Leigh, S. 1981. 'What is concept learning in science theory?' *Australian Science Teachers' Journal*, 27(3): 15–20.

Pope, M. and Keen, T. 1981. *Personal construct psychology and education*. Academic Press, London.

Posner, G., Strike, K., Hewson, P. and Gertzog, W. 1982. 'Accommodation of a scientific concept: towards a theory of conceptual change.' *Science Education*, 66: 211–27.

Preece, P. 1976. 'Associative structures of science concepts.' *British Journal of Educational Psychology*, 46: 174–83.

Preece, P. 1978. 'Exploration of semantic space. A review of research on the organisation of scientific concepts in semantic memory.' *Science Education*, 63: 546–56.

Ravetz, J. 1971. *Scientific knowledge and its social problems*. Clarendon Press, Oxford.

Redeker, B. 1980. 'The difference between the life-world of children and the world of physics: a basic problem for teaching and learning mechanics.' Lecture given at the Universitat-GH-Pderborn.

Ross, K. 1980. 'Language barriers to concept development.' PhD thesis, University of Leicester.

Rumelhart, D. and Norman, D. 1981. 'Analogical processes in learning.' In Anderson, J. (ed.) *Cognitive skills and their acquisition*. Lawrence Erlbaum Associates, Hillsdale, New Jersey. pp. 335–60.

Runciman, W. 1983. *A treatise on social theory*. Cambridge University Press, Cambridge.

Ryder, N. 1982. *Science, television and the adolescent*. Independent Television Authority, London.

Salmon, P. and Bannister, D. 1974. 'Education in the light of the personal construct theory.' *Education for Teaching* (Summer), 25–32.

Schaefer, G. 1979. 'Concept formation in biology: the concept of "growth".' *European Journal of Science Education*, 1: 87–101.

Schutz, A. and Luckmann, T. 1973. *Structures of the life-world*. Heinemann, London.

Shayer, M. and Adey, P. 1981. *Towards a science of science teaching*. Heinemann, London.

Shipstone, R. and Gunstone, R. 1984. 'Teaching children to discriminate between current and energy.' In Duit, R., Jung, W. and van Rhoneck, C. (eds) *Aspects of understanding electricity*. IPN, Kiel, pp. 287–97.

Smith, E. and Lott, G. 1983. 'Teaching for conceptual change: some ways to go wrong.' In Helm, H. and Novak, J. (eds) *Proceedings of the international seminar on misconceptions in science and mathematics*. Cornell University, Ithaca, NY, pp. 57–66.

Sneider, M. and Pulos, P. 1983. 'Children's cosmographies: understanding the earth's shape and gravity.' *Science Education*, 67: 205–21.

Solomon, J. 1983a. 'Learning about energy: how pupils think in two domains.' *European Journal of Science Education*, 5: 49–59.

Solomon, J. 1983b. 'Learning about energy.' PhD thesis, Chelsea College, University of London.

Solomon, J. 1983c. 'Messy, contradictory and obstinately persistent.' *School Science Review*, 65: 213–16.

Solomon, J. 1984. 'Prompts, cues and discrimination: the utilization of two separate domains of knowledge.' *European Journal of Science Education*, 6: 277–84.

Solomon, J. 1985. 'Learning and evaluation: a study of school children's views on the social uses of energy.' *Social Studies of Science*, 15: 343–71.
Solomon, J. 1992. *Getting to know about energy*. Falmer Press, Lewes.
Solomon, J., Black, P., Oldham, V. and Stuart, H. 1985. 'The pupils' view of electricity.' *European Journal of Science Education*, 7: 281–94.
Strauss, S. 1983. 'Engaging children's intuitive physics concepts via curriculum units: the case of heat and temperature.' In Helm, H. and Novak, J. (eds) *Proceedings of the international seminar on misconceptions in science and mathematics*. Cornell University, Ithaca, NY, pp. 292–303.
Strauss, S. 1986. 'Human development and education.' Unpublished paper presented at Tel-Aviv University.
Sutton, C. 1980. 'The learner's prior knowledge: a critical review of techniques for probing its organization.' *European Journal of Science Education*, 2: 107–20.
Tenney, Y. and Gentner, D. 1984. 'What makes water analogies accessible: experiments on the water flow analogy for electricity.' In Duit, R., Jung, W. and Rhöneck, C. (eds) *Aspects of understanding electricity*. IPN, Kiel, pp. 311–18.
Tiberghien, A. and Delacote, G. 1978. 'Conception de la chaleur chez les enfants de 1 à 12 ans.' In Delacote, G. (ed.) *Physics teaching in schools*, Taylor and Francis, London, pp. 275–82.
Tulving, E. 1976. 'Ecphoric processes in recall and recognition.' In Brown, J. (ed.) *Recall and recognition*. Wiley, New York.
Viennot, L. 1979a. 'Spontaneous reasoning in elementary dynamics.' *European Journal of Science Education*, 1: 203–21.
Viennot, L. 1979b. *Le raisonnement spontané en dynamique élémentaire*. Hermann, Paris.
Viennot, L. 1983. 'Natural tendencies in analysing students' reasoning.' In Helm, H. and Novak, J. (eds) *Proceedings of the international seminar on students' misconceptions in science*. Cornell University, Ithaca, NY, pp. 239–44.
Watts, M. and Zylbersztajn, A. 1981. 'A survey of some children's ideas about force.' *Physics Education*, 15: 360–5.
Wellington, J. 1991. 'Newspaper science, school science: friends or enemies?' *International Journal of Science Education*, 13: 363–72.
Wells, L. 1984. 'The development of pupils' understanding of current electricity.' MSc. thesis, University of Oxford.
West, L., Pines, L. and Sutton, C. 1983. 'In-depth investigation of learner's understandings of scientific concepts and theories.' Occasional paper, University of Leicester.
Whorf, B. 1956. In Carroll, J. B. (ed.) *Language, thought and reality: selected writings of Benjamin Lee Whorf*. MIT Press, Cambridge, Mass.
Wynne, B. 1992. 'Sheep farming after Chernobyl: a case study in communicating scientific information.' In Lewenstein, B. (ed.) *When science meets the public*. American Association for the Advancement of Science, Washington DC.
Ziman, J. 1991 'Public understanding of science.' *Science, Technology and Human Values*, 16: 99–105.

Chapter 2

The relevance of Piaget to research into children's conceptions

Joan Bliss

INTRODUCTION

Research into children's ideas about science and mathematics – whether known under the title of 'alternative frameworks', 'misconceptions', 'preconceptions', etc. – has at least one important characteristic in common with the work of Piaget: it takes the child's view of the world seriously. Piaget was one of the first to put forward the notion that children construct their own knowledge, this knowledge being seen as different in kind from that of an adult, evolving and changing over the years.

Why then has Piaget gone, at least for the time being, out of favour? One reason may be that the way in which Piaget has been taught, particularly in education: too often boiled down to a stage-naming exercise illustrated by a few over-simplified examples. This does mean, unfortunately, that some of the more fundamental ideas of Piaget which could be important for education never see the light of day. Much of this problem is, of course, a wound inflicted by Piaget on himself, as his writing is both voluminous and opaque.

A second is that towards the end of the 1970s a wave of well articulated criticism crossed both the United States and Britain and with this the social scientists' and educationists' love affair with Piaget reached both a critical and a turning phase and began to fade away.

The aim of this chapter is not to defend Piaget against his critics or to expand on his ideas so as to do them justice – the latter job being impossible in the space available. By reporting these critiques and discussing them briefly my goal is to bring out some of the lesser known but extremely important ideas of Piaget's theory. In this way I shall show what his work has to offer to science educators: where it presents problems, and what it has in common with recent research in this area. Before looking at the critiques it is better to start by simply saying what Piaget saw to be the goal of his work, and what were the more important influences on his thinking.

ORIGINS OF AND INFLUENCES ON PIAGET'S IDEAS

Piaget was interested in how knowledge develops, how it changes and what the laws are that govern these changes: in Piaget's terms – genetic epistemology. As Piaget (1972a) wrote: 'Genetic epistemology, then, aims to study the origins of various kinds of knowledge, starting with their most elementary forms, and to follow their development to later levels up to and including scientific thought.' Now, if knowledge does develop, where are the more elementary forms of knowledge to be found? To most people, with 60 years of Piaget's work in the background, the answer is obvious: in children. Yet why choose children? Why not choose different sorts of adult, or why not compare societies that are recognizably different?

For Piaget, the development of knowledge is seen as the result of individuals constructing their own knowledge. Furth (1969), describing Piaget's view of knowledge, writes

> knowledge is an operation that constructs its objects . . . [O]n the level of the theory of knowledge . . . knowledge is neither solely in the subject, nor in a supposedly independent object, but is constructed by the subject as an indissociable subject–object relation.
>
> (Furth 1969)

Later, writing about how Piaget envisages that people come to know things, Furth went on to say: 'Intellectual knowledge is thus an activity in the creative sense of the term. It does not merely act on things. It transforms them and turns them into objects of knowing.'

Why did Piaget view knowledge in this manner? Answers to such questions take us back to earlier stages of Piaget's career. He started as a biologist with a philosophical bent during the years 1914–18 when the horrors of war challenged many people's ideas and beliefs. An early work in the form of a novel, *Recherche* (1918), is a semi-autobiographical account of a young man's search to understand the relation between science and faith, and his quest for true knowledge. Precursors of many of Piaget's later ideas are to be found in this volume. For example, ideas from Bergson's *L'Evolution Créatrice* about the biological problem of adaptation, together with the notion that biology offered powerful models of explanation, inspired him.

In the last part of *Recherche* Piaget considers the definition of life and is here inspired by the work of the French biologist Le Dantec. For instance, the organism is seen as having a constant tendency to develop through assimilation and imitation, 'with every organisation tending to conserve itself, this as a result of the equilibration between the part and the whole' (Gruber and Voneche 1979). Already, the powerful concepts of assimilation, accommodation (referred to by Le Dantec as imitation) and equilibration find their origins.

Although biology and philosophy were important formative influences on Piaget's thinking, his work in psychology was to be an important turning point. In 1919 he went to Paris to work in Alfred Binet's laboratory. Spending his mornings in the study of philosophy and logic, he turned his attention in the afternoons – at the suggestion of Simon – to the standardization of some of Cyril Burt's reasoning tests. But Piaget's attention soon shifted from the answers children gave to test questions to their reasons for their responses. Slowly Piaget developed a method of talking with and questioning children, which was later to become known as the clinical interview. But, more critically, Piaget realized that children's thinking differed importantly from that of adults.

Gradually the influences of biology, philosophy and psychology were coming together to give an impetus to drive his work towards the understanding of 'knowledge'. As Wolfe Mayes (1972) says,

> Piaget who started life as a zoologist compares his approach to that of the embryologist. He claims that the study of child development may throw light on adult thought structures, just as embryology has brought to light analogies of structure in the animal kingdom. He believes that a careful study of intellectual activities at their simplest level (in the child) will enable us to obtain a better understanding of the structure of adult thought.
>
> (Mayes 1972)

It is in this manner that psychology became for Piaget a way of studying epistemology empirically. It must be remembered that in this context Piaget is not directly concerned with children as people, with their individual differences or with their problems of adaptation to various environments, or with the role of different kinds of experience: his concern is with the 'epistemic subject'. Piaget (1968) distinguishes between two types of subject: 'structuralism calls for a differentiation between the *individual subject*, who does not enter at all, and the *epistemic subject*, that cognitive nucleus which is common to all subjects at the same level.'

Influencing Piaget's ideas on the psychological front was the work of J. M. Baldwin whose 'genetic logic', as Piaget says, 'gives a penetrating insight into the construction of cognitive structures'. But the work of James, Flournoy, Dewey, Durkheim and Freud all contributed in one way or another to Piaget's insight that the only way to answer his epistemological questions was to turn to genetic psychology.

In his foreword to *The Language and Thought of the Child* in 1923 Piaget says, 'I hope in a few years' time to produce a work dealing with child thought as a whole, in which I shall again take up the principal features of child logic and state their relation to the biological factors of adaptation'. At his death in 1980 Piaget was still seeking this goal.

CRITICISMS OF PIAGET

Many people first had an overview of Piaget's theoretical ideas and research findings through John Flavell's comprehensive book published in 1963. Although the book contained an excellent and insightful critique of Piaget's work, this was neglected in favour of the possibility of being acquainted – in one volume – with Piaget's work (Brown and Desforges, as will be seen later, base some of their criticism on Flavell's ideas). The main thrust of Flavell's critique concerned the notion of stage, and he wrote at that time a question which stuck in many people's minds: 'Can the construct of stage really serve any theoretical purpose other than to mislead us . . . ?'

As research on Piaget's ideas developed in America, so did criticism with some of the more important critiques being summarized in Siegel and Brainerd's (1978) *Alternatives to Piaget*. It was, however, Brainerd's article (1978) on the stage question in cognitive development that stirred many researchers to Piaget's defence. The essence of Brainerd's critique is that Piaget's model for stage theory, although it claims to be explanatory, does no more than describe age-related changes in behaviour and fails on almost all of Piaget's own criteria as an explanatory model.

In criticizing Piaget's model Brainerd essentially makes a two-pronged attack. First, he claims that if a stage model is to be explanatory it must describe some types of behaviour that change, and must suggest some antecedent variables that cause the change. Both the changed behaviour and the variables responsible for change should be able to be measured independently. Brainerd goes on to argue that, while Piaget's theory satisfies some of these requirements, procedures for measuring these two factors independently do not exist.

Secondly, in the absence of such procedures Brainerd turns to the five criteria for stage definition given by Piaget (1955): that is, invariant sequence, cognitive structure, integration, consolidation and equilibration. Brainerd attempts to show that the consolidation and integration criteria are simply restatements of the sequencing criterion; that the structures in the cognitive structure criterion are simply task descriptions without mappings between structure and subject's performance; and that the research findings reviewed do not tend to confirm the idea of successive equilibration levels.

The policy of the journal in which Brainerd's article appeared is to invite commentaries on articles by peers in the same and related fields, publishing articles and commentaries in the one edition, thus providing a forum for debate. Among the many commentaries, surprisingly many of them in sympathy with Piaget's work, David Olson's managed to capture the very distinctive differences in Piaget's and Brainerd's approach to problems:

> Brainerd argues that Piaget has constructed a descriptive theory but failed to construct an explanatory theory of intellectual development. Specifically, he (Brainerd) focuses upon a few of the considerations that

may be relevant to transitions between stages and tackles the problem of translating Piaget's structuralist descriptions into a set of independent variables manipulable by a behaviouralistically oriented psychologist. Not surprisingly, the enterprise fails, and, not surprisingly, Brainerd attributes the failure to Piaget. I, too, regard it as a failure but attribute it to Brainerd, not because he makes poor translation but because he naively believes the translation is possible, even urgent, in cognitive psychology. I shall argue that Brainerd espouses a view of scientific explanations that most productive branches of human sciences . . . have abandoned.

(Olson 1978:197)

In other words, Brainerd's criticism attempts to reduce a structuralist view of behaviour to an empiricist-positivist view. For Brainerd, scientific explanations consist of empirically demonstrated causal relations between independent and dependent variables, together with a behaviourist view which denies meaningful status to internal states. For a very long time Piaget was almost alone in not accepting such a view.

Two of the more prominent English critics were Brown and Desforges. They first looked at the relationship between Piaget and education (1977) and then in 1979 launched a more extensive criticism of Piaget's ideas from a Popperian point of view. They argue that while Piaget's theory would be successful if judged on the criteria of parsimony and breadth of application as well as of fruitfulness, they feel that, 'this body of criticism clearly suggests that the theory, where testable, proves inadequate . . . More seriously it is in many respects untestable.'

They in fact revert to the four major criticisms levelled at the theory by Flavell in 1963:

a) methods of data collection;
b) the relationship between thought and language;
c) the very limited reference to individual differences and effect of experience;
d) the over elaborate treatment of structure.

Brown and Desforges' examination of structure led them to a criticism of the structuralist notion of stage, seeing it as no more than 'definitional'. They also regard the notion of 'horizontal decalage' as being used to explain away any potential conflicts arising from evidence of asynchronisms in the appearance of predicted sequences of behaviours within a stage. They add that on-going research seems to be progressing without recourse to the notion of stage. In other words, in their opinion the notion of stage is both unnecessary and presents too many conceptual problems. They add, like Brainerd, that Piaget's stage model is not an explanation of cognitive development and that he offers no account of how structures evolve from stage to stage.

These and other criticisms suggest a need to look in more depth at three areas:

a) at methodological issues in terms of the relationship between psychology and epistemology;
b) at the sense in which Piaget can be considered both as a structuralist and a constructivist;
c) at how Piaget's work relates to science education.

PSYCHOLOGY AND EPISTEMOLOGY

An important methodological issue was that of the relationship which existed for Piaget between epistemology and the psychological formation of ideas, because psychology was to provide for Piaget a dynamic theory of knowledge. As Piaget (1972b) said,

> If all knowledge is continually in the course of development and consists in passing from a state of lesser knowledge to one which is more complete and effective, then it is clearly a matter of understanding this development and analysing it as accurately as possible.
>
> (Piaget 1972b)

It is important to stress that almost all Piaget's investigations stem from some philosophical issue about the structure of knowledge and not, as is commonly believed, from a psychological concern about children themselves as individuals.

Although there is not the space for a discussion of such philosophical issues, a few instances are given here. Thus, for example, while influenced by Kant's ideas and more particularly his *a priori* categories of object, space, time and causality, Piaget commented that 'his [Kant's] *a priori* forms were much too rich' and he turned them into areas of empirical investigation, thus giving birth to one of the earliest studies of the cognitive development of infants. Whitehead and Russell's fundamental ideas in the *Principia*, where they sought to define the ordinals in terms of classes of classes by one-to-one correspondence, constituted one of Piaget's starting points in thinking about the child's concept of number. Piaget also asked whether the child's spatial operations developed in conformity with the historical order of their 'construction' (Euclidean, then projective and finally topographical) or followed a different but perhaps more fundamental order: as it turned out, topology appeared to be the most primitive for the child. Piaget's discussions with Einstein, on the primacy of the concept of speed or of the concept of time, provided another fruitful area of study. Such a list could be continued at length.

PIAGET AND STRUCTURALISM

What did it mean to Piaget to be 'structuralist'? The very term has, until recently, been foreign to Anglo-Saxon thought, with psychology in particular dominated for the first half of Piaget's career by the behaviourist philosophy within which the issues a structuralist would raise were simply defined out of existence as meaningless. On the other hand, modern structuralist psychological theories, in cognitive science, linguistics and artificial intelligence, appear so unlike those of Piaget (who did see the value of these new ideas) that the deeper similarity is missed.

Structuralism allowed Piaget to get away from the tendency to reduce whole behaviours to their 'prior elements', allowing him to see what various seemingly heterogeneous behaviours had in common. Piaget (1968) describes structure in the following way,

> As a first approximation, we may say that a structure is a system of transformations. In as much as it is a system and not a mere collection of elements and their properties, these transformations involve laws: the structure is preserved or enriched by the interplay of its transformation laws.
>
> (Piaget 1968)

The three key ideas of a structure for Piaget are wholeness, transformation and self-regulation. Wholeness refers to the idea that the elements making up the structure are subordinated to the laws of the structure. In other words the laws of the structure are more than the sum of the properties of the elements that make up the structure. Secondly, the laws of structure must by their very nature be structuring and so they are simultaneously structuring and being structured. Thirdly, self-regulation entails self-maintenance and closure: that is, transformations inherent in the structure never lead beyond the structure and always engender elements that belong to it and preserve its laws.

Piaget saw it as important to describe structures in formal terms and took his ideas for formalisms from two important sources. First, from Felix Klein and his Erlanger Program, which changed traditional representational geometry into one integrated system of transformations, using the notion of group which combines both transformation and conservation. Second, from Bourbaki, the French structuralist mathematician, whose programme of work was based on three parent structures, or as Piaget says, 'three not further reducible sources of all other structures'. These structures were algebraic (example, mathematical groups); order (example, lattices), and finally topological structures (example, neighbourhood).

Moving away from this mathematical view of structure to a more psychological one, Piaget holds that behaviour at every level reveals some aspects of restructuring, where, for Piaget, structuring is identical with knowing. As Furth (1969) says,

The main point for Piaget is that behaviour at all levels demonstrates aspects of construction which derive at least partly from the behaving organism's intrinsic structure and that this structuring aspect is identical with meaningful knowing behaviour . . . More precisely, when Piaget observes the knowing aspects of a behaviour, he aims at uncovering the structuring capacity of the organism, namely, the inner structure that underlies the knowing response at a particular developmental level.

(Furth 1969)

PIAGET AND CONSTRUCTIVISM

Piaget, then, believed – as did Kant and as does Chomsky – in the importance of hypothesizing mental structures which would account for processes of thought. But Piaget needed to account for the growth and transformation of structures, and so structuralism was not enough for Piaget. As Margaret Boden (1979) puts it, 'Empiricism [for Piaget] describes growth of knowledge in terms of genesis without structure, whereas rationalism offers structure without genesis'.

So Piaget is distinguished from other structuralists by the fact that not only was he interested in describing structures but that he wanted to produce a developmental or genetic structuralism to describe how such structures evolve. Initially Piaget labelled his own position as 'interactionism' in as much as it is through the interaction of the individual with the environment that intellectual schemes and operations are created, which, in turn, further the interaction with the environment. Later, Piaget was to call himself a 'constructivist' when discussing the problem of the genesis of thought structures.

Piaget's central metaphor for adding genesis to structure is biological. It is useful in understanding his biological metaphor to take his definitions of assimilation and accommodation – central to his theory of equilibration – and to look at his use of them in describing how intelligence functions. Thus Piaget (1978a) writes:

First Postulate: Any scheme of assimilation tends to feed itself, that is, to incorporate outside elements compatible with its nature into itself. This postulate assigns a driving force to the process and therefore must assume activity on the part of the subject, but by itself it does not imply the construction of novelties . . .

Second Postulate: The entire scheme of assimilation must alter as it accommodates to the elements it assimilates: that is, it modifies itself in relation to the particularities of events but does not lose its continuity . . . This second postulate . . . states the necessity for an equilibrium between the assimilation and the accommodation in order for the accommodation to succeed and remain compatible with the cycle, modified or not.

(Piaget 1978a)

Assimilation and accommodation are two sides of a coin, the fundamental and complementary processes that take place simultaneously in any act of adaptation. Thus the organism, through the continual functioning of these two processes, tends towards better forms of equilibration and in this same manner generates new intellectual structures.

In discussing equilibration Piaget (1978a) (in a revised version of his first theory of equilibration published in 1957) says,

> the passage of imbalance or of imperfect forms of equilibrium to 'better' forms implies at each stage the intervention of new constructions, themselves determined by the requirements of compensations and equilibrations. In such a model the equilibrium and the creativity are thus more antagonistic but closely interdependent.
>
> (Piaget 1978a)

In other words, periods of imbalance and disturbance are as important in the development of knowledge as are moments of equilibration.

Piaget describes three levels of equilibration from a very local type to a more generalized kind. Aware that this model still remains very descriptive he goes on to explore how equilibration and re-equilibration function through compensating regulations. These regulations consist of two types of feedback loops – negative feedback or correction, and positive feedback or reinforcement. Any regulation is a reaction to a disturbance, which may be of two kinds – either due to resistance of objects or to gaps which leave requirements unfulfilled: that is, an insufficiency of 'schemes'. Less abstractly, 'a gap becomes a disturbance when it indicates the absence of an object, the lack of conditions necessary to accomplish an action, or want of knowledge that is indispensable in solving a problem' (Piaget 1978b).

Two further features of Piaget's ideas about the environment help shed more light on his version of constructivism. First, the environment is not there to stimulate the child – the initiative is with the child, responding to those features which are meaningful to him by assimilating them to existing thought structures and by simultaneously modifying those thought structures to make assimilation possible. Second, the environment is 'non specific' – the child can develop his ideas anywhere, anytime. It is not so much the objects themselves in the environment that count, but the child's activity in acting on those objects.

This second point is often misunderstood as Piaget saying that the 'environment' does not count. Piaget does, in fact, distinguish two types of activity – physical and logico-mathematical. When talking about physical activity, Piaget says children are paying attention to the environment, noticing attributes of objects, features of situations, etc. All of this provides them with specific knowledge about the world they live in.

But there is a second logico-mathematical level of activity, which is the basis for the construction of the child's intellectual structures. The often cited example will help to illustrate the point. A child arranges a row of pebbles in a straight line, counts them and finds there are ten. He rearranges the pebbles in a number of configurations, each time finding that the result is ten. What he has learned is that the number is invariant regardless of the transformation. More crucially, Piaget, in interpreting this type of activity, emphasises that it is the child's actions that are important not the objects or their attributes. The pebbles could have been replaced by tennis balls, pencils or Coca-Cola bottles and the result would have been the same. These generalized types of actions become mental operations through what Piaget called a process of 'interiorization'.

The importance to Piaget's theory of the notion of logico-mathematical activity for the account of the genesis of structures cannot be emphasized enough. Furth (1969) says,

> Piaget also uses the term 'reflective' abstraction (for logico-mathematical) since he considers the abstraction in the manner of an internal feedback that progressively enriches the internal structure. The organism reflects on its own co-ordinating activity, not in an introspective, self-reflective sense, but in a self-regulatory and self-expanding sense. The abstraction, as a feedback, is an internal regulation mechanism; and as an internal enrichment, it becomes the principal source of growth of the operative structure. This growth takes the form of an internal increase where on a higher plane later structures subsume or 'reflect' earlier structures. Operative growth is thus not a cumulative addition of externally imported elements.
>
> (Furth 1969)

So for Piaget the child must make or construct his own logical ideas. Piaget prefers the idea of invention or construction rather than that of discovery since the ideas do not exist 'out there', and, having no prior existence, are unable to be discovered by simply being exposed.

Furth (1969) commenting on Piaget's stance, says,

> the result of Piaget's 'radical constructivism' is his resolute refusal to take objectivity in any but a constructivist sense. A thing in the world is not an object of knowledge until the knowing organism interacts with it and constitutes it as an object.
>
> (Furth 1969)

In other words, Piaget's whole emphasis is on the constructive activity of the mind in the formation and interpretation of experience. Let Piaget (1968) himself describe his position, particularly as the quotation also valuably summarizes his own philosophy:

> These pages contain an account of an epistemology that is naturalist without being positivist; that draws attention to the activity of the subject

without being idealist; that equally bases itself on the object, which it considers as a limit (therefore existing independently of us but never completely reached); and that above all sees knowledge as a continuous construction.

(Piaget 1968)

CONSTRUCTIVISM AND ITS IMPLICATIONS FOR EDUCATION

As has been shown, criticisms of Piaget in psychology have mainly tended to focus on the stage/structure notions in his theory. However, researchers in science education have shared with Piaget his constructivist approach to learning. Driver (1982), while seeing Piaget as representing the developmental perspective on learning, also places him within the constructivist tradition, saying, 'In as far as he makes the assumption of the active participation of learner in the development of his or her own thinking, Piaget is a constructivist'.

Another basis sometimes given for constructivist approaches is the psychology of George Kelly (1955). Gilbert and Watts (1983) characterize Kelly's view of concept as 'actional' and say, 'Thus, as Kelly would argue: conceptual development can be seen as a continuous, active, creative process of differentiation and integration of local conceptual domains. Nothing remains static or unchanged.' Such words suggest that Kelly's idea of construction is being understood in a way which is at least superficially not unlike Piaget's.

There are, however, differences between Kelly and Piaget, in particular that Kelly integrates the affective side of the individual into his picture. Also, whereas Piaget focuses on the construction of knowledge common to all individuals, Kelly looks at construction at a level that would generate different results from person to person. A further essential difference is that Kelly is concerned with the 'conscious self-regulation' by the child of his own construction. While 'self-regulation' is a fundamental feature of structuralism, Piaget thinks the very opposite about the consciousness of self-regulation; according to him the child is only aware of the results of his actions and not of the structures that organize them.

In any case, the 'lived' (or conscious) can only have a very minor role in the construction of cognitive structures, for these do not belong to the subject's consciousness but to his operational behaviour, which is something quite different. Not until he becomes old enough to reflect on his own habits and patterns of thought and action does the subject become aware of structures as such. If, then to account for the constructions we have described we must appeal to the subject's act, the subject here meant can only be the 'epistemic' subject, that is, the mechanisms common to all subjects at a certain level, those of the 'average' subject.

(Piaget 1968)

Thus the constructivist position increasingly taken in science education research can derive its origins from Piaget or from Kelly. It is important to distinguish the difference in meaning of constructivism for Piaget and Kelly because their two different conceptions lead to quite distinct views of 'what knowledge is', which, in turn, produce very different implications for research and for classroom practice.

Starting from Kelly the focus will be on the individual and on the uniqueness of each person's construction of the world and the different construct systems each will develop. Pope and Gilbert (1983) argue that such a view, 'lends support to teachers who are concerned with the investigation of student views, who seek to incorporate these views within the teaching learning dialogue, and who see the importance of encouraging students to reflect upon, and make known their construction of, some aspects of reality'.

Osborne and Wittrock (1985) spell out some of the difficulties that such an approach would present for teachers, particularly the interpretation of the technical complexity of Kelly's ideas into a language more accessible to teachers. Putting aside for the moment the difficulty of communicating Kelly's ideas, such an approach also requires the teacher to be a 'diagnostician' of cognition, discovering each individual pupil's construct system. The problem then arises as to whether there are as many construct systems as there are individual pupils or whether similarities exist between construct systems in the same way as some children can be seen to have similar personalities. Whatever the answer, to view science teaching as a cognitive diagnosis task is to give a different and more complex meaning to the job of teaching. If teachers are to do such a job successfully they would need both a different training as well as a great deal of information about children's informal ideas. At present, research into children's conceptions still takes a very traditional form, sampling children over an age range, with very few longitudinal or in-depth studies of children. This is not a criticism of Kelly's ideas but of the more general area of research into children's ideas about science whose philosophical basis is Kelly's work.

Piaget, on the other hand, has looked widely across individuals in order to describe at a more general level the development of knowledge and the laws that govern it. Piaget is not concerned with the individual or with those differences that distinguish one person from another. In studying what he calls the epistemic (or average) subject Piaget provides us with a general picture, domain by domain, of how a particular idea develops, with, in principle, all individuals following the same evolution. It must be stressed that children are essentially a means of studying the development of knowledge, the average child being the vehicle of the study. But the picture is not quite so simple because no two individual's developments are alike in term of pace, varying due to factors such as maturation, learning, social influences, motivation, etc., even though the pattern of their development is the same.

So the difficulty of translating Piaget's work into educational practice is that of moving from the epistemic subject to the individual subject. Differences between individuals, effects of experience, motivation, etc. are, for Piaget, the study of psychologists. The translation of Piaget's work into educational applications therefore needs to be undertaken with care, school and schooling being concerned with real individual children.

Two further difficulties with Piaget's work are:

a) that there are few longitudinal studies, looking at the development of a given notion in a particular child over a number of months or years, and
b) that there has not been a great deal of research which attempts to look at a particular child's reasoning over a number of areas in order to get an overall picture of that child's 'operational potential'.

The research described in (b) would allow a more complete picture of the relationships between the developments of the different areas of knowledge described by Piaget.

LIMITATIONS OF PIAGET'S THEORY FOR SCIENCE EDUCATION

When researchers or curriculum developers in science education turn to Piaget's theory for guidance there are a number of areas – extremely important to them – where Piaget has little to offer. These are as follows:

– focus of the research: absence of descriptions
– limitations of the research: restrictiveness of descriptions
– constraints on the application of the stage model.

Focus of the research: absence of descriptions

What Piaget considered as fundamental areas of knowledge, for example, conservation of quantities such as weight and volume, are now considered by science and mathematics educators as essential parts of the school curriculum. Indeed the findings of Piaget's developmental psychology have provided guidelines for various curriculum development projects, for example, Schools Council Science 5–13, Nuffield Mathematics 5–13, Science Curriculum Improvement Study and many others.

However, in spite of 60 years' work, when his research is looked at in detail, domain-specific descriptions of pupils' ideas about areas in secondary science are very limited. Andersson (1984) says:

> But although Piaget and others have described the development of reasoning in such a comprehensive manner, the model does not tell us, for instance, what conceptions the pupils have of electricity, heat, light, matter, etc. before they begin science lessons. This is because Piaget and

others have been interested in the development of reason in general. Our interest lies in a specific subject area. We must therefore to a large extent find out about the pupil's initial position by focusing research activities on this problem.

(Andersson 1984)

Lastly, Piaget did not start to explore the realm of causality, with ideas relevant to the secondary science curriculum, until the late 1960s and early 1970s. Part of his reason was that he believed it essential to first understand the construction of an individual's mental operations, because '[e]xplaining a physical phenomenon must presume the use of such operations because the search for causality always ends up in going beyond the observable and in having recourse to inferred, therefore operational, connections' (Piaget 1977).

Piaget's work in this area has attracted little attention, mainly because the more complete studies are only published in French with one shortish book, *Understanding Causality*, summarizing them all, translated into English. In addition, not all the studies mentioned in the book have been published, so readers have difficulty in following them up.

Limitations of the research: restrictiveness of description

Piaget's main work on formal thinking appeared in 1955 (translation 1958) with the description of this stage in terms of operational schemes, not in terms of domain specific descriptions as for the earlier stages. For example, isolating and controlling variables, combinatorial, correlational, proportional and probabilistic schemes are some of those described. A reasonable criticism of such a list is that it looks very similar to the sorts of processes involved in what could be described as a 'scientific approach' to a problem. To say that all the thinking of young people and adults should fit such a restricted set of criteria is to give a limited, and perhaps arid, picture of what could be called 'thinking beyond a concrete operational level'.

However, it could be argued that Piaget's 'formal thinking schemes' might be a suitable description for a subset of all the possible processes that make up the structure of the thought mechanism of the 'formal thinker'. What many researchers are presently striving towards is a more adequate description of thinking in domain specific areas beyond the age of about 14 years, as well as a more comprehensive description and/or model of formal thinking.

Constraint of application of stage model

Studies by Piaget himself, and replications of the model by other researchers, have revealed several limitations in the application of the stage model to educational problems. There are two of particular importance for science education.

First, Piaget himself, during his work on causality, found that he had difficulty in applying his stage model to his data. Commenting on this, he said:

> Consequently, as we began to doubt the existence of stages in this evolution (cause and effect) we had to undertake a much greater number of research studies than anticipated, so diverse were the fields to be explored. Furthermore, each new analysis threatened to contradict as well as complete some of the preceding ones since, let us repeat, the causal explanations depend more on the objects than on the subject.
>
> (Piaget 1977)

Piaget argued that to talk of causality was to presume that objects exist in a real world outside us. The real world can thus resist the way in which an individual attempts to understand it, and he envisaged that the development of explanations in causality might not present the same pattern as the development of ideas in other domains. Piaget may have been getting a glimpse of some of the difficulties involved in making science intelligible to young people.

A second source of concern for anyone involved with secondary education is recent research on the age at which children attain formal operations. Generally speaking, studies have shown that only a very small percentage of children reach the formal stage by 15 or 16, that is, by the end of compulsory schooling. For example, according to Shayer, Kuchemann and Wylam (1976), less than 20 per cent of children in English comprehensive schools were in the late formal stage at age 16.

One of the basic premises of Piaget's stage theory is that the order of appearance of stages is constant, but that the age at which an individual attains any stage will vary, depending on factors such as maturation, learning, motivation, social environment, experience, etc. As mentioned earlier, the move from the epistemic to the ordinary individual is a difficult one, and the extent to which such factors could affect attainment is still largely unknown, most of the research in this area being carried out in non-western cultures where yet other factors are at work.

Piaget (1977), discussing the problem of the attainment of formal operations wrote:

> Our third hypothesis would state that all normal subjects attain the stage of formal operations or structuring if not between 11–12 to 14–15, in any case between 15 and 20 years. However, they reach this stage in different areas according to their aptitudes and their professional specialisations: the way in which these formal structures are used, however, is not necessarily the same in all cases.
>
> (Piaget 1977)

OTHER LIMITATIONS

Piaget's work has a number of other more general limitations which, although not having an immediate relevance to science education, are important in terms of whether or not a theory has applications in a wider educational context.

Piaget's formalisms

What is best known about Piaget's work is a qualitative but somewhat restrictive description of the stages of cognitive development. This rarely, if ever, touches on the formalization of the psychological structures in terms of logico-mathematical structures – many people wondering even about its relevance. Such formalizations, of course, do have a long-term significance because an adequate model of 'thinking' would by its very nature generate new research. But for a teacher this is rather an indirect source of help and information.

Many attempts, all problematic, can be made at formalizing a structure, but it may, by its very nature, be difficult to formalize. The inability of theoreticians to 'produce formalism' does not deny the validity of the structure itself, it just makes it much harder to produce good research. This line of argument would attempt to meet Brown and Desforges's criticism of the 'untestable' nature of Piaget's theory.

Piaget's suggested formalisms have been criticized by many. Karmiloff-Smith (1978), commenting on this problem, says

> Piaget's formalisation merely reflects the state of the art in the 1950s. Since then, Piaget and his colleagues have considered other formalisations . . . [w]ith the shift of emphasis from logical operations to physical causality and more recently to the procedural aspects of goal-orientated behaviour
> . . .
>
> (Karmiloff-Smith 1978)

My own view on Piaget's most well known and still used formalizations is that part of the problem is that the use made of mathematical structures is hardly sufficiently intimately connected with the material – thinking – for which they supposed to account. Formal thought has by its very nature the ability to be reflexive, and so can by thinking about itself modify thinking. The resources Piaget deploys, namely, propositional logic, group theory, lattice theory, etc., are further inappropriate because they describe structure by the simultaneous existence of a related set of relations – they are 'frozen' mathematics. Formalisms such as those based on recursive methods could be more promising, a point further developed below.

Equilibration and explanation of structure transformation

Piaget's new conceptualization of the equilibration theory, sketched above, has up to the moment attracted little commentary. Brainerd's (1978) commentary would seem to be based on the earlier work. However the criticism he makes is one that is frequently found in the literature and so needs examining. Brainerd interprets a manifestation of the equilibration criterion (one of the criteria for stages) as giving rise to a development in spurts with 'these spurts preceded and followed by periods of less rapid change'. In other words, development is seen as a discontinuous process. Inhelder (1962) was very aware of the existence of this problem:

> A theory of stages remains incomplete, however, as long as it does not clarify the contradiction between two concepts of development – the one stressing the complete continuity, and the other the absolute discontinuity of stages. . . . Namely, that in the development of intellectual operations, phases of continuity alternate with phases of discontinuity. Continuity and discontinuity would have to be defined by the relative dependence or independence of new behaviour with respect to previously established behaviour.
>
> (Inhelder 1960)

In fact, in development Piaget sees each new procedure as dependent upon the ones that have gone before – as they emerge from them – but once constituted then independent of the former ones and serving as the starting point for the construction of new procedures. In other words, a type of discontinuity exists as illustrated through the change to different procedures, but in a continuous process.

The issue of discontinuity then is not one of abrupt spurts as Brainerd supposes, but is rather one of the independence of qualitatively different new behaviours from the earlier ones that generated them. For example, the reasoning of a 5 year old 'non-conserver' is clearly very different from that of a 7 year old arguing cogently in favour of the invariance of substance. However, if one child were to be followed through this period the change would be gradual with precursors of the later stage in the earlier one, with much continuity in the total development.

Piaget's new model, while containing a great deal more detail and sophistication in its attempt at explaining equilibration and re-equilibration still needs to be thought through and worked out empirically in terms of tasks looking at children's changing behaviour. Perhaps more important, what still seems to be necessary are models that can represent a more complete link between Piaget's model of equilibration and his description of structures.

> Assimilation is therefore nothing else but the incorporation of objects into schemes (already established schemes or ones in the process of becoming) and schemes constitute the product of assimilation (previous or present) . . .

A similar circle is present at a higher level between concept and judgement: the concept or representational scheme is a product of judgements while the judgement or representational assimilation is either an incorporation of data into concepts or a relation of concepts to each other.

(Piaget 1977)

While it is easy to say that assimilation leads to schemes and schemes lead to assimilation, to model this process is much more difficult. It is perhaps in Artificial Intelligence that the most promising work of this kind is going on. Schank's (1982) *Dynamic Memory* reads at times very much like Piaget, particularly when he says:

The theory is a simple one. For every event that we process we attempt to relate it to what we know, that is what we have previously processed and stored in memory . . . Our theory then, is that there are a variety of structures in memory, each abstracting out features of an event in such a way as to make that structure general enough to be of use in representing information from distinctly different events that are similar to the extent that they can share elements of the same structure. We thus get a hierarchical sequence of structures, each responsible for part of the processing action and thus part of the memory storage. The higher level the structure responsible for processing, the greater its generality and hence the greater the possibility for learning across contexts.

(Schank 1982)

Schank claims that these structures both guide processing and storing information – not unlike Piaget's functional and structural aspects of intelligence. For Schank, not only do they account for our ability to learn and to generalize, but also – and important for teaching – they account for the reason that we get confused and forget. Those working in artificial intelligence and Piaget share some of the same goals, namely the understanding of how we acquire knowledge and how knowledge is transformed. The models used in artificial intelligence are no less mathematical than Piaget's, but they begin to exploit the mathematics of procedures, and procedures acting on procedures, as was suggested above.

Stage model and the notion of 'decalage'

Brown and Desforges (1979) in referring back to Flavell's criticism of the stage concept write:

It is difficult to test Piaget's notion of 'stage' since the sequence described seems to be no more than definitional. Second, it is a notion protected by safety clauses such as 'task resistance' and 'horizontal decalage', such that any potentially conflicting data can be explained away.

(Brown and Desforges 1979)

For the critics, 'decalage' is an all embracing construct that can permit almost anything to happen and so discussion in this section will focus on a brief examination of this idea.

The classic example of decalage is where children are asked – on different occasions for each – whether the substance, weight or volume of two balls of plasticine remain invariant in spite of the shape of one of the two undergoing changes. In each of the tasks the structure of the arguments given by children is similar when applied to the different domains, although the age at which children can give these arguments differs from task to task. Results generally show that by about 7 years of age, children can conserve substance, and that at about 8 or 9 conservation of weight is acquired, but that invariance of volume is much harder, with the majority of children reaching this at about 12 or 13 years.

Piaget (1947) describes the constitution of concrete operational structures but is careful to stress that while children are able to use logical reasoning in some contexts this is not true of all contexts – it is here that the notion of 'horizontal decalage' is introduced. He goes on to argue that concrete operations are not dissociated from the material on which they operate and, as a consequence, they are constructed domain by domain before actually reaching a truly complete generality.

Odom (1978), like many others, suggests that this argument does not constitute an explanation, going so far as to say:

> It should be emphasised, however, that decalage is not a theoretical construct and in no way provides an explanation or account of any aspect of psychological development. It is a descriptive term that summarises the relation between (a) differences in the performance of various age groups and (b) differences in information contained in problem solving tasks that have the same solution requirements.
>
> (Odom 1978)

Many critics of Piaget have stressed that he did not study sufficiently the context in which a task is set, which could be another important factor in understanding 'decalage'. Donaldson (1978) particularly makes the distinction between formal, or what she terms 'disembodied thought', and a type of 'human sense' thought. Thinking that is to do with people – their goals and intentions – and patterns of events in familiar contexts is sustained by this latter type of 'human sense'. Thus conclusions of our thinking do not conflict with things we already know or believe. Thinking that has been 'prised out of the old primitive matrix within which originally all our thinking is contained' is necessarily disembodied thought since it seeks a way of expressing form or logical structure beyond the bounds of meaning and content.

Other critics, for example Miller and Lipps (1973), Hall and Kaye (1978) and Cowan (1984), have looked more carefully at the cognitive demands of tasks – a concept possibly similar to the notion Piaget used of 'task resistance'. An example of this type of analysis refers to the well known areas of conservation and transitivity tasks. Miller and Lipps (1973) argue that, in conservation tasks, objects undergo transformations, whereas in tasks demanding transitive reasoning there are no such transformations, and they put forward the idea that:

> [h]owever equivalent the underlying logical systems for the two concepts may be their psychological application may differ. Application of principles of conservation may always be more contingent on and hence more susceptible to disruption by physical knowledge and physical feedback.
>
> (Miller and Lipps 1973)

It is analysis and criticism of this kind that, in fact, shows the importance of passing from Piaget's epistemic subject to the individual child. They also reveal the importance of the need for a careful analysis of the object, almost an epistemology of the object. Piaget (1947) briefly acknowledged this problem when he said 'the reason for these decalages is naturally to be found in the intuitive characteristics of substance, weight and volume which help or hinder the operational construction'. However, the majority of Piaget's work emphasized the importance of the activity of the child rather than the nature of the object. Only the study of causality brought this point home to him.

SUMMARY OF PIAGET'S CONTRIBUTION

One way of summarizing what has been argued in the chapter is to ask whether it would, in fact, be important for someone starting to do research on children's informal ideas to know about Piaget.

From a methodological point of view, Piaget established a tradition. He went into schools and talked informally to children; he usually devised some interesting activity or task for the child to do as the focus of the conversation; but above all he listened to and valued what children said. This approach, known as the clinical method, has now been widely adopted, but unfortunately is sometimes not carried out with as much care as Piaget himself insisted on.

Epistemological concerns were the focus of Piaget's work and not psychology for its own sake. His essential quest was to understand knowledge – what it is and how it develops. More than this he wanted to know what types of knowledge were essential to our view of reality, with each of these informing an area of research. So Piaget's main concern was to trace how these various areas of knowledge developed, with children illustrating development rather than speaking in their own right. Thus much of his research describes in detail children's reactions to many hundreds of ingeniously conceived tasks within specific knowledge domains: for example, number, space and geometry, and physical quantities, to name only a few.

Fundamentally what Piaget's work showed was that children's ideas about the world are importantly different from those of the adult, and certainly from those of the science teacher, and that if 'knowledge' is so evidently an evolutionary process, then all the stages leading up to it must be vital to the child. Thus the way in which children understand the world at any given moment, though to adults it may appear wrong, or strange, or even childish, is of great importance to them. Each new step in understanding is a necessary phase in its evolution; each new insight is like a springboard to the next stage.

Piaget was interested in universals, in knowledge that was common to all individuals and in structures that would allow him to hypothesise mental links between very different conceptual domains. For Piaget, an individual's thinking about reality was determined by his or her present mental structure.

It is crucial to distinguish between the idea and discovery of structure and the way in which it is formalized. Many, not satisfied with Piaget's structural models, have shown that they are not adequate representations of thinking. Such criticisms do not argue against structuralism but against the particular model chosen. Research is still going on around the issues of the nature of development, and problems of discontinuity or continuity.

In the past much research in mainstream behaviourist psychology investigated small localized problems and so was not sympathetic to Piaget's structuralist approach. Present day research into children's conceptions follows a similar pattern, often presenting the reader with a catalogue of children's responses to particular tasks in areas of science. While each set of responses is interesting in its own right, these and other findings need in some way to be charted and organized according to some more general principles so as both to get a better grip on those that are valid and to be able to judge where to go in further research. While some sort of constructivist approach, when more clearly defined, gives us a view of how children get their ideas, we need to make a leap beyond this – of just the kind that Piaget made originally – to see how these ideas form some sort of coherent picture.

Central to the whole of Piaget's work was the biologically inspired idea of an equilibration function that would generate cognitive structures: individuals interact with the environment, assimilating new and different realities to what they already know, and by so doing modify their own way of thinking to adapt to the newness of the situation – the unknown becoming known. So, for Piaget, knowing is an activity and, therefore, all knowledge is a construction. As pointed out earlier, many researchers in the children's conception field also share a constructivist approach in as much as they assume that 'learners actively generate meaning from experience' (Driver and Erickson 1983).

Piaget is, however, careful to distinguish two kinds of activity and thus two kinds of knowledge: first, knowledge about the physical world itself and then knowledge about how to make sense of the world – how to solve problems, how to organize reality, etc. – derived not from objects but from the child's co-ordinated actions on objects. These actions are then interiorized to become 'internal mental schemes' and it is here that Piaget shares with present-day cognitive psychologists, although postulated many decades before, the idea of inner processes of the mind directing intelligent behaviour.

The idea of 'self regulation', which comes from Piaget's equilibration model, is often quoted by researchers in the field of children's informal ideas to be the basis of a second shared assumption, that of 'children as learners . . . responsible for their own learning' (Driver and Erickson 1983). This interpretation attributes to children a greater awareness of consciousness of their own learning than Piaget himself would have done. For Piaget, children's consciousness extends to two levels only – to the goal they wish to attain and of a global intention to reach the goal; and, secondly, to the result, whether success or failure, of trying to reach the goal. It does not extend to consciousness of the structures, and schemes that generate the strategies for reaching the goal. This interpretation has very different implications for classroom practice.

CONCLUSION

The discussion of this chapter, in weighing up the Piagetian contribution, has necessarily been retrospective. In conclusion, it may be useful to reflect briefly on some future directions.

Trivially, learning involves an interaction between a person and a thing to be learned. Perhaps in reaction to older learning theories, which could be seen to have concentrated too much on 'what has to be learned' at the expense of the learner, recent constructivist accounts of learning might be said to have reversed the imbalance. Attention is centred on the pupil and on the nature of the pupil's constructions, while that which the pupil's construction concerns – namely, some part of science – is pushed into the background, being seen as 'the pupil's experience of science in school'.

By contrast, teachers of science know, even if only intuitively, that different parts of science present difficulties which differ both in level and in kind. The work of Shayer and Adey (1981) deals with this and with the relation of learner to thing-to-be-learned, mapping the relation between levels of competence and demand – these levels being adapted from Piaget's account of stages. I want to suggest that, in addition, there may be important and fundamental differences in kind which are not captured by distinctions such as formal/concrete, abstract/nonabstract or beyond/within immediate experience. Such differences would relate to the actual content of the ideas to be learned, in particular to their degree of challenge to the 'world view' or constructions of the learner.

Piaget himself, it seems to me, ran into essentially this difficulty when he tried to extend his work to the development of notions of causality. The case is not quite parallel, since Piaget was concerned with understandings arising from unschooled experience, and my present argument concerns the pupil in relation to schooled knowledge. However, whereas in the studies based on logical categories, Piaget could at least attempt to understand children's responses in terms of *a priori* categories, in the realm of causality he confronted their different and individual ideas about how the real world works, not merely their general conception of 'causation'. 'To talk of causality is to presume that objects exist in the real world' (Piaget 1974).

As mentioned earlier, the kinds of research questions raised by most present work in pupils' conceptions pay little attention to any analysis of the science itself. It is asked whether one method or another may lead pupils to change their conceptions, but rarely are questions asked about what kind of object is a given part of science, seen as something about which a person may construct new ideas.

Part of this ignoring of the essence of the science to be learned is the too easy equation which is sometimes drawn between the 'pupil as scientist' and the scientist as scientist. Science is not merely what a given scientist thinks. More to the point, science feeds on itself in building its new constructions, so that what results is an elaborate and complex structure, very far from a codification of immediate experience. Consider briefly one or two examples. Motion, seen as pushing, pulling, passing and throwing connects with common sense; motion seen as Newton saw it as needing no explanation at all undercuts everything we know. At a less cosmic level, many might accept a viral theory of the common colds, but still want to attribute a given cold to having got cold and wet.

It seems to me that a great merit of Piaget was that he took the growth of epistemology seriously, asking how it came about that people generally come to see the world as they do. What remains is to take no less seriously the processes by which people may change, or may resist changing, their ideas about the world. Different parts of science differ in the degree and manner in which they offer to reshape our deepest ideas. To neglect to pay attention to this aspect is as wrong as it was to neglect the active human intelligence which seeks, in learning, to deal with it.

REFERENCES

Andersson, B. 1984. 'A framework for discussing approaches and methods in science education.' Paper presented at 'Educational Research Workshop on science in primary education', Council for Cultural Co-operation. Edinburgh, September 1984.

Boden, M. A. 1979. *Piaget*. Fontana Modern Masters, London.

Brainerd, C. J. 1978. 'The stage question in cognitive developmental theory.' *Behavioural and Brain Sciences*, 2: 173–213.

Brown, G. and Desforges, C. 1977. 'Piagetian psychology and education: time for revision.' *British Journal of Educational Psychology*, 47: 7–17.

Brown, G. and Desforges, C. 1979. *Piaget's theory: a psychological critique*. Routledge and Kegan Paul, London.

Cowan, R. 1984. 'On what must be – more than just associations?' Paper presented at USC–UAP, 11th Interdisciplinary International Conference on Piagetian Theory and the Helping Professions.

Donaldson, M. 1978. *Children's minds*. London, Fontana.

Driver, R. 1982. 'Children's learning in science.' *Educational Analysis*, 4 (2): 69–79.

Driver, R. and Erickson, G. 1983. 'Theories in actions: some theoretical and empirical issues in the study of students' conceptual frameworks in science.' *Studies in Science Education*, 10: 37–60.

Flavell, J. H. 1963. *The developmental psychology of Jean Piaget*. D. Van Nostrand, Princeton, NJ.

Furth, H. G. 1969. *Piaget and knowledge: theoretical foundations*. Prentice-Hall, Englewood Cliffs, NJ.

Gilbert, J. K. and Watts, D. M. 1983. 'Concepts, misconceptions and alternative conceptions.' *Studies in Science Education*, 10: 61–98.

Gruber, H. E and Voneche, J. J. 1977. *The essential Piaget*. Routledge and Kegan Paul, London.

Hall, V. C. and Kaye, D. B. 1978. 'The necessity of logical necessity in Piaget's theory.' In Siegel, L. S. and Brainerd, C. J. (eds) *Alternatives to Piaget*. Academic Press, New York.

Inhelder, B. 1962. 'Some aspects of Piaget's genetic approach to cognition.' In *Thought and the Young Child*, monograph of the Society of Research in Child Development. Serial no. 83, vol. 27, no. 2, pp. 19–40.

Karmiloff-Smith, A. 1978. In 'Open peer commentary on C. Brainerd's article on cognitive stages.' *Brain and Behavioural Sciences*, 2: 173–213.

Kelly, G. A. 1955. *The psychology of personal constructs*. W. W. Norton, New York.

Mayes, W. 1972. 'Translator's introduction.' In Piaget, J. 1972 *The principles of genetic epistemology*. Routledge and Kegan Paul, London.

Miller, S. A. and Lipps, L. 1973. 'Extinction of conservation and transitivity of weight.' *Journal of Experimental Child Psychology*, 6: 388–402.

Odom, R. D. 1978. 'A perceptual salience account of decalage relations and developmental change.' In Siegel, L. S. and Brainerd, C. J. (eds). *Alternatives to Piaget*. Academic Press, New York.

Olson, D. 1978. In 'Open peer commentary on C. Brainerd's article on cognitive stages.' *Brain and Behavioural Sciences*, 2: 173–213.

Osborne, R. and Wittrock, M. 1985. 'The generative learning model and its implications for science education. *Studies in Science Education*, 12: 59–87.

Piaget, J. 1918. *Recherche*. Le Conforde, Lausanne.

Piaget, J. 1923. *Le langage et la pensée chez l'enfant*. Delachaux et Niestle, Neuchâtel et Paris.

Piaget, J. 1947. *La psychologie de l'intelligence*. A. Colin, Paris.

Piaget, J. 1955. 'Les stades du développement intellectuelle de l'enfant et de l'adolescent.' In *Symposium on 'Le Problème des Stades en Psychologie de l'Enfant.'* Presses Universitaires de France, Paris.

Piaget, J. 1968. *Le structuralisme*. Presses Universitaires de France, Paris.

Piaget, J. 1972a. *The principles of genetic epistemology.* Routledge and Kegan Paul, London.

Piaget, J. 1972b. *Psychology and epistemology: towards a theory of knowledge.* Penguin University Books, London.

Piaget, J. 1974. *Understanding causality.* W. W. Norton, New York.

Piaget, J. 1977. 'Intellectual evolution from adolescence to adulthood.' In Wason, P. C. and Johnson-Laird, P. N. (eds) *Thinking.* Cambridge University Press, Cambridge.

Piaget, J. 1978a. *The development of thought: equilibration of cognitive structures.* Blackwell, London.

Piaget, J. 1978b. *Success and understanding.* Routledge and Kegan Paul, London.

Pope, M. and Gilbert, J. 1983. 'Personal experience and the construction of knowledge in science.' *Science Education,* 67: 193–203.

Schank, R. C. 1982. *Dynamic memory.* Cambridge University Press, Cambridge.

Shayer, M., Kuchemann, D. E. and Wylam, H. 1976. 'The distribution of Piagetian stages of thinking in British middle and secondary school children.' *British Journal of Educational Psychology,* 46: 164–73.

Shayer, M. and Adey, P. 1981. *Towards a science of science teaching.* Heinemann, London.

Siegel, L. S. and Brainerd, C. J. (eds) 1978. *Alternatives to Piaget,* Academic Press, New York.

Chapter 3

Minitheories: a preliminary model for learning science

Guy Claxton

INTRODUCTION

To assume that people's scientific intuitions directly reflect the nature and structure of their prior knowledge – their 'alternative frameworks' – is to be guilty of a gross oversimplification of their psychology. There remains prevalent in the 'alternative frameworks' research the lingering Piagetian notion that an experimenter's questions act as a dipstick with which we can assess the level and nature of someone else's cognition. In developmental psychology it is now widely recognized that this is not so (see, for example, Bryant 1982; Donaldson, Grieve and Pratt 1983). Being a subject in an 'experiment', however informal it may be, is a novel social and cognitive experience, that demands the selection or construction of knowledge and of knowledge-manipulation and expression procedures. What subjects reveal, therefore, is not 'what they know' or 'how they think': we never catch them simply manifesting their prior knowledge. All we see – all we ever *can* see – is their mobilization and application of that knowledge in a situation that embodies an unprecedented question, and in which a unique nexus of opportunities, priorities, abilities, constraints and personal history is present.

Thus, in interpreting what students say and do when asked questions or solving problems about science, we cannot ignore the processes they choose to use. It follows that we cannot ignore either the nature of, or the influences on, the decision-making procedures they employ to make that selection. And at this point we are forced to acknowledge all the personal, social, motivational and emotional factors that form the essential 'ground' from which the 'figure' of a student's intellectual performance emerges. What we are all too keen to interpret as a sturdy 'alternative framework' need be no more than the ephemeral reflection of a purpose-built and tentative attempt to cope with the social and intellectual demands of the present moment. Indeed, as I shall argue in detail, the robustness of a student's performance is itself a variable quality that depends on the stance and strategies they have decided to adopt.

This problem has been occasionally raised. For example Driver, Guesne and Tiberghien (1985) argue, on the basis of an extensive review of 'alternative conceptions' research, that

> one of the problems involved in investigating children's ideas is devising ways of probing thinking which enables [sic] us to sort out the status of the responses we obtain; distinguish between these ideas which play a significant part in the thinking of individual or group and these which are generated in an ad hoc way in response to social pressure to produce an answer in an interview or test situation.
>
> (Driver, Guesne and Tiberghien 1985)

This worry is made all the more real by the work of Hughes and Grieve (1983), who have shown that children will readily give adults answers to bizarre or nonsensical questions such as 'which is heavier: yellow or red?' Clearly these answers cannot exhibit stable knowledge structures, but rather show the ways in which obliging children will fabricate responses.

The alternative conceptions researchers have seemed to assume that if you get the same kind of answer from a number of different children, then this problem can safely be ignored: from a commonalty of response they think it safe to infer the stability or reality of each individual framework. But unfortunately this will not do. We can just as well infer that children tend to *manufacture* responses in the same kind of way, in the heat of the moment. We could even suppose that they have similar implicit theories, and that similar coping strategies generate from these implicit theories similar kinds of answers, without it following that the answers themselves reflect the underlying theories in any direct, or easily interpretable, way.

What is needed, therefore, is a conceptual framework within which to explore the 'alternative conceptions' data, that takes this difficulty into account. In particular a useful approach must be a dynamic rather than a static one. It should show how knowledge is mobilized and used in order to meet on-line demands. And it should show (or at least make some suggestion about) how knowledge is itself developed and modified in the process of trying to answer novel questions. It is the intention of this chapter to map out such an approach using the central notions of 'minitheories' and 'learning strategies'.

EVERYDAY KNOWLEDGE

The ideas that young people have picked up about the world seem to have a number of fairly obvious characteristics. First, they are piecemeal. Instead of the one big supertheory that the research scientist aspires to, in which many seemingly disparate phenomena can be brought under the same abstract, explanatory umbrella, the everyday 'theories' of young people are fragmentary and local. Many 'minitheories' are developed in response to particular experiences, predicaments or needs, that work well enough on their home ground, but whose limits of applicability – what Kelly (1955) called a theory's 'range of convenience' – may be rather circumscribed.

What strikes us about much everyday behaviour, in school and out, is the situation-specificity of ways of acting or thinking (Lave 1988). Apocryphal stories abound of people who can add up at the bowling alley but not in the classroom, who can remember copious details about cricket matches but not about history, or who are kind and generous out of school, but surly and withdrawn within it. Both what we are able to do, and how we communicate and think, seem to be dependent very often on the situation. Young people in particular can display wild inconsistencies when they (frequently for no apparent reason) tip over from one minitheory to another. For example, someone might have quite different ideas about wood (in the context of plant growth) and wood (in the context of fuel) (Barker and Carr 1989). The way they use the notion of 'energy' might be entirely different in the two cases. Yet these inconsistencies mostly go unremarked, or, when noticed, are certainly not treated as a problem. 'Oh, that's *different*', we say, and sail on (Kirkwood, Carr and McChesney 1986).

The second feature of our everyday knowledge seems to be that these minitheories contain a whole package, not just of content but of process (Claxton 1990). In the anecdotal examples above it is apparently rather general cognitive operations – recall, manipulation, problem-solving, speech – that vary from occasion to occasion. It remains an open (and contentious) question whether there are cognitive skills that are genuinely multipurpose and content-free (see Fodor 1983), but certainly much of the time the way knowledge is stored and used seems to depend on the circumstances.

What are the typical contents of one of these packages? When a particular minitheory is accessed and 'loaded', like a computer programme, what functions of the person can be thereby set? First, various *predictions* can be made about what follows what within the scenario. These predictions may not surface as such, but rather in the form of intuition, impulse, apprehension and response. The programme makes available a specific set of habits whose effects can be anticipated. Secondly, these may be associated within the domain with a characteristic set of *attitudes*, such as 'I am useless at this', 'I like this person' or 'school is boring'. These determine the stance we take towards events, and the kinds of judgements, opinions and moods we are likely to produce. Thirdly, there are forms of *description* – ways of conversing about the domain, the kinds of words used and explanations offered, and so on. Finally, the minitheory may contain sub-routines that influence our very *experience*, the way we perceive what is going on, in addition to the way we react to it. The food tasted fine until someone said it was puppy – and now even the smell of it is nauseating. It is one of the commonplaces of psychology that our perceptions do not precede our interpretations: they *are* our interpretations (e. g. Gregory, 1966). The five aspects of a minitheoretic package – the Situations to which it applies, together with the Predictions, Attitudes, Descriptions and Experiences that it produces – form the convenient acronym SPADE. This model is elaborated and justified in my book *Educating the Inquiring Mind* (Claxton 1991).

METAPHORS FOR LEARNING

The question we wish to approach is: how does this patchwork landscape of special-purpose programmes react to novel events? What techniques do people possess for coming to terms with or mastering phenomena that, when they first arise, are not covered by any existing SPADE? And specifically we wish to answer this question with respect to that particular domain of novelty called *school science*. What strategies are available to the young learners, and what determines which one they select? But before we can tackle these questions head-on, we need to equip ourselves with two simple metaphors for thinking about the problem. One is an image for the structure of our knowledge landscape; the other for its activation and utilization.

You can think of minitheories as amoebae, masses of them, living on a plane surface that represents our experience. The 'body' of the amoeba represents so to speak its capacity – its contents, and the operations of prediction, action, etc., that it makes available. How big an amoeba reflects how *general* it is: the extent of the domain of experience to which it applies. And its location on the surface refers to the nature of that domain. Each amoeba 'lies on top of' that domain of experience to which it is currently assumed to be applicable. Within this picture, learning can occur in a variety of ways. The capability of an existing amoeba can be altered, so that attitudes or reactions in that domain change. Or an amoeba can shift its ground, so that the circumstances to which it applies, its 'range of convenience' expands or contracts. Or a new amoeba can be 'born' – a new minitheory constructed to account for phenomena in a new domain.

Elsewhere (Claxton 1990) I have elaborated this particular metaphor further. One particular modification we might note here is to introduce fuzzy boundaries. The amoeba image presupposes that there is a clear distinction between where a knowledge-module applies and where it does not: the boundaries of a real-life amoeba are (relatively) well defined. But our knowledge is often not like that. We are frequently uncertain about whether this is a 'this' sort of situation or a 'that' sort. (How should I behave in a group interview? *Is* it an 'interview'? To whom do I address my remarks? Should I try to be super-critical, or pleasant and relaxed?) Thus it often makes more sense to think of a minitheory as shading off into uncertainty or ambiguity, *except* in those areas where we have good reason to suppose that it doesn't apply (because we have been told, or tried it out). This refinement enables us to talk of another form of learning which involves *sharpening* the boundary, rather than *shifting* it. A good deal of our everyday learning involves the automatic adjustment of the limits of applicability of what we know, by sharpening and shifting (Rumelhart and Norman 1978).

The complementary metaphor involves imagining a cross between a jukebox and a microcomputer. Our minitheories are now the discs that are stored, and they are filed according to a specification of the situations in which they are to be 'played'. When we are in familiar territory, an event comes along, we punch the buttons E7, and the appropriate disc is loaded and run. The package of attitudes, knowledge and reactions that we have learnt to use 'in physics lessons' or 'tea-time' or 'playing snooker' is activated, and then what happens within each scenario is interpreted in terms of that 'programme'. *What we learn from an event thus depends on which particular stance we happen to have adopted for dealing with it, or the particular programme that happens to be running already when it occurs.* If the same learning opportunity arises within two different scenarios, the way we react to it may therefore be quite different. For example, the same information might be reacted to as 'interesting and thought-provoking' if it appears in a *Horizon* programme we are idly watching on TV at home; but as 'boring old biology' when presented by a teacher at school. And, what is more, the learning that accrues from watching *Horizon*, because it is recorded on the 'Horizon' disc, may not be activated and retrieved later when the 'school' or 'examination' disc is running.

In a useful extension of this image, we might imagine that the jukebox has a special collection of records that are selected by experiences called 'Quite Unusual'. When we do not have a minitheory that can be called up, with a fair degree of confidence, to deal with the situation, we can switch in one of these special-purpose 'learning strategies'. These strategies are of different sorts (Claxton 1984, 1990), but we might suppose that some of them are designed to get more information by exploring or investigating the phenomenon, while other, complementary ones, can be used to generate good guesses or working hypotheses about how we might tackle it. When we are in such a learning mode we are not *committed* to our responses and points of view, but rather treat them experimentally, being attentive to their outcomes, whether anticipated or not, constantly looking to see whether this approach helps us to achieve comprehension and mastery or not.

Both these models emphasize, as a crucial aspect of our knowledge, the specification that is always attached to it of the circumstances in which it is to be used. Amoebae do this with the ideas of location and boundaries; the jukebox does it with the buttons that have to be pushed before any record is selected. We need now to be a little more precise about what we mean by 'circumstances'. Obviously we are referring to the perceptual features of the current situation: but we need to include the perceived *demand characteristics* of the situation as well. To make a selection in a jukebox, you commonly have to press a combination of buttons – say a letter and a digit.

We might say that the letters correspond to specifications of the situation *as it is*. We look out, decide what sort of situation this is, and press E, let us say. But we also need to specify what we want to achieve, and in what way; what resources we have available and what possible risks we must avoid; what constraints are placed on us, and how important it is that different outcomes are achieved. Only when we have computed this second part of the specification can we go ahead and press 7, say, and make our selection. No selection can be made unless one of each kind of button is pushed – cue *and* goal, possibility *and* desirability, antecedent *and* intended consequence. (See Allport (1980) for the psychological background to this point.) As we shall see, this second part of the specification is particularly crucial when we are confronted with a *learning* event. Whether we choose to engage with it or not, and if so how, and to what level, are decisions that critically determine both the attitude that a pupil (or anyone else) takes to the event, and the learning outcome.

One important part of the 'goal' specification concerns the kind of performance that is anticipated. What is learnt is influenced by the learners' expectations, at the time of learning, of the manner in which they will eventually be required to demonstrate what they know. If the learner is 'set' to be learning for a traditional, written examination, she will take something different away from a lesson than the learner who is principally interested in building her own cloud-chamber. The intent to acquire an intuitive mastery of X will extract a certain learning from an event; aiming at the ability to discuss X critically will have a different effect.

A learner's success in learning in a particular mode (rational-analytic, perhaps, as against intuitive-spontaneous) thus depends not on some hypothetical general ability, but on whether they have, in the repertoire of learning styles and strategies they bring with them, an existing programme that generates the desired kind of outcome. This is of some relevance in the science lesson. Science teaching not only has a particular subject-matter, about which, as we know, children have all kinds of preconceptions; it has a particular 'medium' that values or requires learning outcomes of certain kinds, and rejects others. Children may have much knowledge about the physical world, but it is embedded, often, within an entirely different set of ways of expressing it, and purposes which it was learnt in order to achieve.

GUT, LAY AND SCHOOL SCIENCE

As a useful (though limited) approximation, we might group the minitheories that a child deals with in school into three clusters, which we might call 'gut science', 'lay science' and 'school science'. (In addition, we might note a fourth cluster, 'scientist's science', of which both school children and school teachers are largely ignorant, but which seeps into schools, over time and in a simplified form, through textbooks and the syllabuses set by the public examination boards.)

Let us illustrate these types of knowledge from the general area of dynamics. (I am grateful to the late Roger Osborne for permission to use sections of Osborne (1984) here, where he elaborates on an earlier, unpublished paper of mine in which I explore these ideas.)

Gut dynamics

Einstein is reputed to have stated that even a physicist learns half his or her physics by the age of three. Much of this is dynamics, and it is largely 'gut dynamics'. Through trial and error this learning occurs in the home and is based on direct experience rather than language. The active efforts made at a young age to comprehend the world enable children to make predictions about what will happen, for example, to an object thrown from the high chair or kicked along the kitchen floor. Gut dynamics is about the tangible world and influences motor skills and perception.

The collection of minitheories constituting 'gut dynamics' tend to be unarticulated and not necessarily conscious. Rather they are shown in a person's spontaneous reactions and intuitive judgements and tested against 'does it work?' and 'is it useful?' 'Gut dynamics' provides the individual with the ability to interact physically with the world whether it be for work or pleasure. Sport is largely played using 'gut dynamics'. Examples of 'gut dynamics' for many people would include their experience that heavy things fall fastest, things need a push to get them going, you have to keep pushing to keep things moving, and rubbing causes things to heat up and wear out. (See Chapter 7 in this volume.)

Language is very much second place to experience in terms of gut dynamics. Where it is involved it either recounts physical facts (e.g. 'hit the ball closer to the top of the bat and it will not jar so much'), or it encapsulates generalizations such as those used as illustrations in the preceding paragraph.

Lay dynamics

Unlike gut dynamics, which is based on direct experience, lay dynamics is based in the form and content of the language the child grows up to speak and the accounts and images of experiences conveyed by those with whom the child comes in contact, the media, and the authors of the books he or she reads. These ideas may be accepted passively, sight-unseen, and gradually, so that the child may grow up not even realizing that they are there. The wealth of visual and verbal information that the average child receives – for example from *Star Wars* and *Space Invaders* involving force fields and time warps, NASA pictures and *The Paul Daniels Show* involving weightless astronauts and feats of magic – provides him or her with a mixed-up store of fact, fantasy and belief related to dynamics. This store is quite extensive even before the child reaches school and may be held quite independently of 'gut dynamics' and not related to it.

Examples of lay dynamics would be the idea that 'astronauts are weightless in the space shuttle' (NASA pictures); 'oil reduces friction and hence reduces wear' (TV advertisement); 'space travel requires powerful engines at all times' (*Star Wars*); 'the force of the explosion can be seen in the damage' (TV News); and 'the force field kept him out' (science fiction story).

Lay dynamics provides an individual with knowledge that can be used to provide entertaining conversation and is of practical use in so far as its maxims are not 'old wives tales'.

School dynamics

In the school setting dynamics is primarily Newtonian dynamics. It appears to many beginning physics students to apply to a strange world of frictionless slopes and pulleys, uniform gravitational fields and point masses, and rigid light rods and massless strings of uniform tension. Even in the laboratory, air tracks, air tables and air pulleys imply an attempt to demonstrate some fantasy world set apart from reality.

While gut dynamics builds on experience and lay dynamics builds on vernacular language, school dynamics has a linguistic and mathematical superstructure of its own. Sometimes it is counter-intuitive; for example, a car moving at a steady speed around a circular path *is* accelerating and this point is not open to question. The knowledge is articulated, consciously and deliberately transmitted and received, and, if understood, forms a highly coherent set of ideas. A variable amount of active and self-directed experimentation is possible, but the experiences often tend to show the limitations of the idealized theories rather than providing supporting evidence for their viability. Examples of school physicists' dynamics to contrast with the gut and lay dynamics discussed earlier include: things accelerate towards the earth at 9.8 ms^{-2}, an object moving at a steady speed has no net force acting on it, and the force of gravity acts on the astronaut in orbit accelerating him or her toward the centre of the earth.

Children's 'gut science' has been acquired through experience and is expressed in unreflective, unpremeditated action. Their 'lay science' has been acquired through informal, but mediated, sources such as family, friends and the media, and commonly comprises a store of 'amazing facts' that can be traded and discussed with others as a means of exploring or establishing friendships. In neither of these domains are the 'school science' demands – for rationality, logic, coherence, rigour, precision and explanation in terms of a limited set of agreed, technical concepts – of much importance. What is important about 'gut science' is that it *works:* it stops you getting burnt and falling over. It doesn't matter at all how piecemeal or situation-specific the minitheories are, or how well you are able to articulate them. What is important about 'lay science' is that it gives you practical advice about when to plant the radishes, or how to load your camera; and that it gives you intrinsically interesting things to talk about. Lay science works well when it enables you to have an animated conversation in the playground. It doesn't matter whether your understanding is accurate, or whether you could write it down, or whether there is an inherent contradiction between what you are saying now and what you said yesterday. But to be good at school science you have to be good at acquiring, manipulating and transacting knowledge in a very particular kind of way, that for some children is initially quite alien, and persistently hard to grasp.

LEARNING STRATEGIES

Let us look in a little more detail at how and when learning happens. On the minitheory view, there are two main types of learning: that which involves modification of an existing module, and that which involves the creation of a new, purpose-built minitheory to deal with a new domain of experience.

Of the modification type, there are again two sorts: learning that produces a change in the content of a record, and learning that involves rewriting the 'heading' (Morton, Bekerian and Hammersley 1985) of the record so that it is assigned to, and activated by, a modified domain of experience. As we saw before, this kind of learning may also result in a sharpening of the boundary of a minitheory, so that its sphere of influence becomes delimited more precisely.

We can visualize these kinds of learning in terms of our amoeba analogy (with the embellishment that these amoebae fade away at the edges rather than ending abruptly). The amoebic landscape, seen from 'above', looks haphazard. There are areas of experience that are entirely covered by a patchwork of theories; there are areas that are partially covered, with 'holes' in them corresponding to experiences that are not currently within the purview of any minitheory; there are places where the theories 'overlap', thus offering two different points of view about the same range of events; there are little minitheories, big minitheories and metaminitheories that subsume or enclose a variety of more specific packages.

Imagine a phenomenon that occurs on the margins of an existing minitheory: that is to say, it is adjacent to it, but there remains some uncertainty about whether this minitheory actually applies or not. The most obvious approach is to act on the basis of this minitheory, and see what happens. The amoeba tentatively pushes out a pseudopodium to 'engulf' the new experience, so that predictions, actions, etc., become available. If the predictions turn out to be accurate, and the actions therefore successful, the boundary will remain extended so that it now includes or subsumes this new domain. If the application of this process-package is not successful (you assumed that the milk wouldn't boil over but it did; you treated this teacher like other teachers, but she responded quite differently), then the boundary is withdrawn, sharpened and clarified, thus reducing the risk of making the same mistake again. Having done this, though, the experience itself remains unaccounted for: it now lies in a very definite hole.

If there is another adjacent minitheory that can be extended to cover this case, then that is likely to happen. Its application will probably be somewhat tentative, however, following the failure of what had been assumed, *a priori*, to be a better candidate for the job. But if now there is no perceptually related minitheory that could be tried with any degree of confidence at all, then it may become necessary to establish a new package to deal with this puzzling domain.

There is a number of strategies that a learner may possess for generating new minitheories, of which imitation, questioning and analogizing are three of the most important. If you do not know how to act with respect to a new situation, you can watch how someone else deals with it. Or you can ask someone. Or you can find an existing minitheory that may serve as a template from which to design the new one, but which suggests itself not on the basis of perceptual or motivational characteristics, but by virtue of structural or relational similarities. Such a minitheory is an analogy.

STRATEGIES FOR LEARNING SCHOOL SCIENCE

Accretion, integration and creation

We can now summarize some of the considerations we have reviewed, and see how they apply in the particular case of learning school science. First, children come to many topics already equipped with conceptions, attitudes and habits that are potentially relevant. Second, these prior learnings can be grouped roughly into 'gut science', which operates predominantly within the domains of perception, spontaneous action and intuition, and 'lay science', which manifests in informal expressions of knowledge and belief about nature. Third, this knowledge is in general piecemeal and frequently tacit. Fourth, these knowledge/skill/attitude packages, or minitheories, are located with respect to the occasions, purposes and response modes to which they are currently held to be applicable. Fifth, there is a special group of minitheories that are activated in the face of significant strangeness. These fall into two main categories, of which the first are strategies for the elaboration of existing minitheories, and the second are strategies for the creation of new minitheories.

Let us now explore the science students' options in a little more detail. The basic decision, given that a student has committed him/herself (even weakly) to learning *something*, is whether to treat this new knowledge as an extension or elaboration of pre-existing gut and lay knowledge, or whether to start a fresh minitheory. It appears that this is a decision that it is easy to get 'wrong', in the sense that the ensuing strategies turn out not to deliver the anticipated outcomes. One example, not uncommon, is the learner who hopes to get by, to do enough to get an exam pass and keep out of trouble, and who elects to do so by trying to stick the new knowledge, concepts, terms and styles of knowledge-manipulation onto their existing minitheories about heat, light, nutrition or whatever it may be. There are unanticipated hazards with this, however. Although many of the key terms are familiar (work, force, speed, compound, solution, etc.) they are now given new, counter-intuitive meanings that are easily lost or confused *if they are not stored and used in a separate domain.* Children who activate gut and lay science in a science lesson are in danger of flooding their minds with myths, usages and associations that are actually inappropriate and distracting. In the context of school science such associations are mere 'noise', a nuisance to student and teacher alike. School science tries to create a coherent, integrated conceptual structure, and it is a mistake to site it on top of the fragmented and shifting quicksand of everyday experience and discourse. The student who successfully masters school science (from the point of view of passing exams) has mastered a logical, linguistic and investigational style that is foreign to the domains of gut and lay knowledge, where reasoning needs to be neither explicit nor coherent. The attempt to embed school science in this amorphous framework is misguided even if it sticks, because the processes for using and displaying knowledge that already pervade this package are not those that will generate good grades in public examinations. The style, at the very least, will be too loose-weave and chatty for the examiners' taste. (Exactly the same problem is experienced by many Masters' students in education as they try to grapple with the social sciences. Either they adopt an inept and stiff scholasticism, or they all too frequently lapse into woolliness and anecdote. Only a few such students manage to acquire a style that straddles both relevance and rigour. And their exam papers reflect it.)

One of the problems of using prior conceptions as a basis for learning is illustrated by the old horticultural analogy for education. Branches divide into twigs, and twigs grow leaves as a result of an internal need of the whole tree for nutrition. And the *pattern* that the tree grows into is influenced by an interaction of this tendency with external influences and constraints like the proximity of other trees, the direction of the sun and the prevailing wind, and so on. If the inner impulse toward growth is absent (or blocked in a particular area), the only possibility for 'quasi-learning' is to stick twigs on with glue and tie leaves on with cotton. A kind of teaching that attempts to do this is literally hard graft. And a learning strategy that aims for this sort of accretion or aggregation of particles of information around a pre-existing minitheory is sub-optimal, because it achieves accumulation without functional integration. Such knowledge is fragmentary, hard to retrieve and therefore unlikely to be 'called' by signals of its potential relevance. It is, we might say, merely a heap of granular 'microtheories'.

Nevertheless accretion is one possibility that is open to a science student as a kind of falling-between-the-stools of 'elaboration-and-integration' of an existing minitheory, on the one hand; and setting up of a new module – planting a *new* tree – on the other. In the repertoire of learning strategies, accretion represents Cognition's Last Stand, to be used only when understanding is prevented (by shortage of time or the difficulty of the information); where piecemeal recapitulation of undigested subject-matter is possibly sufficient to achieve the goal; and where its use is sanctioned and even promoted by the ethos and rhetoric of the milieu. To the extent that these three conditions obtain in school, as they often do, students are likely to adopt accretion as a major strategy, but they are then vulnerable to discovering that it fails to live up to its promise, or to deliver the goods.

At the other extreme, there exists the possibility for formal scientific knowledge to effect a radical transformation in understanding that supplants, transcends or embraces pre-existing gut and lay conceptions. In common with accretion, this kind of learning can be seen as operating with, and on, a prior minitheory, though of course the outcome is very different, comprising a broadening of perception, an enhancement of competence and a deepening of understanding. The premises of a minitheory are changed, so that a pervasive shift in attitude towards phenomena within that domain occurs. Some of the 'alternative frameworks' literature seems to advocate this sort of learning, but while drawing overdue attention to the benefits of such united and evolutionary forms of learning, it has ignored or underestimated the costs, as we shall see in a moment.

The other type of strategy we can consider here is the creation of a new minitheory. In the science classroom the pivot around which the novel module comes to develop is provided, most frequently, either by definitions or analogies. In physics the hydraulic metaphor of electricity, and the elastic billiard ball metaphor that underlies the kinetic theory of gases are two key analogies, while in basic mechanics the verbal and algebraic definitions embedded in Newton's laws of motion are likewise pivotal. Representational frameworks are set up 'in space' as it were, and are subsequently or concurrently mapped onto experimental evidence that is mostly reported to, and sometimes generated by, students. The intention is that larger patterns of coherent and structured understanding will build up around these core images or formulations.

In addition, before we move on to the next section, we consider one other very important class of strategies in the science students' repertoire of ways to deal with lessons: those that enable them to avoid, deny, or escape from the learning opportunities presented. The option for a child not to learn is an ever-present one, and, as we shall see in a moment, an essential influence on the developing cognitive and emotional stance towards science.

A cost–benefit analysis of deciding how to learn

The question that faces science students, not once but over a period of time, is how to approach the learning task in such a way that the learning that accrues is sufficient and appropriate to their own needs, and can be successfully undertaken given their present strategies and resources. Let us look at some of the considerations that need to be weighed up. They include at least the following: What am I studying science for? Do I want to get by with as little trouble as possible? Do I sincerely want to pass exams? Is there a reasonable chance (as assessed by myself and others) that I can do well if I try? Do I judge (largely from the messages emanating from the teacher) that I need to *understand* what I am doing, or will I be required to *recapitulate* knowledge with only minimal manipulations? Do I have out-of-school knowledge, skills or interests that seem to be relevant and helpful? How good am I, on past evidence, at remembering things I don't understand? Do I find difficult ideas challenging or threatening? Does it look as if the amount of time required for me to do well will crowd out other pleasant and necessary activities from my life? And then there are other, more social, considerations that affect the way the task is tackled. Do I like the teacher? Do I trust her? Do I want to please her? Who are the other students? What is the class ethos? Will I be laughed at for being a 'swot'? Are there enough like me to provide safety-in-numbers against this disdain? Do I want to be liked by people who are impressed by bravado and defiance? Is it possible to reconcile working hard *and* being seen as a rebel? Are there any attitudes, positive or negative, at home, concerning my choice of science? Are there any incipient signs that following my interest in science will take me away from my roots? Will I enjoy, or can I put up with, being a girl in a predominantly man's world? What is my image of a 'scientist', and how do I feel about being seen in that light?

These considerations are answered, weighted and integrated for the most part tacitly. But the complex computation happens nonetheless and issues in policy decisions about the espoused goals, amount of effort, learning styles and attitudes, to be adopted to deal with physics or chemistry or biology. Over time a cognitive, emotional, motivational and social stance towards science is evolved. A programme is compiled that is loaded and run every time the learner steps through the laboratory door. For some children this will be a minor modification of the general 'school' programme, simply setting values of relevant parameters to do with the particular teacher's questioning style, where to sit to avoid being picked on, and what special means (gas taps, squeezy bottles) are available for having fun. For others, on the whole the more successful or the more motivated, the science package will be purpose-built to respond to the specific demands of the situation.

But within the context created by these long-term decisions, choices remain. When confronted with a demonstration or a theory that appears, or is asserted, to be in conflict with a student's prior expectations, he or she has several options as to how to react, and which is selected depends on an intuitive though rational decision about the pros and cons of each. We can now give a simplified illustration of this process. Let us consider the four responses of *declining* the invitation to learn; *accreting* the new information in a way that neither acknowledges nor resolves the conflict; *creating* a new minitheory, so that the conflicting information is deemed to be 'about something different' (thereby treating the conflict as only apparent); and *restructuring* the existing gut/lay minitheory so that a full understanding and resolution of the conflict results.

The benefits of declining are that the risk of failing and the effort of trying are removed; that alternative non-learning strategies with attractive pay-offs (like mucking about) can be activated instead; that hostility to the teacher can be released through disdain for the subject matter ('it's stupid'); and that generally security and predictability are preserved. The cost is continued incompetence, and the forfeiting of either integrated understanding or exam success.

The benefits of accreting are that sufficient facts and detail may be accumulated to keep the teacher happy and maintain invisibility, while not having to think; and that, in the event of failure one can claim in mitigation that 'I tried'. The cost is the inability to use the information on occasions and for purposes that do not exactly coincide with those that provided the context of acquisition. The knowledge is as functionally inert as a heap of cogs.

The benefits of creating are that the conflict is removed without gut/lay understandings being disturbed, the embarrassing information being transported to its own special 'township'; and that knowledge in the new domain does not become diluted or contaminated by inappropriate out-of-school connotations. The cost is again a lack of impact of the knowledge on everyday life (the policy of apartheid preventing the two cultures learning about and from each other).

Finally, the benefit of restructuring is an understanding of the conflict, and integration of the two domains into a higher-order theory. Such an understanding straddles the intellectual and the everyday and allows each to inform and enrich the other. The costs can be severe, however. It may take a long time, and/or considerable research, experimentation and thought, to achieve. This investment may actually be counterproductive in terms of more mundane goals like passing tests. A student who really gets her teeth into something may be perceived by a teacher – despite her rhetoric – as a pest, draining the teacher's valuable time with what seem like zany or irrelevant questions. There may be costs in terms of peer-group or family approval, and so on. To undertake this sort of learning, in which previous certainty is called into question and if necessary abandoned or reordered, a student must need to or want to quite badly. In school this kind of commitment to deep and coherent understanding is rather rare, and is not fostered by the demands of exam syllabuses and the fragmented nature of the standard timetable.

The decision-making process becomes more complicated still when we feed into it the other relevant considerations that were illustrated at the start of this section. The decision to learn in one way or another (or not to learn at all) *depends on situational demands, situational constraints, personal goals* and *personal resources.* Of each learning strategy we must ask: is it likely to deliver the kind of answer I am being asked to come up with? (Does it generate the requisite response mode, or depth of understanding?) Secondly: am I free to pursue it? (Am I likely to get the amount of time or support that this strategy requires?) Thirdly: is there a good chance that it will solve a problem that I care about? (How will the outcome fit with my priorities?) And fourthly: am I skilled enough at using this strategy, or relevant substrategies such as metaphorical or logical thinking, or mnemonics? (Do I have the necessary contacts, or techniques, or patience?) This last consideration – the evaluation of personal resources – obviously calls for as much metacognitive back-up to the learning processes as possible. Overall, therefore, if a strategy or strategy-type is at a low level of competence, or does not offer learning of the required type, or is debarred by situational constraints or lack of requisite resources, then the cost-benefit assessment of that strategy will be low and it is unlikely to be selected.

CONCLUSION

The alternative conceptions research has been primarily concerned to elicit and represent the *content* of schoolchildren's pre-existing knowledge about science. But this approach, while a necessary starting point, is of limited utility, for two main reasons. First, we can never be sure that particular tests, such as those used by alternative conceptions researchers, which are unprecedented in the child's experience, are revealing long-term stable features of what the child knows or thinks. Establishing content through experimental enquiry is inherently problematic. Secondly, the content approach lacks any coherent model of the *structure* of knowledge representation and the *dynamics* of knowledge change.

For both these reasons the content-focused approach is not likely to generate powerful recommendations concerning pedagogy. The main purpose of this chapter has been to present and explore a complementary point of view that highlights structure and structural change. Minitheories are theoretical entities, that are to be evaluated in terms of their ability to help us generate explanations, and formulate interesting questions, about learning in the context of school science. They are, so to speak, moulds, made of a material that has certain intrinsic properties, which can be filled with a whole range of different contents. It is my present contention that it is these intrinsic properties of organization and deformation that largely determine how learning occurs, and therefore how it is to be facilitated. It is interesting and important to have some inkling of what children think. But in planning better teaching, it is at least as important to be able to represent to ourselves how thinking changes, and what implicit options a learner has for dealing with novelty in different ways.

In one of the simple cases we have looked at, students may choose to extend an existing minitheory to cover the novel case. Whether this extension generates the 'right' answer depends on which mini-theory happens to have been selected, and that depends on many factors, transient and trivial as well as long-term and structural. It is also possible for a selected minitheory to generate the 'right' answer to a specific question, where it would have given 'wrong' answers to any one of a dozen other questions that might have been asked. Thus in this case students do not 'have' an alternative (or even a mis-) conception; they *make* an application that may or may not turn out to be an appropriate one. It is *our* misconception if we assume, from one or two 'wrong' answers, that a student 'holds' an alternative theory that is in 'conflict' with the received theory of textbook science, which is resolved when one 'wins' and the other 'loses'. It is at least a start towards a more sensitive and accurate interpretation of the situation if we construe it more as the amicable negotiation of the appropriate limits or boundaries of both theories, each of which has an as yet ill-specified domain of situations and tasks to which it is legitimately and successfully applied. The students' classroom performance and apparent difficulties are symptomatic of the procedures they have chosen, rightly or wrongly, in order to work towards a negotiated settlement. This choice is influenced quite as much by how they feel about the subject and the teacher, their image of themselves, and what they want to do with their lives, as it is by what they know about nature. This fact may be inconvenient for a teacher who wishes to have a clear-cut, articulated recipe for how to teach. But progress will not be made by ignoring truths that are a nuisance.

REFERENCES

Allport, D. A. 1980. 'Patterns and actions: cognitive mechanisms are content-specific.' In Claxton, G. L. (ed.) *Cognitive psychology: new directions.* Routledge and Kegan Paul, London.

Barker, M. and Carr, M. D. 1989. 'Photosynthesis: can our pupils see the wood for the trees?' *Journal of Biological Education,* 23(1): 41–4.

Bryant, P. E. 1982. 'The role of conflict and agreement between intellectual strategies in children's ideas about measurement.' *British Journal of Psychology,* 73: 243–51.

Claxton, G. L. 1984. *Live and learn: an introduction to the psychology of growth and change in everyday life.* Harper and Row, London.

Claxton, G. L. 1990. *Teaching to learn: a direction for education.* Cassell, London.

Claxton, G. L. 1991. *Educating the inquiring mind: the challenge for science education.* Harvester/Wheatsheaf, Hemel Hempstead.

Donaldson, M., Grieve, R. and Pratt, C. (eds) 1983. *Early childhood development and education.* Blackwell, Oxford.

Driver, R., Guesne, E. and Tiberghien, A. 1985. *Children's ideas in science.* Open University Press, Milton Keynes.

Fodor, J. A. 1983. *The modularity of mind.* MIT Press, Cambridge, Mass.

Gregory, R. 1966. *Eye and brain.* Weidenfeld and Nicolson, London.

Hughes, M. and Grieve, R. 1983. 'On asking children bizarre questions.' In Donaldson, M., Grieve, R. and Pratt, C. (eds) *Early childhood development and education.* Blackwell, Oxford, pp. 104–14.

Kelly, G. 1955. *The psychology of personal constructs.* Norton, New York.

Kirkwood, V. M., Carr, M. D. and McChesney, J. 1986. 'LISP (Energy) – some preliminary findings.' *Research in Science Education,* 16: 175–83.

Lave, J. 1988. *Cognition in practice: mind, mathematics and culture in everyday life.* Cambridge University Press, Cambridge.

Morton, J., Hammersley, R. H. and Bekerian, D. A. 1985. 'Headed records: a model for memory and its failures.' *Cognition,* 20: 1–23.

Osborne, R. 1984. 'Children's dynamics.' *The Physics Teacher,* 22: 1–23.

Rumelhart, D. E. and Norman, D. A. 1978. 'Accretion, tuning and restructuring: three modes of learning.' In Cotton, W. J. and Klatzky, R. (eds) *Semantic factors in cognition.* Lawrence Erlbaum, Hillsdale, NJ, pp. 37–54.

Chapter 4

An alternative conception: representing representations

Terry Russell

> In psychology as in physics there are no pure 'facts' if by 'facts' are meant phenomena presented nakedly to the mind by nature itself, independent respectively of hypotheses by means of which the mind examines them, of principles governing the interpretation of experience, and of the systematic framework of existing judgments into which the observer pigeon-holes every new observation.
>
> (Jean Piaget: Introduction to *The Child's Conception of the World*)

INTRODUCTION

'Alternative conceptions' research activity and debate appear to hold together as a conglomeration with a shared interest in content (the concepts or subject matter of science) and expected utility (the promotion of more effective learning). Much of the research undertaken relates to the understanding by older children of objects and events in the physical world, often within the subject- or content-based divisions demarcated by the local secondary science syllabus. More recently, research attention has extended to the elementary years (see, for example, Osborne *et al.* 1990, 1991; Russell *et al.* 1991). In the desire for a more scientifically literate community, Ausubel's exhortation that attention must be paid to 'preconceptions' before attempting intervention is being seriously heeded. This movement suggests an increasing sensitivity to the outcomes of science instruction and is to be welcomed. Yet the content-centred direction that research has tended to follow might be construed as evidence that the necessity for a broadly based and pupil-centred philosophy is not always a fundamental assumption. A common view is that alternative conceptions are rather embarrassing ideas conceived the wrong side of the blackboard. There are few explicit or common assumptions concerning psychological development or genetic epistemology evident in the various studies which cluster around this research area; theory-related research tends to be a rarity. The content emphasis has permitted a body of research to grow without a clear theoretical underpinning and without the establishment of links with existing research in other areas.

In the spirit of Piaget's words quoted above, a systematic framework will be presented which attempts to encompass the various sources of children's representations of the physical world, and the possible relationships between these sources. Such a framework might permit an observer to 'pigeon-hole' the increasing volume of reports of children's expressed beliefs. Incidentally, but equally important, such a system-atization may also serve to reveal the predilections of researchers as evident in the particular kinds of knowledge representation which they are disposed to investigate. The guiding values behind this paper are that research into children's thinking should be a broadly based and coherent activity that does not lose sight of complex human qualities when engaging with young human subjects. To avoid pedagogical tunnel vision, an overview of the field which is both analytical and integrative will be attempted. Such an ambitious aim implies that the posited relationships can be discussed only in broad terms, with a brief consideration of some promising directions for research.

ALTERNATIVE TO WHAT?

The orientation of the 'alternative conceptions' position tends to be broadly constructivist, but this general viewpoint may generate activity at three different levels of interest: sociological, anthropological and psychological. For the science education community, the constructivist position is predominantly sociological in perspective. Most simply stated, this orientation accepts that significant numbers of pupils may actively develop 'conceptions' or 'frameworks' which are 'alternative'. That is, the construction of meaning or understanding may have personal legitimacy but not universal social currency. This broadly shared view may be the total base upon which research is conducted. It is a view which may represent progress in science education thinking (or even revolution in some quarters), yet there are reasons to doubt its sufficiency.

The anthropological view is much broader, being concerned to investigate not so much differences within a society as differences between cultures. One of the earliest uses of the term 'alternative conceptions' in the literature derives from a cross-cultural orientation (Tulkin and Konner 1973). The kinds of explanations forwarded to explain cross-cultural differences – for example, an ethnological perspective which describes the pressures of natural selection and the survival value of knowledge of animal behaviour to hunter-gatherer communities (Blurton, Jones and Konner 1976) – are likely to be at the level of total life-style, rather than the particular behaviours relevant to specific learning outcomes of interest to educators. Nevertheless, the debt remains to anthropology and cross-cultural psychology for highlighting the importance of the cultural relevance of particular content to cognition (see, for example, Cole and Scribner 1974, and Luria 1976).

The important additional contribution of a psychological perspective to research into children's ideas arises particularly where multiple representations of the same external phenomena exist within the same individual, perhaps serving different purposes, occasionally competing and confusing. All three possibilities of 'alternative' conceptions – cultural, sociological and psychological – must be considered in any attempt to understand the learning outcomes (the mental constructions, concepts or representations) manifested by the learner.

As well as describing learning outcomes as possible multiple-representations, the onus is on the techniques of psychology to describe something of the dynamics of knowledge acquisition, and application. Of particular concern will be the issues of how novel representations are encoded; the factors governing the retrieval and deployment of one representation rather than another competing form, as governed by contextual cues etc.; and, finally, the integration of multiple representations which might be described as the development of an individual's sense of meaning or understanding.

The components of any epistemological model need to be developmental and dynamic, not static descriptions, and this point is a challenge to the sufficiency of Ausubel's recommendation. The value of the advice is not in doubt, as far as it goes, but if the information gained about pupils' knowledge systems consists of content-based descriptive inventories, there will be no obvious guidelines in attempting to move towards a dynamic teaching/learning enterprise. The overriding idea which will be explored in the following sections is that particular content and modes of constructing meaning may interact in a variety of ways, and that given concepts may be acquired most effectively via one of a variety of modes of learning. To use medical terminology, the epidemiology of commonly occurring pupil representations will be of interest; even more valuable will be some insights into aetiology. Crucially, diagnosis must be linked to treatment. The present state of knowledge might be described as one in which the emphasis is on the collection and treatment of symptoms rather than the understanding of the system within which symptoms are produced. The incidence of particular representations may be relevant to establishing priorities in attempting intervention, but insight into the origins of the formation of representations is perhaps more important. Most important of all to instructional intervention will be an understanding of the modes of information processing (encoding) which lead to the storage of particular types of representation.

One of the great strengths of the alternative conceptions movement is that it has not been laboratory-based; though conducted within science subject disciplines for the most part, pupils soon reveal the diversity of sources which contribute to or limit their understanding. This strength also poses difficulties for any attempt at overall modelling, yet to be useful to the task of promoting more effective learning (i.e. the development of mental constructions which map onto the physical world with the best available predictive and explanatory value) the broadest context of learning must be embraced. For example, for all its merits, the Genevan focus on operational structures will be found too narrow to explain many learning outcomes, especially when figurative knowledge and social transmission (with its implicit historical dimension) impinge.

There are, of course, alternative views within the 'alternative conceptions' movement. This need not be a cause for consternation. It is appropriate that theories referring to mental phenomena should be reflexive. Scientists and pupils alike can be regarded as actively constructing models, meaning and knowledge, while the educational research community looks on. Educational researchers select and collect samples of the actions and interactions of the other two groups, actively constructing yet a third set of abstractions: representations of the representations. In the sense that the broad theoretical position predicts 'alternative' views, heterogeneity under its own banner need not be problematic. (In a sense, *all* representation of intangible mental phenomena are candidates for the alternative conceptions label). Nonetheless, a classification which overcomes clear contradictions is desirable.

The discussion which follows will be essentially an analytical exercise within a classification system which permits parts to be related to the whole. This may permit the total complexity and richness of learning outcomes to be handled in manageable research chunks without losing sight of a possible overall picture. In the general unravelling of the epistemological plait, it will be the psychological strands which are of particular concern. One outcome of the exercise might be to permit some perspective on the question as to whether the 'alternative conceptions' orientation implies the adoption of existing psychological systems in a new content area (science education), or whether this research activity is actually enhancing our psychological understanding by promoting novel explanatory systems for new phenomena. The unravelling may be expected to reveal strands which are the proper concern of the applied cognitive developmental psychologist, and other no less important areas which are more appropriately researchable through other disciplines. At that point, the 'alternative' label will have served its purpose.

Certainly, arguments about whether we are dealing with *pre*conceptions, *mis*conceptions or *alternative* conceptions have no particular psychological importance once it is agreed that at all points in development and whatever the culture and social status of the possessor, what we are concerned to know more about is the construction of mental *representations*. That these representations can have alternative forms is from now on taken as axiomatic.

SOURCES OF REPRESENTATIONS

On the basis that the source and mode of information flow is an important consideration, how is the totality of experience to be divided into a meaningful but manageable classification system?

Representations from direct experience or by cultural transmission

The two main origins of experience impinging on the individual are the first-hand impressions of sensory input from the physical world, and the second-hand relaying of experience from the culture which the individual inhabits. This distinction will guide the first cut, and gives us the picture presented in Figure 4.1.

Representations from direct experience and from cultural mediation are described as sources which can be independent of one another, but which may also overlap. The assumption is that individuals may encounter perceptual experiences which are unique, or which are independent of cultural influence; representations from such sources are located in region a. In contrast, as the result of child-rearing practices and the multiplicity of socialization processes through which conventional knowledge is transmitted, the representations in region c become available. The phenomena to which representations in region c refer have not been available as direct experiences to the learner. Their mode of acquisition might primarily be through an unselfconscious diffusion, a cultural osmosis gained from immersion in what has been called the 'vernacular environment' (Silberbauer 1981).

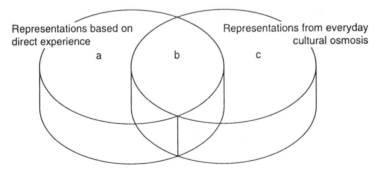

Representations based on direct experience

Representations from everyday cultural osmosis

a   b   c

Figure 4.1 Sources of knowledge representation available to an individual from direct sensations and cultural mediation

In region b are located those representations of phenomena possessed by an individual which are both directly experienced and culturally labelled. If direct experience were always to confirm cultural experience, and vice versa, a mapping between the two should be possible. However, it is not assumed that such mapping is an invariable cognitive activity. Representations of the same phenomena derived from different sources may have the potential to combine (perhaps with the phenomenological experience of creative insight or 'understanding'); that they also have the potential to remain separate (psychological alternatives) is also accepted. For this reason, Figure 4.1 is shown as having depth as well as surface features.

The assumption that integration of knowledge about the same phenomena does not automatically take place is not always made in an instructional situation. A description of how such integration may take place is crucially important in psychological terms, and will be considered later.

Ultimately, although very much concerned with intangible mental activity, the description presented in Figure 4.1 is materialist in the sense that all representations of the material world are assumed to result from interactions between the learner and the environment which lead to physical changes in the state of the nervous system. This does not preclude the notion of the individual reflecting upon 'internal' sensations and gaining new insights, but the phenomenology of these insights is probably most consistently interpreted as the reorganization or consequences of existing impressions. The role of maturation of the nervous system is not seen as contributing to the construction of representations per se, but may result in an increased capacity to handle incoming information. In this interactive sense, maturation may be highly relevant to learning. A final point to make about an individual's 'hardware' is that similarities in the physical construction of the nervous system of *Homo sapiens* must to some extent limit, if not determine, the range of possible constructions available. Coupled with similarities in the environment in which individuals are likely to be located, striking similarities in their representations, as well as the possibility of idiosyncratic outcomes, are to be expected.

Sensory input from the material world, often with the human sensitive range artificially enhanced by machinery, is the scientist's raw data. Various representations of objects and events having varying degrees of 'goodness of fit' are constructed and promulgated, so long as their predictive and explanatory utility is the best available for the user's purpose. The better the fit or mapping of the representation to the physical world, the better the 'understanding'. A representation capable of only partial mapping to reality, and consequently capable of only partial prediction and explanation, implies only partial understanding. It follows that an 'understanding' is inviolate until used; it must be put into action in order to be challenged or validated.

To some extent, direct sensory experience will be channelled so far as it is mediated by the expectations which an individual learns to share in the process of acculturation. But this acculturation need not be seen as a total submission of the individual to the cultural milieu. The relationship between the individual and culture is as subtle in psychological terms as it is described to be in politics, sociology and anthropology. Novel impressions and combinations of sensory input, unique interactions of experience and percept, suggest that innovative representations remain a constant possibility. The recognition of cultural impact on an individual's perception of the world can stop well short of the idea of complete cultural determinism.

This brings us to the consideration of the other main source of experience impinging on an individual, which is the culture within which socialization occurs. Variations in terms of location and time are self-evident. The social milieu offers or imposes a range of ready-made templates for classifying or condensing the multiplicity of sense impressions to which an individual *may* be exposed. Direct sensory exposure is not actually a prerequisite for the assimilation of this type of knowledge at second-hand. Various modes of communication, including spoken and written language, behaviour sequences, two- or three-dimensional icons or symbols, as well as other forms of abstract notation having their own rules and conventions, allow information transfer. Once the internal logic of the information transfer system has been learned, knowledge which is independent of the recipient's direct experience becomes available and manipulable. Experience can be shared, compared, recorded and accumulated beyond one person's experience in a single life span. It is also possible for 'knowledge' shared by a culture but having no basis in terms of the physical world to be transmitted, as with astrology, for example. The templates a culture uses for classifying experiences may be thought of as having varying degrees of probability of being adopted by an individual but need not be considered mandatory, either when they are designed to map on to the material world, or when they represent a shared fantasy.

The description of knowledge acquisition presented so far is capable of considerable refinement, but even in this elementary form where the most basic assumptions are exposed for consideration, some criticisms relevant to the body of alternative conceptions research can be offered. By way of justification for the argument from first principles assembled so far, some exploration of relevance to the research debate will be undertaken at this point. The cultural dimension of the model will then be extended to include formal instruction in science, and discussion will shift from an exposition of principles to a consideration of the heuristic value of the elaborated representation, and the possibilities of generating operational research questions.

The acceptance of the postulates outlined above implies a challenge to some assumptions or descriptions related to learning explicit or implicit in some reported studies. The first criticism, and perhaps the one having the broadest relevance, is the failure on the part of many researchers to note not just the implications of, but even the distinction between, presenting subjects with actual physical objects or events, and the variety of possible representations of those objects and events (e.g. written or verbal descriptions, diagrams, photographs, line drawings or other formal notations including algebraic or mathematical). While assessment using any of the possible modes may be legitimate, there is no justification for regarding them as interchangeable and equivalent alternatives. Science assessment programmes have demonstrated the sensitivity of children's responses such as context, content and presentation and response modes (Russell *et al.* 1988). The suggestion that a 'complete' understanding should embrace all modes is an arguable position, but it does not follow that success in a particular mode can be generalized; success would indicate a necessary but not a sufficient contribution to 'complete' understanding. This is an important point when the context of this type of research is considered, for with the distrust for assessment of regurgitation of rote memorization and the pursuit of 'understanding', creative researchers may invent the most ingenious of unfamiliar situations with which to confront children. Yet if 'understanding' is agreed to equate with the possession of a representation having explanatory and predictive value, this representation must be acquired, stored and retrieved for use from memory. Memory is indispensable to cognitive functioning; it is the form, the adequacy and the utility of what is stored in memory which needs to be questioned and probed.

A second area of criticism suggested by the above description concerns the use of terminology which obscures attempts to understand knowledge *acquisition*, even as it describes representational outcomes. One such usage, the description of some kinds of learning as 'spontaneous', can be traced to Piaget, and is not uncommon in the work of those influenced by him, (e.g. Viennot 1979). The notion of spontaneous learning is as suspect as the ideas of spontaneous combustion or spontaneous generation; all are 'spontaneous' only in so far as we are unaware of or do not feel the need for, a causal explanation. The only way in which 'spontaneous' learning can have any place within the assumptions presented is in the belief that physical maturation itself generates knowledge of the world – a quite eccentric proposition. Piaget's researches might well be interpreted as supporting the idea of an increasing information processing capacity with maturation, but only through *interaction* with the physical world. More likely, the use of the term 'spontaneous' is not intended to have this literal sense, but to make a distinction between the outcomes of controlled, formal, self-conscious pedagogy and learning *undirected* by external agents. The issue is confused by the fact that the so-called 'spontaneous' outcomes are frequently contaminated by instruction, with the resultant constructions being hybrids of the two sources.

Another term in current use which avoids a causal description of the learning process is 'gut' learning. The use of this term does not constitute a late challenge to Aristotle's view of the heart as being the centre and source of thought and sensation, or the current view that the brain is the organ more likely to be the seat of these functions. The intent of the description is no doubt metaphorical, and successfully identifies the 'flavour' of learning which is other than self-conscious and explicit. But for research purposes, or to guide educational intervention, the invocation of such a term is less helpful since it offers no guide on where to start to operationalize. A psychologically more precise description of learning outcomes is usually possible, and more appropriate. If a given learning outcome was not truly believed to have been mediated by the gut, then how was it achieved? If by direct sensation, then what sensory modality was likely to have been involved and what physical property of the environment? Though we accept the literary licence, we know that Biggles never *really* flew with the seat of his pants, but no doubt had considerable experience in interpreting visual, auditory, tactile and kinaesthetic feedback from his aircraft; if we are concerned to have a better operational understanding of learning, detailed descriptions in terms of the latter terminology are likely to have greater utility.

A third area of general criticism concerns interpretations which neglect the wide cultural milieu of the learner. For example, the recapitulation notion of the genesis of alternative frameworks is sometimes given credence. This idea echoes the biological principle of ontogenesis repeating phylogenesis; the modern-day learner, it is suggested, re-enacts in the course of personal intellectual development, the sequence of ideas as they have evolved historically in the formulations of a succession of eminent forebears. This idea might have some plausibility in certain circumstances but the thesis can have no general applicability.

In terms of the present discussion, a culture absorbs and transmits important new ideas through language, metaphor and other media. The culture (and the individuals which comprise it) in which a novel formulation is advanced is itself changed by that formulation. This cumulative factor makes the possibility of a modern learner starting at the same point as Aristotle remote. (Piaget suggests it might be possible to trace a personal development paralleling historical development within the subject matter of algebra – possibly a content area sufficiently removed from everyday cultural usage and impact to remain relatively virgin territory.) We might assume for instance, post lunar landings, *Star Wars*, etc., that the poetic Moon images of the nursery are receiving a powerful challenge from photographic and cinematographic images, despite the constancy of the directly perceptible evidence.

Representations from formal instruction

So far, a single broad division (with some overlap) between knowledge acquired or confirmed by direct perception and culturally transmitted knowledge has been described. Although it has been shown that even in these broad terms there are possibly important implications to be drawn for science education research into children's representational systems, some refinement is possible by the superimposition of a region designating those representations transmitted by schooling and formal instruction. Of course, schooling and instruction are activities which take place within a culture. The division is made to emphasize the distinction between those representations which are adopted implicitly, informally, and those which, through schooling, are more likely to be formally presented and self-consciously accommodated. This distinction is justified because the sources of knowledge representation seem to imply different epistemologies.

Formal instruction is one particular source of the knowledge base which a culture may provide for its members. In order to highlight the particular relationship of formal instruction to the knowledge sources already discussed, it is not represented as being entirely subsumed within the cultural region. In Figure 4.2, the area of consciously apprehended representations from formal instruction is like a pseudopodium, extending interpretations into regions often unfamiliar to the wider culture from which it burgeons.

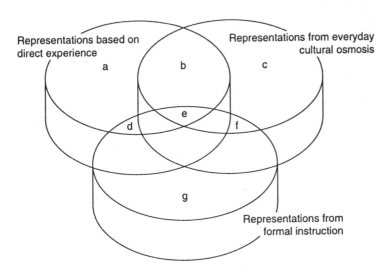

Figure 4.2 Sources of knowledge representation: from direct experience, by cultural transmission and from formal instruction

The mechanisms of information transfer employed by formal instruction are likely to be quite unlike the osmosis between the learner and everyday vernacular culture. It is also likely that formal instruction will on occasions be concerned with phenomena which are outside either the direct experience or the more general culturally transmitted experience of an individual. On other occasions, the phenomena will be acknowledged and represented within all three sources. When this occurs, there is a possibility of the three sources contributing to an integrated representation, or alternatively of three discrete representations of the same phenomena serving different purposes. The worst possible outcome might be when attributes of a representation appropriate to one source are inappropriately applied to another. Figure 4.2 offers the possibility of a taxonomy which might permit the classification of descriptions of phenomena elicited from learners in the following terms:

Region a: Representations from direct perceptual experience. To cite the extreme case, such intuition would comprise the total of the feral child's knowledge system. The same range of perceptual experiences would be available to more domesticated human observers, but would comprise only a portion of their knowledge systems. To take the example of the Earth's moon, its luminosity, variable shape and position are perceptually available as direct experience.

Region c: Knowledge transmitted by vernacular osmosis alone, as in region c, will not be available to intuitive confirmation. For example, a culture may represent the moon as having feminine gender and mystical or poetic powers; these powers may be capable of inducing romantic or 'lunatic' behaviour. Myth, metaphor and language are likely to be the predominant modes of transmission. Representations are likely to change within a culture over time and to differ between cultures. To take an example from a group at the extreme of cultural isolation, a belief is reported among Kalahari hunter-gatherers that the moon controls menstruation (Lee 1979).

Region b: Direct experience may be congruent with some conventional wisdom; for example, the phases of the moon as indicators of auspicious times for fishing may be confirmed without recourse to any formalization of the links between moon, tides and fish behaviour.

Region g: Formal instruction presents elaborated representations of phenomena which may be outside the range of direct perception and are only described by a specialized vocabulary. Properties of the moon such as its geological history, gravitational force and reflective surface are only available to the majority of learners through formal instruction. Notations involving quantification are likely to be used extensively here: for example, the distance from the Earth, orbit, velocity, mass, volume, surface area, etc.

Region f: Formal instruction and the vernacular environment may have representations of a phenomenon which is outside an individual's experience. An eclipse of the moon would be explained scientifically by reference to the orbits of the Sun, Moon and Earth. Marshall Thomas (1959, p. 35) reports a Gikwe-Bushmen belief that 'the eclipses of the moon are caused by lions, as on very bright nights a lion may cover the moon's face with a great paw, giving himself darkness for better hunting'.

Region e: Formal instruction, direct experience and cultural transmission may on occasion all represent the same phenomena: for example, an explanation of tides and fishing outcomes predicted by conventional wisdom experienced directly and explained by a formal model of the moon's gravitational effects.

Region d: Formal instruction might encourage an individual to re-interpret direct perceptual evidence. The representation of the moon might consequently be transformed from disc to sphere, from light source to reflector, from an ethereal car-chaser to a cosmic mass of predictable orbit. Region d is (metaphorically) well trodden by educators in the search for direct experiences which may be presented to children before being re-interpreted using the constructs of science.

REPRESENTATIONAL SOURCES AND RESEARCH PREDILECTIONS

For the purposes of exploring the heuristic potential of the model, a single conceptual area – ideas about the moon – was used as an illustration throughout the previous section. There is no intention to imply that all concepts could be located in an equivalently widespread form. Representations may be located in a single attribute set (a or c or g), in one of the double attribute regions (d or f) or in the triple-attribute region, (e). It is of interest to explore how various schools of research can be linked with particular sources of knowledge representation. This relationship will be explored in the present section.

Representations from direct experience

In his introduction to *The Child's Conception of the World*, Piaget makes a very clear statement of his interest in the whole region labelled a in Figure 4.1, with an emphatic exclusion of region b:

> [there] are two very different types of conviction among children which need to be distinguished. Some are . . . influenced but not dictated by the adult. Others, on the contrary, are simply swallowed whole, either at school, or from the family, or from adult conversations which the child overhears, etc. These naturally have not the slightest interest.
>
> (Piaget 1929, p. 28)

Piaget's genetic epistemology postulates the gradual development of particular types of internal representations – operational structures – which model in logical terms transformations in external reality. His deliberate attempts to avoid the influence of science education or cultural influences might not be immediately apparent to a reader of the later work, *The Growth of Logical Thinking* (Inhelder and Piaget 1958), as a result of the physics and chemistry problem settings which are discussed there. Understanding achieved through the support of culturally transmitted representations were of 'not the slightest interest'. (The misapprehension that Piaget's intention was to describe learning outcomes from pedagogical roots may have fuelled unjustified criticisms.) Although the development of operational structures may be facilitated or promoted by teachers or parents, social intervention is not a necessary precondition for their emergence.

Direct experience and formal instruction: competing representations

A well-known piece of research conducted by Viennot on children's reasoning in dynamics – students' explanations of the forces acting on a ball as it is thrown into the air and falls back to the ground – is a suitable example here (Viennot 1979). Viennot's work bears some influences of the Piagetian tradition. The term 'spontaneous reasoning' (criticized above) continues Piaget's usage. However, a major difference is that Viennot *is* interested in pedagogical considerations. Her research is concerned with difficulties or interferences between competing representations in region d; that is, between impressions gained through direct experience and the alternative representations promoted through formal instruction. Region a is of interest in that it is seen as a likely source of conflicting or competing representations derived from intuition (direct sensation). As Viennot puts it,

> even in physics where most people would imagine that they know nothing they have not been taught, we all share a common explanatory scheme of 'intuitive physic' which, although we were not taught it at school, represents a common and self-consistent stock of concepts.
>
> (Viennot 1979)

Viennot's immediate objective is simply to *describe* students' thinking and contrast these descriptions with the representations offered by formal teaching in elementary dynamics, where 'many of the ideas taught contradict very common kinds of spontaneous reasoning'.

There is no attempt to explore psychological aspects of knowledge acquisition, but the potential which some percepts may have to dominate and suppress other types of reasoning is noted. Motor schemas already present in the learner, internalized as enactive imagery, may have a direct and vivid 'common-sense' quality. Perhaps also for most individuals' most frequent needs, this type of representation works well enough. So it survives and is propagated. (To extend the possibilities of the argument: sufficiency of explanation may become common usage; common usage may become 'common-sense'. The potential for *three* competing representations is then established, as in region e of Figure 4.2.)

Other examples of a failure to make the counter-intuitive move from sense percept to abstraction are provided by Driver (Driver *et al.* 1984).

Some of the examples of children's thinking described pose an interesting comparison and contrast with the work of Viennot, in illustrating examples of reasoning where pupils are failing to 'take leave of their senses' because they are dominated by a *visual* percept. For example, a resultant mass decrease as the result of combustion is the everyday expected outcome, and the proof might be in an empty coal cellar, or an empty petrol tank. In contrast, formal instruction suggests mass conservation in physical and chemical changes. Driver *et al.* remark, 'It is interesting to note that the questions which were answered correctly by the smallest proportion of pupils were those which called for a scientific interpretation of very familiar situations'. The *context* in which the concept is required to be applied appears to influence which of the competing or 'alternative' representations is recalled from memory and used as an explanation.

Representations from direct experience, cultural transmission and formal instruction

Joan Solomon's work provides an example of a focus of attention on the triple overlapping in region e of Figure 4.2 (Solomon 1983). The development of physics students' conceptions of energy may be influenced by formal instruction, cultural usage and direct experience. While the first representation is in terms of the capacity to do work of a body or system of bodies, the more general usage in the 'life-world' or broader culture is quite different. In the life-world, 'work' has a different complex of meanings. Much energy can be expended in doing no work, while some other kind of work may be so light as to require no energy expenditure or, though exhausting, so pleasurable as to be not considered work at all. The cultural usage competes with formal science usage, often because an apparently shared vocabulary is being used with quite different definitions in each case. Understanding is even further confused by direct sensation. The claim from physics that a body has more potential energy at the top of a steep hill than at the bottom would not be confirmed by the breathless experience of most human bodies. Solomon's interest goes beyond the recording of the various representation to the issue of the recognition of selection for appropriateness for a given context. She also warns that we should not think in terms of 'extinguishing' socialized knowledge:

> Such socialised knowledge cannot ever, by its very nature, be extinguished. Whether or not our pupils become successful in science they must never lose the ability to communicate. It would indeed be a poor return for our science lessons if they could no longer comprehend remarks like 'wool is warm' or 'we are using up all our energy'.
>
> (Solomon 1983)

Representations from cultural transmission and direct instruction

Region f in Figure 4.2 locates another recognizably discrete area of alternative conceptions interest. When Sutton (1980, 1992) discusses knowledge available to children prior to instruction, he has in mind not so much that derived from common perceptions as from shared linguistic and symbolic experience. Like direct perceptual experience, such prior knowledge may either support or interfere with representations from formal instruction. Sutton (1981) draws attention to the way in which the use of metaphor has enabled a number of eminent scientists to bring order to their perceptions, by serving 'the function of non-literal expression at the frontiers of knowledge creation'. He goes on to suggest that:

> metaphorical language, and the imagery behind it, is a major cognitive aid, a means by which new thoughts are begun. The first moves towards formulating a new way of describing some aspect of the world consists in 'seeing it as' something else, and selecting words accordingly. These in turn both persuade the user that this way of talking is of some value, and provoke an exploration of implications.
>
> (Sutton 1981: 219)

For the pupil in the context of formal instruction, the description of being located 'at the frontier' is completely appropriate in the constructivist view of learning, the difference being that knowledge is not so much created as re-created in the classroom. Pupils *actively* interpret the science experiences and language to which they are exposed (sometimes with inadvertently humorous consequences, such as the inclusion of 'frogs born' in the life cycle of the frog). For the child, there may be the added difficulty that the original metaphor, with its complex of connotations, has slowly and subtly aged and died. Only in a historical, cultural, biographical and etymological re-examination can dead metaphors be resurrected.

Representation without the support of direct experience

In contrast to the examples discussed so far, many representations in region g of Figure 4.2 are impossible to approach via direct experience, because of the scale of the observational data involved. The primary data source may be imperceptible because infinitely small (e.g. particle physics), or infinitely large (astro-physics), dispersed beyond the normal human scale of perception by location (species variation) or time (evolution and palaeontology).

Other phenomena are imperceptible to the human sensory range except in their effects (e.g. electromagnetic force). In these cases, there can be no cross-checking with experience. A representation of the universe as evolutionary rather than steady state is based on evidence including extra-galactic radio wave emission. The indirect observational measurements are available to and interpretable by very few. For the vast majority of individuals, including the majority of the science sub-culture, 'knowledge' acquisition in these circumstances calls for an indirect appraisal of indirect evidence and acceptance or rejection of the representation abstracted from that evidence. Access to a radio telescope to check the claim of the increasing incidence of discrete radio sources with decreasing intensity is unlikely to be a component of any school's extra-mural syllabus.

In the circumstances of the sensory information being indirect, for whatever reason, we may suppose that formal instruction utilizes some other bridging system which permits the learner to incorporate knowledge. Two studies, one concerning the conception of the Earth as a cosmic body (Nussbaum and Sharoni-Dagan 1983), the other relating to the particle theory of matter (Brook, Briggs and Driver 1984), will be discussed in order to explore how some of these bridging possibilities that permit operation in region d of Figure 4.2 are used in practice. The first relates to bridges constructed by instructors. The second explores the bridges constructed by learners.

Considering their commitment to 'reception learning' and their conviction that abstract concepts can be acquired earlier than Piaget's work would suggest, it is not too surprising to find the Ausubel–Novak learning model closely associated with Nussbaum and Sharoni-Dagan's (1983) investigation into the acquisition of certain abstract concepts. The experimenters describe five distinguishable notions held by pupils about the Earth as a cosmic body (see Figure 4.3). An audio-tutorial instructional sequence was aimed explicitly at 'cognitive barriers' identified as constituents of the first four representations.

Each pupil received the same total of 80 minutes 'directly relevant' formal instruction over four weeks at a study station within the classroom, where headphones, visuals and hands-on activities were provided. Five weeks after the final instructional session the post-test revealed that about 50 per cent of the experimental group underwent some cognitive accommodation of different magnitudes. (The class gain was estimated as approximately equivalent to 'a couple of years of incidental or spontaneous learning'.) Had

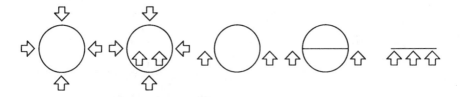

Figure 4.3 Five notions of the Earth as a cosmic body. (The arrows represent assumptions about the direction of the action of the force of gravity)

normal classroom group procedures been available, the authors consider that the outcome effects would have been multiplied.

It is instructive in the context of present purposes to consider the materials used in the post-test in this investigation. These comprised drawings for multi-choice options; a globe marked with land and sea masses; a small figure that could be attached to any place on the globe 'to aid the child in visualising in three dimensions the assumed locations of the persons on the Earth appearing in the two dimensional drawings', a Styrofoam ball with a long straight hole in it, again complementing two-dimensional drawings. The teaching material is not specified but clearly must be similar (but not validly identical) to the assessment material. When the authors refer to 'hands-on experience', they are not referring to hands-on a cosmic body. We may assume they are referring to hands-on a three-dimensional model. The globe is intermediate between the Earth itself and the two-dimensional drawing in psychological accessibility. Finally, verbal propositions are supported and evaluated by reference to the drawings. (It might have been possible in some situations to put another step in this sequence, e.g. enabling pupils to directly perceive the curvature of the Earth which is sometimes perceptible on the horizon over the sea. A good 'teaching example' often uses whatever sensible properties of a generally abstract topic that are available, e.g. Brownian motion or the smell of otherwise imperceptible matter to introduce particulate theory.)

The nature of and conditions for effective information transfer of the particular content under consideration have not been identified by the authors. (Half the subjects showed no evidence of 'cognitive accommodation'; one 'regressed'.) The assumptions outlined in this paper and the techniques described in this investigation seem to reach the closest correspondence when the authors reveal, almost incidentally, their intention to aid the child in 'visualizing' (developing an internal representation of?) in three-dimensions some properties of the planet Earth. Their interpretation, stressing the role of visual imagery, contrasts with the verbal emphasis which is more commonly associated with the reception–learning philosophy, e.g. Novak, Gowin and Johansen (1983):

> Propositions are two or more concepts semantically linked to illustrate a specific regularity, e.g. force equals mass times acceleration. From our perspective, concept meanings are developed primarily in the extent that they are embedded in frameworks of propositions, and hence it is the set of propositions a person has incorporating a given concept that defines that person's idiosyncratic *meaning* for the concept.
>
> (Novak, Gowin and Johansen 1983)

Referring this 'linking' aspect back to Nussbaum's study, it is possible to think of the imagery which is promoted during the instructional sequence as supporting connections between concepts, not two by two, but in a system.

The imaginal model might be seen as providing an 'implicative complex' (to borrow Black's 1968 description of the function of a metaphor) with the aid of which new links can be *generated* as well as described. The lesson for instructional practice from Nussbaum's study might then be inferred to be the promotion of models with as many attributes as possible of the original physical reality; in the present context, a sphere (diminished in size from the original) and a force which, like gravity, causes model people to be attracted to it, e.g. magnetism modelling gravity. The caution that evaluation of this learning must distinguish between testing understanding of the particular attribute of the model, and what the model more generally represents, must be mentioned. In fact, as the next study to be discussed indicates, there is probably a case for evaluation of both understanding the properties of the model and of the application of properties of the model. The sequence of representations in Figure 4.3 as well as being useful summaries *of* children's thinking might be useful supports as discussion material *for* children's thinking. This suggestion implies that a more self-conscious, introspective process of learning (meta-learning) might have some utility.

Remaining in region d of Figure 4.2, but adjusting focus from the cosmic to the microscopic, the study by Brook *et al.* (1983) is concerned with secondary students' understanding of the particulate nature of matter. The emphasis is less with the question of whether instructional objectives have been achieved than with pupils' own hybridized constructions. The authors selected this content area since the idea that all matter is particulate in nature is fundamental to many ideas introduced in the later parts of most science schemes. Using a detailed marking of 300 responses to each of six written questions, supplemented by a further 35 oral interviews, it was found that 20 per cent of pupils included accurate *components* of the particle model in their responses; where pupils studied physics or chemistry, the level was about 30 per cent. About 30 per cent offered responses containing alternative ideas to the accepted ones about particles. Despite a high probability of exposure, the representation which is promoted by science teaching appears to be infrequently adopted.

One point especially relevant to the present discussion, which becomes clear from the investigation, is that the distinctions on which this discussion is based – that is, the modularity of information transfer and the consequences in terms of the epistemological status of various representations – is of little concern to learners. Pupils slip unwittingly and perhaps unnoticed between descriptions of the properties of objects and events in the physical world, and properties of the particular models they receive for the representation of that reality. Consequently (and incidentally demonstrating the active role of imagination in the acquisition of representations) particles may be described as changing in size to explain expansion; as melting in a change of state; as having air or other debris between them (cf. Novak and Nussbaum 1978), etc. The authors hope that the cataloguing in detail of these departures from (or 'alternatives' to) the model which pedagogy intended to transmit may be fed back into a re-examination of practices. It is generally agreed that concept acquisition is a process of gradual accretion, refinement and revision. In this molecular sense, a manual of possible system failure-points is a valuable resource. In a molar sense, the meta-learning awareness of the distinction between real objects and representations of those objects could provide another focus of attention in the learning environment. And this 'learning how to learn' might be found to be as relevant to the practice of teaching as to the practice of learning.

DIRECTIONS FOR RESEARCH

The framework which has been presented to describe different sources of knowledge representation is not intended as a tight and testable structure. Its intention is heuristic, particularly in offering an orientation towards the analysis of a complex set of data. The utility (and in a sense, validity) of this particular organization becomes apparent with the realization that different groups of researchers may also be allocated to the various sectors of the overlapping sets of knowledge sources. Certain rivalries and disputes, e.g. Piaget *versus* Ausubel, may disappear with the acceptance that different sources and qualities of learning are legitimately approached and explained by selecting different kinds of pupil data to explore different hypotheses. For example, learning mediated by direct experience and auto-regulation on the one hand, and learning regulated by an outside agent and verbal transmission on the other. It remains to be discussed how the framework which has been advanced stands in relation to some of the concerns of cognitive psychology.

It is clear that there is no 'off the peg' theory which can do justice to the task of describing the acquisition of representations in their full range and complexity. The problems encountered in intervention studies confirm this. Nevertheless, there are grounds for optimism that a major contribution to our understanding of knowledge representation will derive from the research conducted within the discipline of applied cognitive developmental psychology. The kind of shift that might be possible is from the theoretical and descriptive, with intervention guided by trial and error and the pragmatics of experience, to a dynamic theoretical position. Cognitive psychology occasionally and increasingly acknowledges the need for 'ecological validity': that human subjects' thinking might best be investigated by tasks having some recognizable connection with habitual functioning. Such an orientation can support theoretical development (Baddeley 1982) even in applied contexts. So we have a psychology acknowledging the need for researching 'real' contexts, and the real context of science knowledge acquisition in need of some psychological underpinning. These two forces should be capable of generating a productive outcome. It is of interest to examine, by looking at some particular research, just how fruitful such an outcome may be.

Strauss and colleagues (Strauss 1977, Strauss and Stavy 1982) have consistently found, and explored the nature of, U-shape behavioural growth in children's reasoning on intensivity tasks. Intensive physical quantities can be exemplified by temperature, viscosity, concentration of solution, density, hardness, etc.. To take one example, the concentration of a solution remains constant despite variations in its extensive property brought about by subdividing it. When presented with tasks probing understanding of intensive physical quantity, success rates against chronological age in the range 4–13 years do not confirm monotonic growth. More of the younger children offer a correct solution than do those in the middle range, with rates of success gradually increasing again with older children. The result is a striking U-shaped curve. Two of the seminal investigations used are presented schematically in Figure 4.4. In the 'sweetness' problem, two of three equal starting volumes of equivalent concentration are combined, to be compared with the third. A parallel procedure is adopted for the investigation of the intensive quantity of temperature.

In both tasks, the children at either extreme of the age range 4–13 performed markedly more successfully than those in between. Those children arriving at a correct judgement, both the older and younger ones, used predominantly an identity argument to justify their decisions. The children arriving at an incorrect judgement tended to use a 'direct function' argument, as if the numerator (the sugar) in the ratio had increased, while the denominator (water) had not. The incorrect judgement manifest as a *performance* decrement with age can actually be interpreted as an increase in

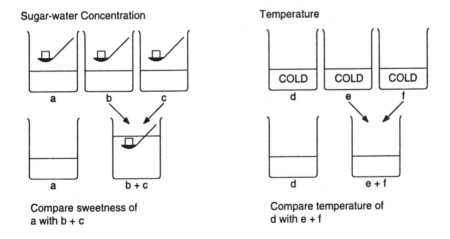

Figure 4.4 Intensivity problems: sweetness and temperature

competence. The reasoning which runs 'adding or mixing leads to more' can be viewed as a faltering step towards quantification of the ratio relationship.

Strauss's empirical work and its interpretation clearly support the general notion of multiple and occasionally conflicting representation of the physical world. Children's early, global representations of concentrations and temperature presumably derived from everyday experiences (mixing drinks, sweetening solutions, mixing paints, running showers, washing hands, and so on) lead to early success in making predictions within these domains. Another representational system, that of functions, possibly emanating from or encouraged by experiences of formal instruction, supersedes the earlier system until the two representations are integrated, and quantification confirms direct experience. The fact that the two representations can exist contemporaneously yet without an intrusive sense of contradiction, suggests some independence of the two domains.

The implications for intervention are interesting. Behavioural outcomes can clearly be misleading; the distinction between overt performance and covert competence is valuable and cautionary. The apparently discrete nature of the domains (with the consequent toleration of what, to the observer, is clearly contradictory) suggests that the promotion of cognitive change through dissonance might not always be an effective strategy. Most salutary of all, though Strauss's data are not longitudinal, it would seem likely that the changes take place over a considerable time-span. The developmental perspective encourages the long and broad view of cognitive change, in contrast to the brief and optimistic teaching exposure which is frequently evaluated within intervention studies. Fortunately, it appears possible to track the process of some representational changes within an individual by rather more rapid procedures.

In the studies reported by Karmiloff-Smith (1984) the representational changes which are tracked are micro- rather than macro-developmental. These changes are not of invariant sequence and irreversible, as those described by Strauss are. Karmiloff-Smith's focus is the more general process of recurrent changes in real time, within an interview lasting about one hour, i.e. 'phases' within micro-developmental representational change. The technique used consists of posing a problem tailored to a child's level of development, so that success can be expected within a single session. The data which provide the clues to internal representations are behavioural rather than the product of introspection and conscious reflection. Actions, corrections, drawings, comments, and so on, reveal the nuances of representational change.

Reviewing a series of interview studies from a range of domains (spatial, mechanical, linguistic, etc.) Karmiloff-Smith advances a three-phase model of recurrent phases in problem solving. Initially, in the *procedural* phase, children are essentially 'data driven', responsive to positive and negative feedback and achieve procedural success. In the second phase, the *metaprocedural,* external stimuli become secondary to internal representations. In this 'top down' mode, children are not as flexibly responsive to negative feedback as previously they were. Previously isolated procedures are integrated, sometimes at the expense of ignoring inconsistent information. The outcome may be a shortfall in procedural success. The *conceptual* phase completes the cycle, with a balance between environmental features and internal representations. The ostensibly identical behaviour to that in phase one is a superficial quality only. The procedural success is achieved as a product of a new representational system. As with Strauss's work, the three-phase model suggests increasing competence masked by behavioural failures. Karmiloff-Smith suggests that while failure generates behavioural change, it is *success* which generates representational change. This is interpreted as a generalized motivation to *control* both the environment and personal representations of the environment. Again, this is a challenge to the dissonance model of promoting conceptual change.

CONCLUSION

This chapter is concerned with the problem of achieving a better understanding of representations, their sources and the ways in which they may interact and change. An attempt has been made to draw a sketch map of some of the broad features of activity in this area relevant to science education. It is suggested that the organizing features outlined help to locate certain areas of relatively discrete research activity. But the pressing need is for some clues as to the dynamics of conceptual change. Some of these clues will be found within the discipline of applied cognitive developmental psychology. Others, no less important, will only become apparent from a sociological or anthropological perspective. There is scope for single or multi-disciplinary research. The parts can only be impoverished by losing sight of the whole, and whatever the approach, a theoretical underpinning is required. There is little evidence that a new psychology tailored to the needs of science education is needed. It seems likely that cognitive/developmental psychology applied to the particular contents which are of interest to science educators has the potential for fruitful and mutually beneficial research activity.

REFERENCES

Baddeley, A. 1982. 'Domains of recollection.' *Psychological Review*, 89: 708–29.
Black, M. 1968. *Models and metaphors: studies in language and philosophy.* Cornell University Press, Ithaca, NY.
Blurton Jones, N. and Conner, M. J. 1976. '!Kung knowledge of animal behaviour.' In Lee, R. B. and Devore, I. (eds) *Kalahari hunter gatherers: studies of the !Kung San and their neighbours.* Harvard University Press, Cambridge, Mass., pp. 325–48.
Brook, A., Briggs, H. and Driver, R. 1983. *Aspects of the particulate nature of matter.*

Children's Learning in Science Project, Centre for Studies in Science and Mathematics Education, University of Leeds.

Cole, M. and Scriber, S. 1974. *Culture and thought. A psychological introduction.* John Wiley, New York.

Driver, R., Child, D., Gott, R., Head, J., Johnson, S., Worsley, C. and Wylie, F. 1984. *Science in Schools. Age 15, Report number Two.* Department of Education and Science, London.

Inhelder, B. and Piaget, J. 1958. *The growth of logical thinking from childhood to adolescence.* Basic Books, New York.

Karmiloff-Smith, A. 1984. 'Children's problem solving.' In Lamb, M., Brown, A. and Ragodd, B. (eds) *Advances in developmental psychology.* Vol. 3, pp. 39–90. Erlbaum, Hillsdale, New Jersey.

Lee, R. B. 1979. *The !Kung San: men, women and work in a foraging society.* Cambridge University Press, Cambridge.

Luria, A. R. 1976. *Cognitive development. Its cultural and social foundations.* Harvard University Press, Cambridge, Mass.

Marshall Thomas, E. 1959. *The harmless people.* Secker and Warburg, London.

Novak, J. D., Gowin, D. and Johansen, G. T. 1983. 'The use of concept mapping and knowledge vee mapping with junior high school science students.' *Science Education,* 67: 625–45.

Novak, S. and Nussbaum, J. 1978. 'Junior high school pupils' understanding of the particulate nature of matter: An interview study.' *Science Education,* 62: 273–81.

Nussbaum, J. and Sharoni-Dagan, N. 1983. 'Changes in second grade children's preconceptions about the Earth as a cosmic body resulting from a short series of audio-tutorial lessons.' *Science Education,* 67: 99–114.

Osborne, J., Black, P., Smith, M. and Meadows, J. 1990. *Primary SPACE project research report: light.* Liverpool University Press, Liverpool.

Osborne, J., Black, P., Smith, M. and Meadows, J. 1991. *Primary SPACE project research report: electricity.* Liverpool University Press, Liverpool.

Piaget, J. 1929. *The child's conception of the world.* Routledge and Kegan Paul, London.

Russell, T. (ed.) with Black, P., Harlen, W., Johnson, S. and Palacio, D. 1988. *Science at age 11. A review of APU findings 1980–84.* HMSO, London.

Russell, T., Longden, K. and McGuigan, L. 1991. *Primary SPACE project research report: materials.* Liverpool University Press, Liverpool.

Silberbauer, G. B. 1981 *Hunter and habitat in the central Kalahari Desert.* Cambridge University Press, Cambridge.

Solomon, J. 1983. 'Learning about energy: how pupils think in two domains.' *European Journal of Science Education,* 5: 49–59.

Strauss, S. 1977. 'Educational implications of U-shaped behavioural growth'. Position paper for the Ford Foundation. Tel-Aviv University School of Education.

Strauss, S. and Stavy, R. 1982. 'U-Shaped behavioural growth: Implications for theories of development.' *Review of Child Development Research,* 6: 547–99.

Sutton, C. R. 1980. 'The learner's prior knowledge: a critical review of techniques for probing its organisation.' *European Journal of Science Education,* 2: 107–20.

Sutton, C. R. 1981. 'Metaphorical imagery: a means of coping with unfamiliar information in science.' *Durham and Newcastle Research Review,* 9: 216–22.

Sutton, C. R. 1992. *Words, science and learning.* Open University Press, Buckingham.

Tulkin, S. R. and Konner, M. J. 1973. 'Alternative conceptions of intellectual functioning.' *Human Development,* 16: 33–52.

Viennot, L. 1979. 'Spontaneous reasoning in elementary dynamics.' *European Journal of Science Education,* 1: 205–21.

Chapter 5

The social construction of children's scientific knowledge

Joan Solomon

It is no longer necessary to argue about whether or not children have out-of-school notions which affect their school learning of science. Research has copiously affirmed the point in ways which have been described in Chapter 1 of this book. Now it is possible to take as our starting point that these notions do exist, that they have pronounced common features (at least within any one culture), that they are multiply held and often inconsistently applied by the children, and that they are remarkably resistant to change by teaching.

The first generation of explanations of the genesis of such notions was curiously scientistic. Perhaps it was because the educational researchers had themselves received a scientific training that they began by attributing a naive scientific method to the children. George Kelly's idea of 'man as scientist' (1955) was expanded until the various ideas of children came to be graced by the name of 'children's science' (Gilbert *et al.* 1980). Each child, such researchers argued, had sense perceptions and experiences from which a series of hypotheses about the world were constructed. The child then compared further experiences with what had been predicted from these hypotheses. Daily life provided plenty of opportunities to check predictions against the results of mini-experiments or unplanned happenings. In this way, such theorists assumed, the child's notions were adapted and refined so that they could be reliably used to explain the common events of the natural world.

The results of research do not entirely support this individual constructivist position. In particular we are faced by three troublesome questions:

1 If children's notions have been assembled in such a logical, almost scientific way, why do school children then have such difficulty in understanding the logical method of science and resist changing their notions in the light of new and compelling evidence?
2 If they have tested their ideas in the different circumstances of daily life why is it that they apply them so inconsistently?
3 If every child is his or her own independent scientist, how is it that within

a cultural group notions are so much more similar than they are across different cultures? (Ross and Sutton 1982).

In this chapter it will be argued that the process by which children construct notions for explaining the meaning of events in their daily life is more social than personal. Illustrations will mostly be drawn from the classroom discussion of children, but also from sociology and from other branches of knowledge. This is possible because the urge to build up common systems for interpreting the world is not confined to the domain of events that could be described by science. It occurs for emotions, for rules of conduct, and for all human concerns about which there is converse. We shall certainly fail to grasp how the public understand science unless these powerful pressures on our powers of interpretation are taken into account. The public, including pupils (even sometimes when they are inside the classroom!), discuss those matters which concern them personally. Since their deepest concerns are bound up with possible action, there is also a strong relation between the social construction of knowledge and the values/behaviour/action complex which touches us all most closely. The recent research into how groups of the public reconstruct the scientific knowledge that is available to them has brought out this 'action aspect of learning' very forcefully (e.g. Jenkins 1990; Wynne 1992; Solomon 1992b).

Thus people, old and young, strive through talk to clothe the bare happenings of their lives, as well as the more difficult information they receive from school and the media, with shared meanings. This, we shall see, is at once both the incentive to talk and also its outcome.

Such a social theory of the construction of knowledge is not new, except with respect to children's learning in science. It stems back to the early work of Mead and Husserl who gave it a rich phenomenological flavour.

> It was the error of the old *tabula rasa* theory of mind, and the associationistic psychology based on this assumption, to argue that we have isolated perceptions, ideas, sentiments, following each other in time, by which our knowledge of the world is built up.
>
> (Schutz 1932)

Any step-by-step logical construction of children's explanations would not be easy to accommodate in this perspective even before the social component is added. The special contribution of Schutz's later work (Schutz and Luckmann 1973) was to incorporate the notions of reciprocal perspectives and inter-subjectivity.

In our everyday 'life-world' it is taken for granted that others see things very much as we do. We may disagree in detail but we will expect to be able to understand each other and to share meanings. Indeed it would be deeply worrying, almost a threat to our sanity, were we to find that others could not follow our simplest ideas, or we theirs. The very essence of our social life, our

understanding of self in relation to others, depends upon
shared familiar notions.

Thus the final picture is one of people, linked by h
experiences', talking together in order to elucidate the
and events, intent on constructing socially acceptable e...
has happened to them and to others. 'Do you get what I mean ....
I meant was ...', we say urgently and frequently because it matters that our
meanings are understood by others.

CHILDREN TALKING

There is no difficulty in applying this phenomenological approach to the
ideas of school children. As they play and chat together children refer to
events they have witnessed and to experiences they have had. During this
gossip they do more than just exchange individual views and argue about
them. Indeed, as we shall see, they very rarely conduct a set-piece argument.
They are simply to be heard reconstructing what they thought, saw or
experienced, thus establishing the general accepted sense of these pieces of
life-world knowledge.

In the introduction to their delightful book *Understanding Children
Talking*, Martin *et al.* (1978) have this to say about the way in which we all –
children and adults – talk through experiences in order to understand them:

> We all need to work through, sort, organise and evaluate the events of our
> daily lives. Sleeping, we do it in dreams, waking in internal monologue
> and relaxed talk.... [W]e hold out to others – in talk – our observations,
> discoveries, reflections, opinions, attitudes and values, and the responses
> we receive in the course of these conversations profoundly affect both the
> world picture we are creating and our view of ourselves.
>
> (Martin *et al.* 1978)

These generalities will now be illustrated from transcripts of class
discussions held during normal physics lessons. In the following extract the
teacher first puts a question and the pupils begin by making their individual
contributions, each one of which seems to be triggered by the one before,
acknowledging it and adding to the socially constructed domain of explanation. Only the last of the line strikes an individual note of disagreement.

    T: 'How do human beings get energy?'
        'From food'
        'From water'
        'Oxygen'
        'Nitrogen'
        'From exercise'
        'By doing exercise'
        'You lose it by exercise'

Now that the sociable consensus had been broken by this last contribution the teacher tried to sharpen the seeming contradiction between getting energy from exercise and losing it by exercise through a class vote of the 'hands up' variety. But the putting of the question and the counting of hands did not stop the exchanges between pupils.

> 'You may lose energy'
> 'It makes your body fit'
> 'Yes, I think *both*'
> T: 'How many people think it could do both? . . . five?'
> 'It improves your muscles but it doesn't actually give you energy'
> 'It makes your body better able to support you'
> 'Energy is in our muscles'
> 'Yes . . . Yes'
> 'Muscles store the energy'
> 'Exercise makes your heart stronger'.

It is true that there were a few recordings which showed angrier exchanges, but this usually occurred where animosity between children was already present on other scores. In this, and most other examples, there was always a kind of unstated pressure to resolve disagreement. Contrasting opinions were sounded out and often two contradictory ones both gained support from the same children. Assertions were not weighed and tested by logic but only paraded, as it were, for social recognition. This was given by adding on another neighbouring piece to the general mosaic of meaning. In the end familiarity wins the day. What is recognized is consensual; what is consensual is recognized; disagreements are either resolved or simply ignored.

At first sight such a description of socially acquired knowledge, which is 'patted' into shape by verbal exchanges, appears to have a fatal flaw. It seems both static and monolithic: worse still it contains little or no room for change and growth. Obviously it would be foolish to embrace a theory in which children are condemned to hold the same majority view for all their lives. How does so gross a thing as social consensus move, change, or develop?

We need to remember that social knowledge is a rag-bag of odds and ends picked up from conversations of parents, teachers, and friends; from the television and magazines. Hence the children find a wide variety of knowledge from which they can choose. If it happens that one particular child has reached a stage at which one meaning or explanation seems more valuable or more widely applicable than another, then it can simply be selected from the existing stock. One way in which cognitive development becomes apparent is in just such different preferences.

But being different is not encouraged by the mores of social interaction. We are thus forced to assume that in a large group such as that of the classroom, consensus will develop at the rate of the average pupils, since new meanings will need reiteration and social confirmation if they are to thrive.

The same study of energy from which the exchanges above were taken (Solomon 1983a) gave an interesting example of this slow change of consensus. A second year group of pupils who have not yet learnt about energy within school, were discussing it in class. Asked by the teacher if a piece of bread lying on the bench had any energy one of the pupils (let us say Mark) volunteered the opinion that it did not have energy because it 'couldn't jump around'. This meaning for energy proved familiar to most of the others who then leapt eagerly into the argument using the same idea to deny that petrol had energy. It is just possible on the recording to hear another pupil (let us say Errol) disagreeing with the idea that energy must be equated with 'jumping around', but it is ignored by the others and his voice fades out with the sentence still unfinished. Meanwhile the rest of the class go cheerfully reinforcing their notion of energy, and swapping jokes about jumping beans!

Two years later it happens that the same group, now in the fourth year and beginning to study energy in their physics class, are asked much the same question about energy. At once Mark began to stake out his previous claim that food could not have energy, but this time the recording shows that he was the one to be contradicted and ignored. There was no detailed argument, no evidence was offered, but Errol can be heard stating that 'energy is *stored* in food' and the others are agreeing with him. This time it is Mark's view which is drowned out and Errol's which is reinforced. The class consensus is established and one week later, in the next class discussion of energy, even Mark can be heard to have changed his mind and fallen into line with the rest of the class. Whether he is already convinced or is merely following the prevailing fashion is not clear. In the terms of the social construction of knowledge we need only conclude that he has added another meaning to the word 'energy' which he may employ during physics lessons.

WORDS AND THEIR MEANINGS

In socially acquired knowledge, items are 'linguistically fixed' (Schutz and Luckmann 1973) by the words used in conversation. What makes this such a difficult but fascinating idea is that the meaning of any word is not single but multiple, dependent on the context in which it is used, variable with the culture of the user, and even shifting with respect to time.

In the extracts quoted in the previous section there have been a number of different meanings for energy. There was the 'active energeticness' of Mark and his friends, the fuel 'store' that Errol mentioned, and the notion of 'fitness' that was the point of argument in the first extract. These multiple meanings can, at times, give rise to contradictions and disagreements. On the whole, however, they are distanced from semantic conflict by being used either in different physical situations or in different social contexts. Meaning is very strongly verbal. It is true that the children in the extracts were referring both to their own bodily perceptions, and to their experiences. Talking, however, is of paramount importance in socially acquired knowledge, not only because words are the vehicles of spoken meaning, but also because the kind of rumination we use to reflect on our perceptions and experiences may also be derived from talk. Vygotsky (1978) set young children some practical tasks of the kind that Kohler (1927) had previously set his apes and reported that the children used a stream of problem-solving speech almost like a tool while they worked. Older children no longer spoke out aloud, but Vygotsky commented that 'Aspects of external or communicative speech turn inward to become the basis of inner speech'. Thus inner and personal meanings are also likely to be deeply verbal. The construction of meaning through language is a lifelong process, which does more than extend and refine the vocabulary and permit social exchanges in a variety of circumstances; it builds up the very picture of reality just as powerfully as does the sum of sensory perceptions and experiences.

> Language arises in the life of an individual through ongoing exchanges of meaning with . . . a coterie of people who constitute his meaning group . . . building up the child's picture of reality . . . inseparable from the semantic system in which the reality is encoded.
>
> (Halliday 1978)

This extract seems to close on a note of strong linguistic relativism. It is one thing to observe children building up their notions of reality through social interactions, another to tie these perceptions unambiguously to a linguistic system. This is the strong position taken up by Benjamin Whorf (1940):

> This fact is very significant for modern science, for it means that no individual is free to describe nature with absolute impartiality . . . all observers are not led by the same physical evidence to the same picture of the universe unless their linguistic backgrounds are the same.
>
> (Whorf 1940)

There can be little doubt that different cultures do vary in how their children speak about common concepts and phenomena. Duit (1981), for example, analysed the different word associations for 'energy' given by children in Germany, Switzerland and the Philippines. It is trivial to find geographical variations, like a lack of reference to electricity and power stations in the Filipino data. It is more interesting to examine the differences across the language divide separating British children from German-speaking ones. Here there certainly are variations which might, at first sight support the Whorfian perspective.

The German word 'Kraft' which is generally translated as 'force', at least in its scientific sense, has almost exactly the same meaning area of fitness and health that our word 'energy' has for the schoolchildren quoted in the previous section. Thus a German patient might complain to a doctor of lack of 'Kraft' where his English equivalent speaks of having no 'energy'. Duit's data from German children shows that this meaning of fitness or 'energeticness' is almost completely missing from the word 'Energie' which is most frequently associated with electricity, rather as our word 'power' might be.

What these data suggest is not so much that what we perceive of the world is inexorably controlled by the language that we speak, but that perceptions, meanings, and the quasi-explanations associated with them may be differently distributed through the common vocabulary.

If we add to this finding the idea that thought is based on the turning inwards of early speech, as Vygotsky described it, we may also expect that it will be the mother-tongue of children which most strongly affects their associations and meanings. The work of Ross and Sutton (1982) supplies data of this kind. Tiv-speaking Nigerians, whether educated in the English language or in Tiv, had similar associations for the words for 'energy' and 'electricity'. A comparative group of English-speaking children gave sharply contrasting groups of meanings for the same words.

No doubt there are many differences in life-world knowledge from one culture to another. Some of these may reflect different styles of living, and different availability of objects of interest for comparison. The effect of language itself is undoubtedly strong, even from a non-Whorfian perspective. The common meanings of the words we use to speak about a situation certainly influence what features of it we will be paying attention to, even if they do not completely over-ride our perceptions. A class of schoolchildren is itself a cultural group, and when they receive information or watch an experiment, the words used will direct their attention – but not always in the sense which that out-group figure, their teacher, had expected.

This can be illustrated from the results of a small test administered to a class of second-year pupils who had just completed a three-week span of lessons on purifying and distilling water. During this time they had filtered suspensions and solutions, and spent a considerable amount of time using distilled water. When asked in the test what the word 'distilled' meant most pupils (14) wrote 'pure' as their answer, and some (3) wrote 'clean'. It seemed from this that the new word had entered the right meaning area of pure/clean/nothing dissolved in it (another answer that was occasionally given). However, this meaning area also contained the notion of 'clear (transparent)' as a life-world concomitant of being pure. Despite their recent experiences of looking at distilled water which was no more clear to the eye than was tap water or a salt solution, the notion of 'clear' as a test for cleanliness and purity, over-rode their own sense perceptions for 4 of the 21 pupils in the class.

Even after the point was corrected by the teacher and also illustrated practically in class, a second test showed that there were still three pupils who wrote 'clear' in their answer to the question. One of these added 'with no bits in it' showing, perhaps, the intention of indicating the purity of the distilled water.

There is a two-way exchange of meanings between science and the everyday vocabulary. While once the major movement consisted of the annexation of common words for special scientific purposes – 'energy' and 'compound' are examples which often perplex children – the reverse process also exists. It was interesting to observe how the child culture, and its mouthpiece the comic, took the word 'atom' or 'atomic' to mean explosive after the first bomb was dropped. 'Black holes' and 'krypton' have both followed in its wake. Needless to say the children then invest these words with new meanings.

Words enter the life-world because they seem a particularly striking metaphor or image. However, as Black (1962) argued, the strong interactive forces between the two parts of a metaphor tend to affect not only the object of comparison but also the term imported to perform this metaphorical comparison. The word 'evaporate' for example is often used as a metaphor for something which disappears completely, as in 'his anger evaporated when she smiled'. As a result of this, children who watch a liquid evaporate during a science lesson have their attention directed towards the disappearing of the liquid rather than the production of vapour. In this way, a metaphorical usage may add a meaning to a word, which in turn affects our perception of phenomena.

TWO WORLDS OF KNOWLEDGE

Using the substance of the last two sections – the evidence of children talking about the concept of energy, and also the multiple meanings of words in general use – it is possible to map out the contrasts between the life-world knowledge constructed by children talking together, and the scientific knowledge that they attempt to learn in their school science lessons. The lists below provide such a map.

Life-world knowledge	*Scientific knowledge*
Social exchanges try to achieve a mutual understanding and agreement.	The aim of debate is to sharpen differences and to confirm or refute rival opinions.
Words used have multiple meanings which are not defined but negotiated socially.	Concept words are unambiguously defined for exact use.
Meanings are dependent on the cultural group and on the physical or affective context.	Concept meanings are symbolic and abstracted from any particular situation.

Apparent contradictions are tolerated. No logical method is thought to be needed.	A tight logical network of concepts and theories is claimed.
This knowledge system is well socialized by daily use with familiar people.	This knowledge is not well socialized since its methods are rarely used and then only by teachers outside the peer group.

The catalogue of the attributes of scientific knowledge is by no means exhausted by this list. It is the life-world way of knowing which is hard to describe in any effective way. When children or adults are challenged about the views they profess or the meanings that they use they may slip uneasily from one meaning to another, or claim that it is 'just common sense'. This comment serves two purposes: it reaffirms the expected consensuality of the view and it also turns away argument. Steven Pepper (1942), who tried to analyse common sense knowledge, wrote perspicaciously that it was 'cognitively irritable'. It is almost as though searching too hard for a rationale for an item of life-world thought will either destroy the thought link, or break the conventions of social discourse. (See the opening chapter of Solomon 1992a for further discussion of this point.)

If these two domains of knowledge – the life-world and the scientific – are really so very different it must follow that once our children have really understood some science they will have access to two different knowledge worlds. It is not really possible that they could be instantly converted away from the everyday way of thought, since they will continue to use it and be bound by its conventions most of the days of the week. Just when they are in the school science laboratory, during those few hours scheduled for thinking in this strictly logical way, they have a choice of perspectives. Shall they use life-world or scientific knowledge?

The co-existence of two domains of knowledge, one formalized and taught to specialists, the other nebulous but widely held, is not confined to ideas about the phenomena of science. Bourdieu (1977), in writing about customs and laws in different primitive communities, points to a very similar divide:

> Thus the percepts of custom, very close in this respect to sayings and proverbs, have nothing in common with the transcendent rules of a juridical code: everyone is able, not so much to cite and recite them from memory, as to reproduce them fairly accurately.
>
> (Bourdieu 1977)

In a primitive tribe there may be little need to cross the divide between everyday custom with its contradictory maxims which are situation-bound ('Too many cooks spoil the broth' and 'Many hands make light work') into the domain of jurisprudence where the law system, operated by experts, is expected to be consistently applied in all the relevant situations. It may be that novice lawyers go through a learning period where they move awkwardly from the arena of what is *considered right* to what is *defined as legal.* Certainly those of the lay public who are involved in legal disputes often find the transition puzzling. This may well be the correct analogy for the schoolchild who starts, uneasily, to learn formal science.

Children will find that some words used in science lessons carry different meanings from those they have in daily converse. This formally defined meaning, and only it, must then be consistently applied during science classwork and homework. The teacher uses a type of argument which is strong and rational rather than agreeable and social. The hardest part of all is that this alien scientific domain of thought is actually applied to the very same happenings that familiar life-world knowledge has previously described, and continues to do, outside the arena of the science laboratory.

MOVEMENT AND DISCRIMINATION

Because life-world knowledge is such a vital part of social discourse we can neither expect, nor even hope, that it will disappear when children begin to learn science. It would indeed be a poor return for the twice-weekly physics lesson if our pupils had to trade in the ability to communicate with others for this slim and specialized knowledge. In this section we will try to review some evidence for how they might attempt to cope with the problem of possessing two domains of knowledge.

Some researchers (such as Gilbert *et al.* 1982) have suggested that a common mode is to amalgamate knowledge from the two systems. Their evidence was collected from fairly substantial individual interviews where schoolchildren of all abilities were asked about their views on subjects about which they might have been taught, to an unknown degree, at some previous time. The work of Viennot (1979), on the other hand, has been applied to students with a more substantial learning background, usually physics undergraduates, and by means of written tests. On the whole this latter work showed that students tended to use *either* familiar life-world notions *or* taught science notions. The question of how and when pupils move from the use of knowledge of one sort to the other is hard to resolve by any single experimental technique.

In the examples which follow the experimental evidence will not be rehearsed in detail since it has all been reported elsewhere. The intention is merely to suggest some of the different research strategies which have been used, and their results.

In one mode the whole class can be questioned about some work they have previously learnt. The discussion 'trails' (Solomon 1985) that they produce often show a sequence of items all inhabiting one domain – usually the life-world – until a single voice referring to scientific usage triggers a sudden change in response. The consensual character of social exchanges serves here to emphasize the abrupt change from life-world thinking to that of science.

If we make the test harder by abandoning the social milieu and speaking individually to pupils, the same discontinuity may also be produced. Often a silent hesitant pupil will maintain that he or she can remember nothing more than some thin outline of life-world knowledge. Then a single cue may switch thought into the domain of science knowledge, and a whole network of meanings, theories and concepts are recollected and furnished with examples which show real understanding. It is a phenomenon that most of us can recollect from personal experience: usually we attribute it to memory retrieval problems. In the context of the present work it suggests the separate storage of items learnt in these two very distinct ways.

Finally, we can even use the clumsier tool of paper tests to catch evidence of transition between the two domains. If verbal triggers are effective moving agents, then the wording of written questions may also elicit different answers from the same pupils. The work of Viennot (1979) has shown this effect: she set substantially the same question about forces on a moving object, cast first in the form of pictures of the trajectories of juggler's balls, and then in the formal terms of abstract physics: 'if two identical masses are acted upon by identical forces . . . '. It was the hard language of abstractions which proved more effective in recalling scientific knowledge than did the more everyday example of thrown balls. Faucher (1983) and others have also reported that students have greater success in mathematical examples than in apparently 'simpler' verbal settings of the same topic.

Table 5.1 shows the type of answers given by pupils who had been taught the same course in physics, when responding to two similar questions on the same school physics test paper. The first question asked for 'examples of energy' – the second for 'changes of energy'. Although the more able pupils generally managed to use abstract generalized expressions such as 'kinetic energy', 'potential energy', etc., in answer to both questions, the data for the less able were interestingly ambiguous. Out of the 24 less able pupils 20 responded to the first question with life-world knowledge by citing a situation in which energy is used, and with abstract knowledge acquired in their physics classes for the second question. Clearly their lack of success on the first question was not due to total forgetting, but to a failure to cross over to the appropriate domain. The wording of the second question had proved more helpful in effecting the transition. Very few pupils gave mixed answers to either question. It seems that, in this context, the amalgamation of knowledge from the two domains was comparatively rare.

These kind of data suggest that the two kinds of knowledge – the one well socialized and illogical, the other specialized, logical, and less often used – may be grouped separately in the memory. Research into human retrieval

Table 5.1 Cross-tabulation of pupils' responses to two question forms

| | | ['Examples of Energy'] | | | |
		Life-World	Mixed	Physics	Total
'Energy Changes'	Life-world	0	0	1	1
	Mixed	0	0	1	1
	Physics	20	4	59	83
	Total	20	4	61	85

systems has reproduced this clustering effect. The clumping of knowledge in the memory seems to depend very strongly on the way in which it was acquired, and much less strongly on its relevant topic content: 'Input conditions for learning have a large effect on recall and almost none on "recognition"' (Tulving 1976).

If the separation of the two kinds of knowledge is a substantial reflection of their different origins, this too may add some confirmation to the social constructivist position. Were the children's knowledge personally constructed from evidence, by essentially the same hypothetico-deductive method as science uses, it might be expected to link on to school knowledge, or be obliterated by a sharper analysis of the same kind. Neither of these effects is observed in empirical research. When students learn the new formalism of scientific thought they store it in a different compartment from that of the familiar life-world thought of daily discourse.

ADDING TO GENERAL LIFE-WORLD KNOWLEDGE

Learning does not finish when we leave our last place of education, although it may be true to say that, in very many cases, the formal character of learning does. Some aspects of informal learning situations have been studied by Lucas (1991) and others. Informal knowledge has been taken to refer to that which is acquired from sources such as television, museums and occasional informative conversations. It is certainly informal as far as its sources are concerned, but it is less clear whether or not its character, as the recipient perceives it, is different in any way from that of school knowledge.

Comparatively little work has been done on this kind of science learning; even less evidence is available to indicate how the recipients evaluate and store such knowledge. Very often the information impinges on the lone viewer or listener; how then is the knowledge received? Does it become a part of the domain of theoretical abstract thought, or can it somehow be transmuted into socialized life-world knowledge? While it is not clear if these alternatives exhaust the possibilities there is now some evidence, albeit rather schematic, from which we may begin to describe the characteristics of these important additions to our knowledge.

There is little doubt that television has had the most marked effect on our cultural knowledge. It has substantially increased the range of information; it has made it more widely available within the population and, most important for the present purpose, it has made the knowledge accessible to children as well as to adults. In the past it has always been the prerogative of adults to mete out to their children those items of the social stock of knowledge that they considered to be suitable at any age. It is true that this parental censorship was never totally effective, especially when the knowledge concerned was available to other members of the child's peer group. Now, however, all kinds of information, notably that about sex or violence, are readily available. In his article 'The adultlike child and the childlike adult', Meyrowitz (1984) uses the powerful image of parents being able to 'walk their children up the staircase of social knowledge' in times which are now clearly in the past.

However, the fact that knowledge is available does not necessarily mean that it is accepted and assimilated. Indeed it is hard to see how all the information that is presented to us in this electronic age could possibly be assimilated. What probably happens is that children and adults alike adopt a 'cafeteria' attitude towards this mountain of knowledge, choosing what they will take on board as their interests and maturity dictate. Errol, in the story of change of consensus told in an earlier section, had apparently found information about energy being stored which others in his class had ignored. The boys who spoke about their television viewing in *Science, Television and the Adolescent* (Ryder 1982) also illustrate this aspect of personal selectivity.

It is not difficult to understand how this television knowledge is then socialized by being 'talked through' with friends. Around almost every corner in the school playground one can hear children rehearsing what they heard 'on the box', comparing views and thus, in the rather heavy terminology of Schutz, 'sedimenting' them in the social stock of knowledge. This process certainly introduces a strong social element into the evaluation of the knowledge after it has been received, but there is also a possibility that something of a social nature may have entered the informal learning process at a prior stage.

Early research into the reception of viewing (McQuail *et al.* 1972) showed that, far from being the kind of easy escapism that it had been considered, television and the characters it portrayed were accepted into the home as a medium for social experience. It was reported that viewers managed to identify with even the most cardboard characters in escapist fiction as well as in more realistic soap operas. This phenomenon was called 'Para-social

Interaction' (PSI). What we are concerned with here is the possibility that informative programmes might also be accepted more as social discourse than as neutral and expert information.

It is certain that television producers attempt to give their programmes interest by putting emphasis on their sensational or controversial nature. Titles such as *The Doomsday Syndrome* and *I'm not ill, I'm pregnant*, given to programmes which were very largely science information based, show one feature which helps to demystify the expert and introduce the possibility of disagreement. The other element is the technique of confrontation between rival witnesses which is thought to make for more exciting viewing. The extent to which these techniques result in the information being received as knowledge open to social negotiation must vary from one person to another.

In a series of group interviews with non-science adults talking about what they had learnt about energy from radio and television, a range of reactions was recorded. For some the demystification process had clearly not succeeded and self-deprecatory comments like 'scientists who know about these things', or 'now only a few people, like physicists, understand' were made. At the other extreme there were those like a non-graduate secretary, who said of a factual programme 'and you get this feeling, sometimes you agree and sometimes you don't'. In such cases it is clear that PSI has mediated the reception of informal information. The knowledge has begun to be socialized even before it has been talked through with other people. Hence television-generated science information may be added on, not to the store of formal theoretical knowledge built up at school and college, but to the general stock of life-world knowledge.

There is one more area open for children's social construction of scientific knowledge which may be of even greater importance than the reception of knowledge from public sources. Paradoxically this is school science teaching itself, the one source from which they might be expected to gain the abstract, context-independent knowledge of science.

There are many children for whom abstract thought systems such as science are foreign and very hard to comprehend, nevertheless their content will usually be received as non-arbitrary and uniquely correct. To this extent at least they will be distinguishable from the knowledge outcome of children's social interaction.

In the modern classroom, however, there is increasing encouragement for the discussion of scientific theory and explanation. For able children there is little doubt that this brings great benefits. It gives greater opportunity for the new theoretical understanding to be rehearsed by teacher and pupil: it extends the process of secondary socialization into the new symbolic ways of thinking.

If the discussion is not supervised by the teacher it lapses, all too easily, into the familiar agreeable discourse that characterizes the social construction of knowledge. In a small-scale inquiry into pupils' learning during their first course on electricity, Kennedy (1983) reported that although there was a disappointing rate of adoption of the taught model of current flow in a circuit, yet within each practical group the various children had all agreed on a common model. This view on how a current flowed may not have been universally applied – life-world notions very rarely are – but it was clear that interactions between the pupils had proved more telling than teacher instruction in the orthodox theory of current flow.

Such results accord well with the classic findings on human group learning (Sprott 1958), where a group consensus emerged whenever there were individual differences, regardless of the correctness of these. It was also shown in the same work that although group members would appear to follow the opinion of a confident expert the individual views would often re-emerge unchanged in subsequent tests.

The next example is taken from the comments of a group of rather less-than-average-ability children who had been learning elementary mechanics by a method which involved a great deal of pupil discussion. On being asked to compare how easy their physics lessons had been compared with those in chemistry (taught conventionally), a large proportion replied that it was 'easy' and 'just general knowledge'. Unfortunately it turned out that the very pupils who were most vociferous in this view were the ones who had fared worst in the end-of-term test (Solomon 1983b). The interview material suggests that the knowledge had been received as no more than alternative meanings to be added to the existing stock of life-world meanings. It was not surprising perhaps that many had failed altogether to perceive that this well-discussed knowledge was claiming a quite different status.

> 'Physics is easy because it's about what you know'
> T: 'You reckon you didn't learn much that was new?'
> 'No'
> T: 'No? How did you know it already?'
> 'Acceleration, I knew what acceleration meant, and about energy, and all that'
>
> . . .
>
> T: 'Is work something you knew about already?'
> 'Yes'
> T: 'Is the word "work" used in the same way in physics as it is in everyday speech?'
> 'Yes because, say, when you get a job or something that's one kind of work. But another kind is when you hold something up'.

This pupil has failed to differentiate between science knowledge and life-world knowledge. Not only are the contents undifferentiated (and incorrectly remembered), it also seems that the two systems of thought have been conflated. This pupil subsequently did very poorly in school and public examinations. It seems likely that a science course such as *Science at Work*, which aims to add to children's general knowledge rather than furnish them with different conceptual schemes, would have been more appropriate for this pupil and others of similar ability.

Children learn social skills long before they come to science lessons. For some the teacher's attempt to supply the alternative view of science amounts to an affront to the social mores. Tasker (1980) quoted a pupil who says:

> But to the teacher there is a distinct difference between our way and [the teacher's] way ... and [the teacher's] way is the right way ... that's what I find hard ... If I could say how a teacher could instruct the class I would say he teaches the theory his way and says it right ... and gets every kid in the class to write down their way of seeing that ... not what he has written – but their way – and puts it all together and tries to get a happy compromise.
>
> (Tasker 1980)

What is really hard to accept is that the scientific consensus is decided by methods of thought which allow of no 'happy compromise'. For our pupils it is harshly uncompromising and thus severely at odds with the system that children and adults use when they construct together the much less rigorous outlines of the social consensus.

REFERENCES

Black, M. 1962. *Models and metaphors.* Cornell University Press, Ithaca, NY.
Bourdieu, P. 1977. *Outline of a theory of practice.* Cambridge University Press, Cambridge.
Duit, R. 1981. 'Learning the energy concept in school – empirical results from the Philippines and West Germany.' *Physics Education*, 19: 59–66.
Faucher, G. 1983. 'The answer is not enough.' *Engineering Education*, 72: 183–4.
Gilbert, J., Osborne, R. and Fensham, P. 1982. 'Children's science and its consequences for teaching.' *Science Education*, 66: 623–33.
Halliday, M. A. K. 1978. *Language as social semiotic.* Edward Arnold, London.
Jenkins, E. 1990. 'Domestic energy resources and the elderly.' Paper given at a conference on Policies and Publics for Science and Technology, Science Museum, London.
Kelly, G. 1965. *The Psychology of personal constructs.* Norton, New York.
Kennedy, J. 1983. 'Children's use of electrical models.' MSc thesis. University of Oxford.
Kohler, W. 1927. *The mentality of apes.* Kegan Paul, Trench & Trubner, London.
Lucas, A. M. 1991. ' "Info-tainment" and informal sources for learning science.' *International Journal of Science Education*, 13: 495–504.
McQuail, D., Blumler, J. and Brown, J. 1972. 'The television audience: a revised perspective.' In McQuail, D. (ed.) *Sociology of mass communications.* Penguin, Harmondsworth, pp. 135–65.
Martin, N., Williams, P., Wilding, J., Hemmings, S. and Medway, F. 1976. *Understanding children talking.* Penguin, Harmondsworth.

Meyrowitz, J. 1984. 'The adultlike child and the childlike adult: Socialisation in an electronic age.' *Daedalus*, 113 (summer): 19–42.

Pepper, S. C. 1942. *World hypotheses*. University of California Press, Berkeley, Calif.

Ross, K. and Sutton, C. 1982. 'Concept profiles and the cultural context.' *European Journal of Science Education*, 4: 311–23.

Ryder, N. 1982. *Science, television and the adolescent*. IBA, London.

Schutz, A. (1932; trans. 1972). *The phenomenology of the social world*. Heinemann, London.

Schutz, A. and Luckman, T. 1973. *Structures of the life world*. Heinemann, London.

Solomon, J. 1983a. 'Learning about energy.' PhD thesis, Chelsea College, University of London.

Solomon, J. 1983b. 'Is physics easy?' *Physics Education*. 18: 155–60.

Solomon, J. 1985. 'Classroom discussion: a method of research for teachers?' *British Educational Research Journal*, 11: 153–62.

Solomon, J. 1992a. *Getting to know about energy*. Falmer Press, Lewes.

Solomon, J. 1992b. 'The classroom discussion of science based social issues presented on television: knowledge, attitudes and values.' *International Journal of Science Education*. 14: 431–444.

Sprott, W. 1958. *Human groups*. Penguin, Harmondsworth.

Tasker, R. 1980. 'Reconsidering the framework.' Occasional paper, University of Waikato, Waikato, New Zealand.

Tulving, E. 1976. 'Euphoric processes in recall and recognition.' In Brown, J. (ed.) *Recall and recognition*. Wiley, London.

Viennot, L. 1979. 'Spontaneous reasoning in elementary mechanics.' *European Journal of Science Education*, 1: 203–21.

Vygotsky, L. 1978. *Thought and language*. MIT Press, Cambridge, Mass.

Whorf, B. 1940. 'Science and linguistics.' In Carroll, J. B. (ed.) 1956. *Language, thought, and reality: Selected writings of Benjamin Lee Whorf*. MIT Press, Cambridge, Mass., pp. 207–32.

Wynne, B. 1992. 'Sheep farming after Chernobyl: a case study in communicating scientific information.' In Lewenstein, B. (ed.) *When science meets the public*. AAAS, Washington, DC.

Chapter 6

A view of 'understanding'

Jon Ogborn

It is so difficult to find the *beginning*. Or, better: it is difficult to begin at the beginning. And not try to go further back.

(Wittgenstein 1977, p. 471)

THE ISSUES

Introduction

There must be something wrong with a way of thinking about understanding how people think which makes it almost an obligation to place so essential a term as 'understanding' in scare quotes. The purpose of this chapter is to present a point of view from which such reservations may seem less necessary, and thereby to suggest what kind of thing is involved in understanding someone else's thoughts.

It is of course often difficult to understand someone else, and there are times when it seems impossible. What the other person thinks may be too strange; may depend on too many unshared assumptions; may run too much counter to one's own view of how things are; and so on. It may also be that the other person does not understand very clearly or completely what he or she is trying to explain. But these difficulties are not the source of the unease which has led psychologists and others to shy away from a direct and unproblematic use of the term 'understanding'. Rather, the difficulties are philosophical in character, deriving from a conceptualization of psychological processes which makes them seem impossible of access in principle.

My chapter is not, however, a philosophical essay. Its purpose is to offer an interpretation of the work of Gordon Pask, whose 'Conversation Theory' derives from a cybernetic approach to cognition. I am not, I think, alone in finding Pask's writings obscure and difficult, perhaps sometimes wilfully so. But I have come to think that they contain a view of what is involved in such activities as 'explaining' and 'understanding' that is potentially of great value in guiding research into students' ways of thinking. The chapter tries to show that there can be a point of view from which some of the philosophical problems are less paralysing, so far as the business of trying to identify students' concepts in science is concerned, and it will describe briefly an attempt to put this point of view to work in such research.

The solipsist tendency

Within the rag-bag of philosophical views which most of us (myself included) carry around with us, inherited from some centuries of Western thought, it is next to impossible to refute arguments to the effect that thoughts and feelings are private in a particularly ultimate way. The rag-bag contains notions such as: that immediate 'sense impressions' are a direct and privileged contact with 'how things really are'; that what is not directly observed is unreal; that the only meaning of a term is its method of verification or falsification. It is a perverse fact that such positivism is so defenceless against solipsism: the more strongly I hold that what I truly know is what I currently can notice, the harder it is for me to claim that it is not all my dream.

I am not equipped, and will not attempt, to analyse these difficulties further. D. W. Hamlyn (1978) expresses very clearly one aspect which will be of importance in what follows:

> Traditional epistemology, since at least Descartes, has tended to present the problems as if they were such that the individual has to solve them by himself without reference to others; it has presented men as solitary centres of consciousness for whom the fundamental problem is the construction of a world including other men, and this as a problem that each man has to solve on his own.
>
> (Hamlyn 1978)

Such ideas have had a lasting effect on the conception of social science, in particular having made it impossible for psychology, for a sizeable slice of its existence, to admit 'concepts' or 'thoughts' as objects of study. They relate to the strong streak of individualism in Western thought, in which 'thinking' is only conceived of as going on privately and invisibly in the head of one individual at a time. They probably also relate to the success of natural science; the very concept of 'objectivity' maps the goal of being dispassionate onto the inanimacy of physical objects. Sticks and stones are held not to tell lies; humans are renowned for the opposite.

To do research on students' own ideas, however, obliges one to have a view about what it is for a person to have ideas, and even more crucially, to be as clear as possible about what is involved in being able to claim that one has discovered something about what those ideas are: *that one knows what someone else thinks.* Different researchers deal with (or avoid) these questions in various ways. A great merit of Pask is that he tackles them head-on.

THE NATURE OF PASK'S THEORY

Pask is perhaps best known for his distinctions between holist and serialist styles of cognition, and the associated distinction between comprehension and operation learning (Pask 1976c). This aspect of his thinking has been thoroughly reviewed by Entwistle (1978).

The underlying theory has, however, been less widely considered, not least because of the formidable difficulties presented by tracing it through the series of books and papers in which it evolves. Further, the theory is not a single entity, but intermingles elements of at least three kinds: a *theory-of-cognition*, an *epistemology*, and a set of *heuristics* for psychological investigation. All derive, in addition, from a relatively unfamiliar and novel cybernetic point of view, and are expressed in a variety of often idiosyncratic formalisms.

From its earliest (e.g. Pask 1961), Pask's work has had two essential characteristics: first, a belief that human thought is to be understood in cybernetic terms, and, second, a determination that any such understanding must capture that which is most human about human thought. It is no accident that this early book concluded with an account of the circumstances in which Pask might consent to be employed by a computer, including stipulating that it should laugh at his jokes!

Pask's thinking, however, differs in important ways from that which is common in cognitive science, artificial intelligence, or information processing psychology. It is distinctive in seeking always the most general conditions needed for any thinking system to function at all, as opposed to proposing detailed models of functioning. The difference is like that between information theory and cryptography: the first considers the necessary conditions for encryption and decoding to work at all; the second develops and elaborates particular ways of doing them. Thus a theory in artificial intelligence or cognitive science may propose some model for semantic memory or for adaptive learning; Pask by contrast takes the cybernetic approach of asking what general kind of system structure and control would be required for any such model to function. Thus what matters about Pask's sketches of kinds of system is their *necessary architecture*. And this can be understood without looking at any programs at all.

The conversation as a minimum architecture

Pask proposes an architecture for the minimum system which could even in principle be imagined as learning and going on learning. A helpful way to arrive at a description of the conversational structure is to take simpler systems, and to ask why they could not possibly serve this purpose. This is done in the next section. The account should not, however, be read as suggesting that the conversational structure is a compound of elementary parts. It is intended as the *least* complex structure one needs to consider seriously; as the cognitive object with which we need to *begin*.

It will be seen that the basic requirements Pask imposes on any structure are that it must accommodate *understanding, learning,* and *the continuous self-maintenance and propagation of knowledge.* In doing this, the theory challenges many of our deepest prejudices, notably that the sole object to be understood is the isolated thinking individual. So deeply ingrained is the prejudice that even Pask's own work is wrongly seen as attributing to individuals 'properties' such as holism or serialism. It cannot be too strongly emphasized that this is a mistake: a conversation is only sometimes to be thought of as 'inside' or as 'a property of' a single person, and indeed Pask's theory incorporates as part of its epistemology a novel account of individuals.

In brief, a conversation is a self-sustaining structure, which has concepts and which has ways of reproducing, as well as of using, those concepts. It has also to have ways of reproducing its means of reproduction.

The term 'reproduction' may be puzzling. Another deeply rooted prejudice which Pask challenges is the metaphor of 'storage' for knowledge. Memory, for Pask, is not recovery from store but is active reconstruction, and it is in relation to this that he builds 'understanding' into the theory. This approach leads him to a similarly based account of cognitive novelty, with evolution arising through reproduction. This part of the theory draws heavily on the more recent theory of self-reproducing automata.

THE CONVERSATION STRUCTURE

In this section, I build up, from successively less and less inadequate system structures, the minimum cognitive structure that Pask calls a 'conversation'. The arguments will be informal, but could all be cast in more formal and rigorous terms. The argument follows closely that of Pask (1975b).

Some inadequate structures

Figure 6.1 shows an extremely simple system. It has a well-defined set of entities on which it operates, which we will call its domain Δ, and a collection of processes of procedures π which operate on that domain. The arrow across the box representing the domain indicates that the procedures do something to the domain.

Real systems which have such an architecture could range from a fire heating a room, a fixed computer program working on data, or a government official following the rule book without exception. Any such system functions only when its procedures match exactly what is required to happen. It functions blindly, without regard to the results of its operations in the domain. Note that we are asking what the system can do, of and by itself, not what it can do in co-operation with other systems (perhaps people).

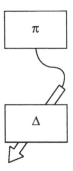

Figure 6.1 Procedures operating on a domain

Figure 6.2 shows the first and obvious improvement: the feedback of information from the domain is provided to the procedures in π which modify or select their effects. Examples include heating systems with thermostats, automatic steering for ships, computer control of industrial plant, or a teacher who modifies work set in accordance with results on previous work. The properties of simple feedback systems are well understood, and Pask's early work explored their possibilities and limitations (Pask 1975a reviews this stage of his development.) That work included several attempts at adaptive teaching systems: for example, computer programs that taught typing skills.

The fundamental limitation of all such systems is that, of and by themselves, they can only cope with foreseen types and ranges of variation in the domain. The thermostat is helpless if the temperature goes outside its range, and pointless if the real problem is that all the windows are open; the computer control program may take very undesirable action in unforeseen circumstances. The essential point is that the control information can only alter parameters of existing procedures, including choosing which existing procedures to use, but it cannot create new procedures.

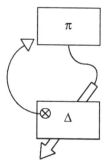

Figure 6.2 Feedback from the domain

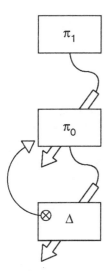

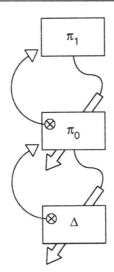

Figure 6.3 Procedure-modifying procedures

Figure 6.4 Procedure-modification with feedback

Figures 6.3 and 6.4 suggest the next two improvements. A new set of procedures π_1, is introduced which can alter the procedures (relabelled π_0) that work on the domain. Figure 6.4 adds feedback from π_0, the domain of π_1, to π_1. The General Problem Solver (Newell and Simon 1972) works rather like Figure 6.3: a set of fixed procedure-modifying rules cast about until they get somewhere. The program HACKER (Sussman 1975; see also Boden 1977 or Boden 1981) is more like Figure 6.4, with a fault diagnosis system which it uses to rewrite procedures it has generated.

Perhaps Figure 6.3 is like a student who cannot do a problem and simply tries all the ways he knows, while Figure 6.4 is more like one who chooses what to do by a diagnosis of why previous attempts have failed. Figure 6.4 would also correspond to a computer programmer developing and improving his program, while one might say that the hypothesis of random biological evolution makes it like Figure 6.3, with no feedback guidance of processes which change the organism-building processes.

No suggestion is intended that the system structures model the examples in any direct way. What is asserted is more abstract: that each system has certain precise possibilities and limitations which mirror those of the examples. In particular, only the structure of Figure 6.4 can evolve step by step so as to develop (other than by chance) new ways of dealing with a changing environment. This is not to say that a given system *will* do so, but is to say that nothing less *could* do so. In saying this, it has to be remembered that the structure diagram must show everything there is. With a suitable *deus ex machina* the simplest system can do a lot.

It is also not asserted that a system must contain physically distinct regions like those shown, but only that the distinctive functions discussed must be available. Just as in a computer, the same hardware may exercise both control and calculation functions (somewhat analogous to π_0 and π_1 respectively), the essential point being that each function has distinct effects and information requirements.

To summarize, a single level feedback system, such as Figure 6.2, powerful though it is, cannot be sufficient for evolving or learning in *unforeseen* ways, because to do that it must make new things it can do. To do that other than by chance, it must have information about what changes to its processes are doing to those processes.

Of course we could sketch more complex diagrams, perhaps with further levels, or with nested structures. The point here is that a structure like Figure 6.4 is the least that will do: we might do more with more, but could do nothing with less.

Self-reproducing systems

Up to this point, there has been a hidden assumption: namely, that the content of the systems is somehow stored in them, either in the way a computer program is stored in memory, or in the way that the function of a thermostat is stored in its physical structure.

This is a place where Pask introduces a radical notion. It is that continued existence of cognitive objects should be looked on as *self-reproduction*, not as 'storage'. This is to apply to the perpetuation of systems the same principle applied to their functioning: that the system should work of and by itself.

This seems perverse, or at least unnecessary, if we hold to the prejudice that whatever one thinks or learns or understands is (perhaps by definition) to be thought of as 'inside' one person. And much cognitive theorizing has been about the nature of various aspects of human storage of information in memory. The 'storage' idea suffers from the objection that it is not protected against accident and damage of storage elements, so that devices like redundancy have to be introduced to explain how humans can possibly remember so well with such frail storage as is offered by neurones.

Pask's idea is that the metaphor is wrong, and that the problem needs to be stated as that of how knowledge and understanding are recreated as the organism evolves and adapts. Seen as a cybernetic problem, the essence of reproduction is the existence, in some sense, of a *description* of the system within the system, just as in biology we are accustomed to the idea of DNA containing a prescription for the construction of proteins and a means of using double strands to 'describe itself' so that it can be replicated.

Figure 6.5 shows a minimum configuration. An example could be a computer screen and its memory map, with the screen drawn from the map and the map taken by sensing the screen. The basic requirement is that the system requires a

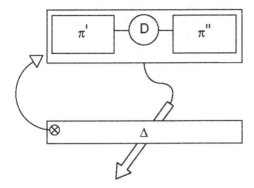

Figure 6.5 Descriptions for replication

description D of itself, and procedures π'' which can use that description to remake its procedures π'. So Pask's proposal is that a thinking individual keeps its knowledge going by keeping on telling itself what it knows.

Conversations

Putting together Figures 6.4 and 6.5 leads to Figure 6.6, which is the structure Pask calls a *conversation*, which he claims as the minimum structure for an entity which can think and learn autonomously. The procedures π_0 which

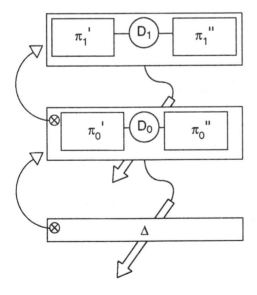

Figure 6.6 A conversation

work on the domain, and the procedures π_1, which work on π_0 are divided into two parts linked by descriptions D_0 and D_1. There could be more complex divisions, but there could not be less than two.

Figure 6.6 could represent a person knowing some area of science. The domain is the set of appropriate material (problems, or apparatus, say) and π_0 what we would call the ability to operate in that domain; π_1 would be the ability to use or alter the previous abilities. The descriptions, at each level, would be knowledge about these abilities which enable them to be sustained and kept in being.

But nothing requires Figure 6.6 to represent one organism. It would serve rather well to describe the community of scientists of a particular kind, which both uses and perpetuates and evolves knowledge of its own kind, so that the (ever-changing) community is a stable adaptive conversation about its subject matter. Pask distinguishes two ways of individuating: m- and p-individuals. An m-individual is a physical entity, whether person or machine, whose boundaries are skin or metal. A p-individual is a cognitive entity with the structure of (at least) a conversation. An m-individual, like a personal computer, is not a p-individual. A p-individual may but need not coincide with an m-individual; so far as people are concerned it is better to think of several p-individuals with distinct stable cognitive structures inhabiting each m-individual. But also, as in the case of cognitive communities, several m- or p-individuals may make up a p-individual, which none of them alone could realize.

CONVERSATIONS BETWEEN CONVERSATIONS

All that has been said so far is that if one chooses to look at 'systems which think' as system mechanisms, they could not have less than this kind of system architecture, regardless of the particular way they work. Claims of this general kind are far from new, particularly in information theory and computer science. What Pask has done, however, is to exploit the ideas to define essential terms such as *concept* and *understanding*, and so as to specify what would count as having evidence of them.

Concepts

To define *concept* Pask asks how two systems would establish agreement about procedures π_0 operating on a given domain. Figure 6.7 shows the relevant structure, in which B is to find out about A's concepts.

When would we say that B shared A's concepts? First, and obviously, they must agree to be talking about the same thing: to have a common domain Δ. If B turns out to be able to do what A can do, do we say that they share the same concepts? Some may wish to, but Pask does not. Two computer programs may function in the same way but be radically different

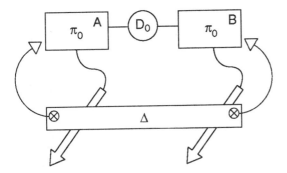

Figure 6.7 Agreement about concepts

internally – one might solve equations numerically and the other by Monte Carlo methods, for example. We may say that B can *imitate* A.

For B to learn A's concepts, B first needs to get from A descriptions D of the procedures π_0A which A uses, and to build from the descriptions procedures π_0B which B can use on the same domain. If B's procedures have the same effect on the domain as A's, we still have to say that B has picked up enough to imitate A. But if B now describes back to A how the new procedures work, and A can construct procedures from them which match A's previous procedures, we will say that B shares A's *concepts*.

Less formally, A tells B how to do things, and both check that B has got it right by B telling A what has been learned. The teacher counts the pupils as having got the idea when the pupil can both do it and say how to do it.

Notice that we neither know nor say that B possesses identically the same procedures as A; the common ground is established at the different level of 'saying how'. Without this level, the two may or may not have the same concepts, but the evidence is inadequate to say that they do.

Understanding

Being able to do what another does, and to say how, is still not enough for us to say that there is a shared understanding. Thus one might teach a pupil how to do long division, but not count the pupil as understanding long division. For that, a level of 'saying why' is needed as well as one of 'saying how'. Figure 6.8 includes this level.

In Pask's terms, what is needed for B to *understand* A is that in addition to sharing the same concepts, they share the same concepts of those concepts. This means that B must get from A in addition descriptions D_1 of how to construct procedures π_1, which reconstruct the procedures π_0. Further, B must be able to give back to A descriptions at that level, for A to check that they do indeed allow A to reconstruct the procedures which A uses.

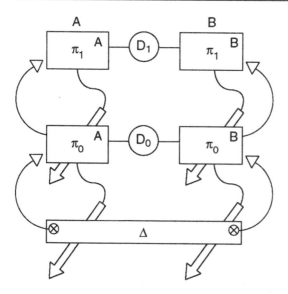

Figure 6.8 Shared understandings

The descriptions are what we call *explanations*. Sharing a concept is to locate a common level of explanation of 'how'. Sharing a common understanding is to locate a common level of 'why', that is to say, of explanations of explanations. Again, nothing is claimed about the *identity* of A's and B's procedures at either level, but only that A and B have in common ways of saying how to do things and of saying why they work. The teacher counts the pupil as understanding if the pupil can teach the teacher both how and why.

Conversation and understanding

Figure 6.8 has, of course, the same structure as Figure 6.6. That is, Figure 6.8, representing the establishing of an understanding between A and B, is the same structure as Pask imposes as necessary for a system to possess and maintain knowledge. Thus in Figure 6.8, if A and B are to keep as well as share understanding, each must be a conversation as well as being a participant in a conversation.

Thus Pask makes the account of memory the same as the account of understanding. In a precise sense, a person teaches himself how to remember. Equally, learning is seen as a form of replication. So Pask would say that to have a stable understanding, and so to maintain a memory of a conceptual domain, a system must do for itself just what a pair of systems must do for one to learn to understand from the other.

THEORY, EPISTEMOLOGY, OR HEURISTICS?

It is clear that Pask's Conversation Theory is a subtle and detailed working out of the simple proposition, 'If you want to know, ask.' But what is the status of this account? Is it to be seen as a psychological theory of knowing of some kind? Is it to be seen as an epistemology, defining when a system counts as knowing or understanding? Or is it a set of heuristics for teaching, learning and remembering; a reminder for example that getting the pupil to teach back to the teacher is an important tactic? It has, I believe, elements of all three (see Pask, 1976b).

Theory

I remain unsure of the sense in which Conversation Theory is to be understood as a psychological theory. This is in part because of its cybernetic character which, as discussed previously, gives it the form of specifying necessary structural conditions rather than mechanisms.

The essential components of the theory are its terms, and a set of theorems taken over from the mathematical theory of self-reproducing automata of the kind, 'If a system is to do X it must have a structure not less powerful than Y'. The terms are the procedures π, which represent how the knowing subject knows; the descriptions D which can sometimes be made accessible, which mediate the continual construction and reconstruction of procedures; and the distinction between (at least) two levels, which correspond to knowing and knowing about knowing.

Much of it can be made to seem to make good practical sense. We do indeed count a child who can do sums by rote, but who cannot say why they are done that way, as having got some idea but not as understanding. We do want to say, 'Yes, but tell me why', both when we grasp how to do something but cannot yet make sense of it, and when we want to see if someone else 'really understands'. We do often say that it was only when we had to teach a topic that we really understood it properly.

Further, memory and understanding do seem to have an organic link. We do find that we easily forget things we learnt to do without learning how to work out how to do them. This we call 'arbitrary' knowledge; that is, we assert that we have no rules with which to reconstruct it, and as a last resort we use 'hacks' in the form of mnemonics, precisely as some kind of procedure to construct procedures. In Pask's account, remembering and understanding are in essence identical.

It may be noted that, although the terms are very different, Pask's theory is rather Piagetian in tone, particularly in the stress on intelligence as activity, and in the conceptual account of memory.

It must be said that the psychological aspects of his theory are developed much further in Pask's writings than has been indicated here (particularly in

Pask 1975b and 1976a). It gives some account of, for example, why much knowledge (such as how to talk English or drive a car) becomes unconscious; of how to measure cognitive loads; of different types of conversational role that can exist; and of how to fit intentions into the theory.

Epistemology

The epistemology contained in Pask's writings makes a radical attack on many current views. A key aspect is that he treats explaining as a behaviour. Thus a classic behaviourist epistemology looks like the self denying ordinance represented in Figure 6.9(a), of counting only observed actions on a domain as possible observations. As we shall show later, Pask also restores the missing experi- menter to this picture.

Certain theories in artificial intelligence would look like Figure 6.9(b), where a computational system is constructed 'alongside' the subject. Where this system is not seen simply as an *engineering alternative* to the subject, but is proposed as a *model* of the subject, there is often serious doubt as to just what aspects of the system are and are not to be taken as modelling features of the subject's working. At least we require such systems to have 'interesting' features: that is, features which we feel (as potential subjects being modelled) are 'something like' what we might do. Tests such as comparing 'talk aloud' protocols with program traces (see, for example, Newell and Simon 1972) look like getting descriptions D from the subject, and seeing whether they can be construed as descriptions of the procedures in the model.

Similar issues arise in recent work on expert systems (see, for example, Forsyth 1984 or Johnson and Keravnou 1984). Here we may think of the user as learning from the system. Early systems could provide very little by way of explanation, being generally restricted to indicating which relations were or were not currently established (that is, a trace of the state of the

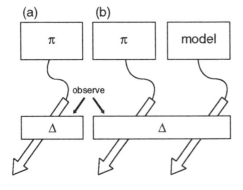

Figure 6.9 Systems and epistemologies

procedures π_0). The need to provide a level corresponding to Pask's level 1 (that is, meta-knowledge) is now widely accepted.

What Pask contributes is an account of the epistemology of experiments designed to elicit knowledge. This epistemology introduces total symmetry into the experimenter–subject relationship. For Pask, the design of an experiment (or of a teaching situation) becomes a matter first of agreeing about a common domain and then of finding means of externalizing descriptions D_0 and D_1 at levels 0 and 1. Figure 6.10 illustrates the conversational structure of an experiment.

The subject and experimenter participate in a conversation. The conversation is split by two interfaces (shaded in Figure 6.10). The vertical interface is the medium or device (be it only air through which sound waves pass) in which the descriptions D_0 and D_1 can be made public as they pass between participants. The horizontal interface is the medium or device with which what either participant does in the domain is made public. The nature of either interface may restrict what can be made public through them, and so limit what the experiment can in principle discover.

None of this makes any assumptions about peering inside the subject's head. The experimenter B, wishing to find out A's knowledge of an agreed domain, asks for descriptions D about how to do things, and then teaches them back to A (by the same process of describing what to do) until A agrees that B has the same concept. B also asks A why the procedures described work, that is, how to reconstruct them if they are 'forgotten'. Again B

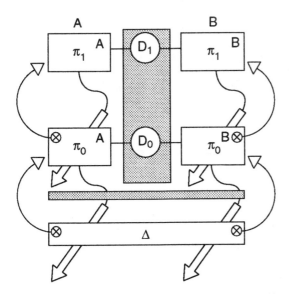

Figure 6.10 Experiment as conversation

teaches these explanations of explanations back until A agrees that B understands A in A's terms. B never 'sees inside' A, but instead A and B come to a stable understanding of one another which has a public dimension in terms of the descriptions given by each.

The actual understanding is reached between B and A, and is not itself a public entity. But B can now claim to understand A, and may attempt in whatever way seems fit to communicate that understanding to others, including readers of research reports.

Heuristics

One may regard the foregoing section as also a set of valuable heuristics for conducting experiments to elicit knowledge, and for organizing effective teaching.

The heuristics for an experiment run roughly as follows. First, provide something to talk about, and ensure that the subject agrees to play the role of subject in regard to this subject-matter. The first is common; precautions to ensure the second perhaps less so. Then provide means of recording questions and descriptions, and actions on the domain. Be sure to ask questions to elicit descriptions at both levels ('how' and 'why'). Finally, teach back the experimenter's understanding, modifying it as A corrects it, until A agrees that B understands A.

Heuristics for teaching (where the teacher is now A) run parallel. The domain needs to be agreed, and both parties must agree to play their respective roles as teacher and learner (so far as the learner is concerned, this means trying to understand – what Ausubel would call 'meaningful learning set'). The essential prescription is to use teach-back from pupil to teacher, to see if understanding has been reached. One may object that these conditions are difficult or impossible to attain, but the point of the conversational approach is to bring out the price which will be paid for not attaining them.

APPLICATIONS

The purpose of this section is to mention briefly how the framework of ideas sketched so far may find applications, particularly in relation to understanding children's informal ideas.

Elicitation

Nancy Johnson (in association with me) carried out a research study into the careful elicitation of children's ideas in arithmetic, with the main aim of testing whether elicitation within a conversation theory framework was possible and useful (Johnson 1983).

Subjects were 12 year old children. Each was interviewed individually for half an hour, at twice-weekly intervals for three weeks (6 interviews). The domain was simple arithmetic. The researcher set out to establish a 'contract' with each child that she wanted to understand how the child understood 'sums'. This agreement was made meaningful by, for example:

- having the child nominate topics to talk about
- bringing back to the next interview material taken from the last, to be checked by the child.

Teachback was used, including the interviewer constructing new examples which, if her understanding was correct, would fit in a predictable way into the child's conceptions (much as a linguist learning a new language would construct and check test examples from the current grammar so as to test it).

The data obtained were treated in two ways. The main effort went into constructing communicable representations of the children's ideas, using both Minsky-like frames and systemic networks (Bliss *et al.* 1983). These were used to address questions both of the merits and demerits of different representations, and questions about how far the children had similar or very different knowledge structures. The second use made of the data was to test their predictive value, both by giving a recognition test of the ideas elicited to a larger sample, and by showing that the data collected could be used to predict the subjects' performances on a standard NFER arithmetic test.

Intelligent tutoring systems

A live issue in the development of intelligent tutoring systems (Sleeman and Brown 1982) is the provision of 'models of the learner'. Particular attention has been given to models of wrong or miscredited concepts or procedures, an early example being the BUGGY system to detect systematic errors in subtraction. This system constructed hypothetical 'bugs' in subtraction algorithms, and attempted to identify those the learner might have by matching the output of the 'buggy' rule with that of the learner.

There are two difficulties with such procedures. One is that the number of 'known bugs' can grow very large (into the hundreds) so that too many trials are needed to discover which might operate. Secondly, from the point of view of the Pask framework, the apparent rigour of the system is illusory: it tests only if its domain output matches that of the subject, not whether it shares the subject's concepts. Success hinges critically on whether the *type* of 'bug' hypothesized is remotely correct.

Theories of children's informal ideas

This book, and much other recent writing (for example, Guidoni 1985, Ogborn 1985, Viennot 1985, Hewson 1985, Osborne and Wittrock 1985), is concerned among other things to clarify what view one would best take of the status of children's informal ideas. In particular, a number of different views have been expressed about what sort of theory may be needed.

It seems certain that a necessary part of any such theory will be some way of giving an account of the ideas children hold, and of representing the extent to which they are more or less structured, and more or less fluid. Some have criticized descriptions of children's ideas for being formulated too much in terms of the scientific world view, and not in terms proper to the child. It seems to me that the framework offered by Pask has some promise as a methodology for eliciting ideas, at least where one is concentrating on individuals.

Although some would regard children's informal ideas as probably deriving simply from misunderstandings (McClelland 1985), many regard them as belonging to some kind of common-sense world view. On the latter view, there arises a crucial problem: common sense is by its nature that which seems obvious, and is difficult to elicit because of the presumption that it is common ground between source and questioner (asked how to read, one may omit to mention the need for light). Here the strong contractual form of Pask's framework for conversational structures may be very important. At the least, one needs a form of inquiry which legitimates asking about seemingly trivial and obvious things (the same problem is also discussed in Chapter 7).

CONCLUSION

Much of the kind of research discussed in this book and in others like it is descriptive. Put simply, the researcher has seen something and is trying to tell others about it, while those who read the research are trying to understand what the researcher means.

The remark may not be as trivial as it sounds. The claim of such research cannot avoid being that in some sense one *understands what someone else thinks*. To communicate its results is at some level to offer to *teach others* what that person thinks.

Such research has an unavoidable need for a way of thinking about its subjects, its problems and its results, within which such notions have a clear and intelligible place. It is indeed difficult to find the right beginning point, neither going too far back into 'sense impressions' or the like as the basic cognitive elements, nor failing to go far enough back behind simply reporting things subjects happen to say. It seems to me that Pask does at least offer one plausible kind of place at which to begin.

Acknowledgements

This chapter is an extended and modified version of a paper (Ogborn and Johnson 1984), which was first published in *Kybernetes*.

REFERENCES

Bliss, J., Ogborn, J. and Monk, M. 1983. *Qualitative data analysis for educational research.* Croom Helm, London.

Boden, M. 1977. *Artificial intelligence and natural man.* Harvester Press, Brighton.

Boden, M. 1981. *Minds and mechanisms.* Harvester Press, Brighton.

Entwistle, N. J. 1978. 'Knowledge structure and styles of learning.' *British Journal of Educational Psychology,* 48: 255–6.

Forsyth, R. 1984. *Expert systems: principles and case studies.* Chapman and Hall Computing, London.

Guidoni, P. 1985. 'On natural thinking.' *European Journal of Science Education,* 7: 133{40.

Hamlyn, D. W. 1978. *Experience and the growth of understanding.* Routledge and Kegan Paul, London.

Hewson, P. W. 1985. 'Epistemological commitments in the learning of science.' *European Journal of Science Education,* 7: 163–72.

Johnson, L. and Keravnou, E. T. 1984. *A guide to expert system technology.* Abacus Press, London.

Johnson, N. E. 1983. 'Elicitation and representation of children's arithmetic knowledge.' PhD thesis, Chelsea College, University of London.

McClelland, J. A. G. 1985. 'Misconceptions in mechanics and how to avoid them.' *Physics Education,* 20: 159–62.

Newell, A. and Simon, H. A. 1972. *Human problem solving.* Prentice-Hall, New York.

Ogborn, J. 1985. 'Understanding students' understandings: an example from dynamics.' *European Journal of Science Education,* 7: 141–50.

Ogborn, J. and Johnson, L. 1984. 'Conversation theory.' *Kybernetes,* 13: 7–16.

Osborne, J. and Wittrock, M. 1985. 'The generative learning model and its implications for science education.' *Studies in Science Education,* 12: 59–87.

Pask, G. 1961. *An approach to cybernetics.* Hutchinson, London.

Pask, G. 1975a. *The cybernetics of human learning and performance.* Hutchinson, London.

Pask, G. 1975b. *Conversation cognition and learning: a cybernetic theory and method.* Elsevier, Amsterdam.

Pask, G. 1976a. *Conversation theory: applications in education and epistemology.* Elsevier, Amsterdam.

Pask, G. 1976b. 'Conversational techniques in the study and practice of education.' *British Journal of Educational Psychology,* 46: 12–25.

Pask, G. 1976c. 'Styles and strategies of learning.' *British Journal of Educational Psychology,* 46: 128–48.

Sleeman, D. and Brown, J. S. 1982. *Intelligent tutoring systems.* Academic Press, London.

Sussman, G. J. 1975. *A computer model of skill acquisition.* American Elsevier, New York.

Viennot, L. 1985. 'Analysing students' reasoning in science: a pragmatic view of theoretical problems.' *European Journal of Science Education,* 7: 151–62.

Wittgenstein, L. 1977. (Editors: Anscombe, G. E. M. and von Wright, G. H.) *On certainty.* Blackwell, Oxford.

Chapter 7

A common-sense theory of motion

Issues of theory and methodology examined through a pilot study

Joan Bliss and Jon Ogborn

INTRODUCTION

The past few years have seen a wide variety of particular research results in pupils' conceptions in various scientific concept areas. (See Solomon, this volume, Chapter 1, for reviews.) These studies share with those in other concept areas a rich set of particular results, but researchers differ as to whether pupils' conceptions represent systematic mental structures or *ad hoc* temporary constructions. Proposed sources include language, kinaesthetic and sensory experience, socialized forms of explanation, even simple confusion. Some take a 'constructivist' position (whether derived from Piaget or Kelly); others view pupils' conceptions as misconceptions arising from defective learning (Gilbert and Watts 1983; Driver and Erickson 1983). However, such broad positions do not so far lead easily to testable hypotheses.

The research discussed in this chapter was our first empirical pilot study of common-sense reasoning which inspired further research and theorizing (Bliss, Ogborn and Whitelock 1989, Bliss and Ogborn 1992, 1993, Ogborn and Bliss 1990). This study was crucial in that it set out to do two things: to construct and refine this first explanatory common-sense theory of motion, and to develop a methodology that allowed the proposed theory to be tested.

A preliminary sketch of such a common-sense theory of motion had already been developed (Ogborn 1985) and is summarized below. These ideas derive from Hayes' (1979) 'naive physics manifesto' which attempts a formalization of ordinary everyday knowledge of the physical world. It is proposed that conceptions of motion derive from schemes which are systematic and can be described as formal structures. The proposed theory makes testable predictions about normal expectations of possible and impossible motions, and about common-sense descriptions of motion and explanations of its causes. Our view would be that these schemes develop early in life, essentially through the internalization of actions, and persist into adulthood.

In this chapter we describe the results of a pilot study that both allows us to look at the validity of the methodology and to examine some of the basic assumptions of the common-sense theory.

Sketch for a common-sense theory of motion

Two basic and related terms of the theory are 'support' and 'falling'. If an object is supported it does not fall; if it is not supported it falls, until it is once more supported. Falling has an initial cause, namely a loss of support, but is a natural motion in that one need not look for a cause (a force or agency) for it to continue, only for a continued lack of support.

Everything needs support, except only the ground, which gives support but is not itself supported. Thus the ground never falls but often stops a fall. Examples of kinds of support include resting on something, being fixed to something or hanging from something. Water and air can also support things (floating), this support often being partial.

To support something needs 'strength' or 'effort' (or both). Thus a shelf supports heavy books by being strong; alternatively an aeroplane or a bird can support itself by its own effort, by flying. People support things (e.g. carry loads) using both strength and effort.

If the strength of a support is not enough it may break. If the strength is enough the support takes (that is, absorbs) the weight of things it supports. We do not have to think of a well supported object having weight, unless the support is liable to break. As a support, the ground is infinitely strong and cannot break.

There can also be partial support. A swimmer may be partly supported by the water, and may make up the rest of the support by the effort of swimming. A partial support means a partial fall, such as sinking. A dropped piece of tissue 'floats' down, partly supported by air.

A law of falling is that, having started to fall, things fall more rapidly the higher up they start and the heavier they are.

For these reasons, movement is conceptualized as taking place either on the ground (or on something supported by the ground), or as taking place in the air, above the ground. Motions which go up or down are distinguished from those which merely 'go along'. In this sense, the 'space' of motions has a preferred direction.

To describe motion further we need two more basic concepts, 'place' and 'path'. An object sitting still is at a certain place relative to other objects – on, under, beside, etc. One kind of motion consists of changing the place of something, as in passing a plate or pushing something aside. Another kind of motion is that in which the object is moving by itself – going on its way. The path it is following, and where it is along that path, is what locates it, not the place it happens to be in at any moment. Motions are judged relative to the ground.

Motions of both kinds require effort, unless achieved by falling. Effort is used to change the place of something; to change the path, including starting and stopping; and to keep going along the path. Any lifting or raising involved requires additional effort. There are three possible sources of effort:

effort of another agent on the object; effort generated by the object; effort *of* the present motion of the object.

Thus if you hand me a book or pass the salt you supply effort *on* the object to change its position. If you kick a ball along the ground you supply effort *on* the ball to start it going, after which it rolls using effort *of* its motion. An athlete running or a car being driven use effort generated by themselves, in order to keep moving and, if they need to swerve or stop, to change path.

The effort needed is larger the heavier the object. The effort to start or keep moving is larger the larger the speed. If place is being changed, the effort is larger the larger the change of position; if path, the larger the effect on speed and direction of path.

The character of each kind of motion depends on the kind of support present. An object such as a bird or aeroplane uses effort both to support itself and to keep itself going. A ball thrown upwards in the air has effort *on* it from the thrower, but uses the effort *of* its motion to rise. When this is used up, since it has no effort to support itself and is not supported, it falls.

The effort of the motion has the special characteristic that it cannot be used to change the path of the same object (otherwise a motion would control itself). An object has no effort *of* motion when it is at rest relative to the ground.

The effort *of* motion is handed on dynamically moment by moment. The present motion makes the coming motion. Where the speed changes little, as with a tennis ball or a dart, motion along the path is easy, with little or no effort being taken away from the effort of the motion. A motion like this uses up little effort, but still employs effort to keep going.

Forces and gravity

Forces, including gravity, are not mentioned as such in the theory, though the general term 'effort' covers some of their possible uses. It is proposed that such terms are added later to the basic natural scheme, gaining properties from the scheme rather than giving their properties to the scheme. That is, people hear such words in use and give them meaning and roles consistent with what they already think.

Since 'force' is a word used to indicate what, among other things, produces motion, we may expect it to acquire many of the properties of effort. In particular, we expect to find a strong sense that force resides in a moving thing, and is used up in keeping motion going or making the object rise.

'Gravity' further illustrates the point. Since falling is, in the scheme, a natural motion whose continuation is a matter of absence of support, not presence of a driving effort, there is initially no need for gravity at all (the ever present needs no accounting for). However, a falling body can deliver effort, and has a motion which continues, so it may be attractive to natural reasoning to invent a supply of effort for it.

The properties attributed to gravity will depend on what it is thought to do. If gravity is thought of as starting off the downward motion of a body, when it loses support, it will be thought of as 'coming into effect' when a ball reaches its highest point. If bodies are thought of as falling at constant speed, the faster the higher they start, gravity needs to be stronger higher up. If they are thought of as falling faster and faster, gravity needs to get stronger as one gets lower. Thus the theory suggests that various views are explicable, and predicts the other beliefs with which they should be associated.

Gravity, and perhaps force, are optional extra ideas in the common-sense theory. That is, changing beliefs about them will not modify any expectation of the theory, but will rather be adjusted or glossed so as to fit in with those expectations.

ELICITING A COMMON-SENSE THEORY OF MOTION

The scientific account of dynamics has evolved so as to be posed in terms which run counter to obvious common sense. By contrast, the common-sense theory is intended to represent the way in which children and adults make sense of their experience in the world, experience which derives from the fact that humans are, among other things, material objects on a gravitating planet with a rough surface and a not very dense atmosphere. The problem with trying to develop a method to investigate such knowledge is that it is so fundamental and primitive that much of it remains tacit.

Many of the situations used in recent research in dynamics are similar to or are derived from school science (for example, Viennot 1985, McDermott, 1984). For our purposes, subjects would need to find the situations presented so that any responses they gave would be in common-sense terms. That is, we felt it important to find ordinary, natural situations that would elicit common-sense reasoning about and understanding of how everyday objects move, and to avoid situations which could suggest that it was 'scientific' responses that were particularly sought. We wanted what the children really did think rather than what they thought they ought to think.

A difficulty is that we would be asking subjects to make explicit things which are so obvious that they normally remain unsaid. Thus to demand explanations of situations that require common-sense reasoning may be to present a contradiction because, by their very nature, such situations often do not need explaining at all. Situations, therefore, had to be such that subjects would feel that it was both reasonable to be asked to explain them, and possible to try to do so.

Thus we needed a world which was 'normal' and 'natural', but in which the rules of the real world could be suspended, so that it was reasonable to ask if the normal rules apply, and in this manner elicit what they are. It seemed to us that comics fitted many of these requirements. Characters in comics are constantly in action: chasing people, running away, climbing up and down things, falling over. Objects also move around, get thrown, fall off things or just stay still. The world of comics is a smaller and more amusing version of our world, some events being realistic and the others funny or fantastic (a character running off a cliff, and staying up for a while by frantic running, before falling). Comics are about the 'fantastic' situated in the real world, and the contrast creates the joke.

We choose four almost classic comics, *Beano, Dandy, Topper,* and *Beezer,* which are still read by almost all children and which have been read by many adults, in albums or when they were younger. The characters in the comics are very much part of children's culture, being so well known that they needed little introduction at the interview.

The aim of the pilot study was to see whether in fact comics were a good choice. Each of the four comics chosen contains about 15 different cartoon strips, thus giving a choice of some 60 stories. Three criteria helped us to select eight or nine to start with, namely: a large number of movements in one story; as much diversity of movement as possible within any given strip; and, lastly, a sprinkling of unusual, unexpected, or original situations. After some initial interviews, the strips were reduced to the most productive four.

Our preliminary analysis of comic strips showed that each story consisted of a number of events; some funny, some bizarre, others startling and yet others quite ordinary. Each event was generally built up through a series of three or four pictures.

Taking such events, the procedure used was first to ask subjects to describe what was happening in each of the pictures making up the event. The subjects were then asked a) to say whether or not certain actions (selected by the interviewer to be of interest) could really happen, and b) to explain why these actions could or could not happen.

We decided to start with children as young as possible, provided they could read. We interviewed individually 14 children between the ages of 6 and 10, about the four cartoon strips, each interview being recorded.

PRELIMINARY RESULTS

We shall select certain features of the theory, and discuss how they are, or are not, reflected in the children's responses. We shall also give examples illustrating methodological difficulties.

Support or fall

Support presents a problem in that nothing 'happens' to objects which are being supported or are giving support so there is no need to question or look for explanations. There are two situations which are easier to examine, each taking the idea of support as a given: first, when the strength of the support is not enough it may break; and second, when the support is taken less for granted, as for example with air when it keeps something up. An example of the first is a drainpipe breaking under the weight of a burglar (Fred, the Flop), and of the second a parachute – first made from an umbrella then a curtain – floating from the top of a house (Plug). In each case the child is asked what is happening, whether it could happen or not, and why.

Support and breaking

Many children noticed situations where something stops supporting something else. For some children the reason is with the object being supported. For example, Lorraine (9 years) says that the drainpipe the burglar is climbing breaks, 'because of his weight (the burglar's)', while Thomas (7 years) says 'it (drainpipe) couldn't take his weight so it broke off'. Others talk about the actual material from which the support – the drainpipe – is made: for example, Scott (10 years) 'it might (the drainpipe might break) if the drainpipe's a kind of plastic, if it is metal I don't think so', or Lorraine (9 years) '(it couldn't happen) because nowadays drainpipes are just metal and he (the burglar) might not been too heavy for it'.

Our interpretation of these children's comments is that they are saying that in order to support something, the support must be strong enough in relation to what is being supported, and that when it is not there is absence of support. As Amal (10 years) said, 'The drainpipe won't hold him'.

In another cartoon strip there is a shelf attached to a wall of a shed on which stands a collection of rather curious objects such as a coal scuttle. Most children made no comment on this situation, which illustrates the problem of cases which are too obvious. Only Nicole (9 years), stopped to explain, 'It's (the shelf) just holding it (scuttle) so that it doesn't fall off . . . umm, it's holding, it's resting, there's bits resting on it. The shelf is pinned on the wall so that you can put things on it without them falling off'.

Partial support by air

In the comic strip about Plug there are two home-made parachutes, the first made from an umbrella and the second from a curtain. Children say that they are not certain whether either of these two parachutes could really work. The majority of the children's explanations involve the air or the wind getting beneath the so-called parachute and acting as a type of support. Some other children attempted to incorporate the idea of partial support in their explanations. The following three examples show how children elaborate their ideas.

Thomas's (7 years) explanation involves the air below or inside the parachute. He says 'because the wind is blowing up and that's going down (parachute) the wind pushes the air into the balloon (parachute) and that makes it fat so that it can float down'.

Sarah (9 years) goes one step further 'because the umbrella pushes it (the air) down and . . . umm . . . the air's trying to pull it (the parachute) up . . . umm . . . so it makes it slow down'.

Chris (9 years) gradually develops his ideas, initially explaining the umbrella as staying up because of the wind, then going on to explain why a parachute stays up 'it's the air. (Where is the air?) It's under the parachute. (Why does it come down in the end?) Because the air got trapped inside the parachute. (But you said the air kept it up, helped it to float, does that same air bring it down?). Yes the air on the top pushes the parachute down but because of the air on the bottom (underneath) it goes down very slowly so the person doesn't get hurt'.

There seem to be two general types of answer: the case of natural falling with partial support from the air, and the case of a downward push, usually from the air, and an upward push from the air trapped beneath.

Falling

For the moment we have not looked at the idea that all things fall that are not supported. However, we have, in some situations, attempted to examine what happens when an object falls. Some children introduce into their explanations the notion of air being a partial support and thus hindering objects in their fall by holding them up, somewhat as the parachute is held up. For example, Thomas (7 years) says that some things like axes and hammers will always come down, 'because they're heavy for the wind to blow up because they are heavier than the wind; because some are so heavy the wind can't take the weight so they just fall down'.

Is gravity important?

Within the common-sense theory it was specified that the properties attributable to gravity would depend on what it is seen as doing. Children talk about gravity in a variety of ways, a few of which are given below.

For Jennifer (9 years) 'if there wasn't gravity, it (parachute) would stay up'.

Amal (10 years) says an object stops going up, 'when the gravity starts pulling it down'. Later when asked about why the character Plug will just fall from the roof, he responds, 'because the gravity will push or pull him. (Push or pull?) Push down. (What is gravity then?) The air'.

Scott (10 years), when asked about things falling, says 'because there's gravity that pushes you down and because you have to come down sometime. (What is gravity?) A load of air that pushes you down'.

One other child, Thomas (almost 7), explains his 'theory' of gravity:

Interviewer What did you say gravity was?

Thomas	It's a kind of shield in the air, a kind of shield, when space comes it sort of disappears, it's like a kind of shield which keeps you down . . .
Interviewer	If we can imagine the earth . . .
Thomas	(Interrupting) It's like a whole load of shields put together but you can walk through them but can't walk up them and they are invisible, umm, you are able to walk through them . . .
Interviewer	They stop when you get to space?
Thomas	Well not exactly when you get to space, the actual shields get weaker and weaker as you get to space.

Thomas insisted in other situations that gravity got stronger and stronger the nearer one got to the earth.

In the development and refinement of the theory it will be necessary to consider whether or not gravity is present in the basic scheme. For the moment free fall is considered as fundamental and gravity is seen as a later addition, rationalized so as to fit in as well as possible.

Motion and effort

Within the common-sense theory, the motion of falling happens because of lack of support, but is then natural. Other types of motion are seen to need some sort of effort either to change the place or path of an object or to keep it going along a path. Three possible sources of effort were postulated: effort of another agent *on* the object; effort generated *by* the object; effort *of* the present motion of the object.

There is a variety of situations in which a ball got thrown, headed or kicked by one of the characters, these being classic examples of effort by someone *on* the object. When the object moves the effort is then that *of* the motion of the object. Amal (10), in the following quotation, is talking about such a situation. A ball thrown up in the air has previously been talked about.

Interviewer	If you throw a ball along rather than up, when will it stop?
Amal	When it hits something or someone catches it.
Interviewer	Supposing there's nothing in the way like on Wimbledon Common or Putney Heath?
Amal	It'll stop after it's lost all that strength after you pushed it.
Interviewer	So if you were to explain to someone about throwing a ball, throwing a ball a certain distance depends on what?

Amal	How far you throw it.
Interviewer	Supposing I say I want to see who can throw the ball the farthest.
Amal	Depends on how your arm pushes it.
Interviewer	When you push it what do you do with the ball?
Amal	You let it go.
Interviewer	But how do you make it go far?
Amal	You are there, you've got some force in your arm.
Interviewer	Has the ball got any force?
Amal	No, it hasn't.
Interviewer	Why does it move?
Amal	Because you gave it force.
Interviewer	Has it got force in it?
Amal	It's just because you've thrown it.
Interviewer	It hasn't got any force in it?
Amal	Yeah, the force pushes it along.
Interviewer	And when it stops, has it got any force in it?
Amal	No.
Interviewer	Where's the force gone?
Amal	It's just come out.

Our interpretation of the transcript would be that for Amal the stationary, 'non-moving' ball has no force, the force coming from the person throwing it – this strength or force starting the movement. Once moving, the ball is different – it has force because it has been thrown and that pushed it along.

In developing the theory it will be important to look at whether or not there is a relationship between the force that initiates a movement and what it is that keeps an object moving; in Amal's interview this is unclear.

In the above transcript, Amal would appear to have two ideas about what happens to the strength or force that pushes the ball along when the ball stops moving. On the one hand, he says that the ball 'lost' all the strength given at the beginning. A little later, however, he states that all the force 'came out' of the ball when it stopped. Lorraine (9 years) also explains what happens to a ball when it is thrown:

Interviewer	How do you throw it (the ball) a long way?
Lorraine	You push it harder.
Interviewer	When the ball stops, why does it stop?
Lorraine	Because it's got no more of your pressure on it.

Thomas (almost 7) is talking about snowballs being thrown at one of the characters, Ginger:

Interviewer	Why do snowballs hurt? Which ones hurt most?
Thomas	The ones that are thrown from a longer distance.
Interviewer	Why do they hurt more?
Thomas	Because they've got time to speed up and when they speed up they hurt more because they come with a lot of hard force.
Interviewer	A lot of hard force. What happens to the force when they hit him (Ginger)?
Thomas	Well it can smash because it's like making a snowman; it will hurt because it's very icy.
Interviewer	But you said they come with a lot of force; what happens to the force when they touch old Ginger, where does it go?
Thomas	Well the force goes back.
Interviewer	Back?
Thomas	It kind of goes back to where it came from so that it doesn't leave a gap because it would have cleared a gap and then it would have to go back to where it came from.
	(Section of transcript omitted)
Interviewer	What about the force in the ball, you said it comes with a lot of force. Is that a different force?
Thomas	It's a kind of force because it's thrown hard, it's the force from your arm.
Interviewer	But does the ball keep it, use it, lose it, or what? What do you think?
Thomas	Well it keeps it and then it uses it for whatever; it loses it when it hits something.
Interviewer	So where does the force go when it hits something?
Thomas	It goes back to where it comes from.

Thomas appears to us to have an interesting 'theory' about the force of the ball. It is almost as though Thomas sees it as a global force that does many things, being 'conserved' throughout, so, although lost on impact, it none the less stays 'conserved' – having to 'go back to where it came from'. (The argument with which Meyer first proposed the conservation of energy was, as it happens, essentially similar to that offered by Thomas.)

In this situation there would seem to be three issues which find expression in most of the children's explanations. First, the act of throwing or kicking an object gives 'something' to the object, for example, some sort of effort. Second, there is some disposition to think that this 'something' tends to stay with the object unless there is a good reason for it not to, as if there is a type of primitive 'conservation'. Lastly, it is not obvious what happens to this 'something', how it gets away, where it goes, etc., when an object is no longer in motion.

In the development of the theory it will be necessary to examine whether or not there should be included in the basic scheme some sort of primitive notion of conservation of 'effort'. Further refinement of this notion is necessary. Is what children consider as conserved or stored 'effort', 'force' or 'cause'? Or do they not make such distinctions at all?

PROBLEMS OF THE COMPLETENESS AND CORRECTNESS OF THE THEORY

Some problems: ideas not within the theory

The transcripts indicate a need to incorporate impacts in addition to motions in the basic scheme. Motions in the theory are considered in terms of 'a change of place of' or 'the path of' an object. However, motions ending produce an 'interaction' between the object that stops moving and the obstacle – object that causes the stopping. Children appear to look for explanations as to why some of these 'interactions' are serious while others are not. We have looked at the two basic interactions, where the object moves with the agent and where, in either case, the object has impact, intended or accidental, on some person or some thing encountered in its path.

Let us first examine the situation of an object moving on its own – possibly an agent starting the motion – where its movement is intended to achieve some impact. The transcripts indicate that children try to understand the relationship between the intensity of impact and the 'effort' of the motion – or the 'stored' effort. There is a good example of such a situation in 'Beryl the Peril': a ball is headed towards something: the ball bounces off the first object and hits a second, bounces off the second and hits a third and so on, creating some damage with each object it hits.

Scott (10 years) said about this situation that the ball moving from object to object did less damage. Asked why, he responded: 'because it's not as heavy. (Not as heavy?) It's being pushed and so it's heavy to start with'. When asked whether the ball would hit each object as hard as every other Scott says, 'No, only one, they wouldn't because as you go on it's going to get slower and slower and it's not going to be so hard'.

Our interpretation of this would be that Scott seems to be saying that the slower the ball the less impact, and so the ball loses its ability to do damage. It looks as though, for Scott, 'stored effort' could be associated with speed; and, although it is hard to say what he means by 'heavy', perhaps 'less heavy' means 'less effort'.

Situations where the agent moves with the object to achieve an impact present issues of a somewhat different kind from those just described. Looking first at the situation described in the commonsense theory, when an object is moved to change its place the effort is generated by the agent with the aim of putting the object in a new location – all the object does is to be supported (for example, passing a plate).

Not all illustrations of this theoretical idea are as simple as the instance of the plate being moved. For example, in some situations the agent generates a lot of effort by moving fast when displacing the object; it appears to us that children may confound the idea of the effort of the agent with that of the effort of the motion of the object. In addition, in many situations the agent is changing the place of the object in order to do something with it: for example, using a hammer to hit a nail. In such cases it would seem as though children look for a possible relation between the intensity of the impact and either the effort of the agent or the effort of the motion of the object.

'Fred the Flop', where Fred is trying to escape from a yard, presents a good illustration of this difficulty. The door needs to be broken down and Fred is charging at the door with a drainpipe in an attempt to do just this. Children were asked why Fred's running helped to break down the door.

Amal (10 years) explained 'because it gives you more strength, gives that (the drainpipe) more strength when he (Fred) pushes it. (Gives what more strength?) The pole, umm, because it (the pole) gives it (the door) a better hit'.

Lorraine (9 years) explains that Fred has decided to run, 'because it'll (the running) give it (the drainpipe) a better push. (Why a better push?) Because it's more pressure on the door'.

Thomas (7 years), who previously said that running fast helps to give you more strength, added: 'then the end of the wood (drainpipe) pushes it (the door) open'. (So who has got the strength, the wood, the man, who . . . ?). Thomas replied immediately, 'the wood', then hesitates, 'er no, the man . . . '.

It will be important to clarify whether what children see as involved in the 'interaction' is the effort of the agent or the effort of the motion of the object, or whether they do not distinguish between the two.

First impressions of the correctness of the theory

Looking, in general, at the ideas outlined in the common-sense theory, there is a broad sense in which the theory appears to be a reasonably good representation of how people think about motion in as much as many of the fundamental ideas do appear to be used as forms of explanation in the situations presented.

Thus we find that for the children interviewed the notion of support is talked about through cases of non-support. They see the need for a support to be strong enough in relation to what is being supported; if not, the support will break and the object will fall. Some children see air as offering partial support so that things which are not supported will naturally fall. Light objects will be stopped from falling for a while by the air, but some objects are too heavy even to get partial support. Clearly, other situations need to be found to look at more taken-for-granted situations of support, such as stationary objects supporting others. Situations relating to the role of the ground in a system of support are also needed.

We also find that when an object is set in motion it is given 'something' and this 'something', whatever it is, stays with the object while it is moving; some sort of conservation. But then, for many subjects, there is the puzzle as to how the conserved or stored 'something' disappears from the object when it is no longer moving.

In this pilot study only a restricted number of situations were looked at and it is, of course, necessary to extend the research to a wider range of situations and subjects. These preliminary findings also suggest that it is important to ask ourselves to what extent the ideas of Intention, Cause, Motion, and Effect are distinct and differentiated. Thus, for example, when a man uses a hammer to hit a nail, to what degree are these four ideas differentiated in this act? Is there an intention, then an original cause and the motion and effect it produces, or is the hammer a 'good thing' which mediates the intention?

The pilot study has shown us that the comics provide a wealth of situations which do in general make sense to the children and provide us with plenty of opportunities to look for common-sense reasoning. Our plan is to take the ideas central to the theory, and to find several realizations of each idea in terms of situations in the comic strips. We shall extend the range of subjects to children as young as possible (perhaps using comics that do not have words), and to a selection of adults. In this way we hope to be able to test both how 'primitive' and how fundamental are the ideas of the theory in terms of natural groupings of explanations of motion and non-motion.

REFERENCES

Bliss, J. and Ogborn, J. 1992. 'Steps towards a formalisation of a psycho-logic of motion.' In Tiberghein, A. and Mandl, H. (eds) *Intelligent learning environments and knowledge acquisition in physics.* NATO ASI Series. Springer-Verlag, Berlin, pp. 65–94.

Bliss, J. and Ogborn, J. 1993. 'Steps toward a formalisation of a psycho-logic of motion.' *Journal of Intelligent Systems,* in press.

Bliss, J., Ogborn, J. and Whitelock, D. 1989. 'Secondary school pupils' commonsense theories of motion.' *International Journal of Science Education,* 11: 262–72.

Driver, R. and Erickson, G. 1983. 'Theories in action: some theoretical and empirical issues in the study of students' conceptual frameworks in science.' *Studies in Science Education,* 10: 37–60.

Gilbert, J. K. and Watts, M. 1983. 'Concepts, misconceptions, and alternative conceptions.' *Studies in Science Education,* 10: 61–98.

Hayes, P. 1979. 'The naive physics manifesto.' In Michie, D. (ed.) *Expert systems in the microelectronic age.* Edinburgh University Press, Edinburgh, pp. 242–70.

McDermott, L. 1984. 'An overview of research on conceptual understanding in mechanics.' *Physics Today,* 37: 636–49.

Ogborn, J. 1985. 'Understanding students' understandings: an example from dynamics.' *European Journal of Science Education,* 7: 141–50.

Ogborn, J. and Bliss, J. 1990. 'A psycho-logic of motion.' *European Journal of Psychology of Education,* 5: 379–90.

Viennot, L. 1985. 'Analysing students' reasoning in science: a pragmatic view of theoretical problems.' *European Journal of Science Education,* 7: 151–62.

Chapter 8

Constructing knowledge from fragments of learning?

Arthur Lucas

INTRODUCTION

As Joan Solomon has indicated in Chapter 1, some workers attribute children's ideas about scientific concepts to the effects of their exposure to the media. In this Chapter, I consider some of these potential informal sources of ideas, concentrating on television and museums. By examining what happens when people encounter such sources we may begin to understand the processes of learning-out-of-school. I draw upon studies reviewed earlier (Lucas 1983, 1991) and work by members of an 'informal learning of science' seminar based at the Centre for Educational Studies (e.g. McManus 1987, 1988; Tulley 1990). Some of the studies discussed have been used to consider methodological points by Lucas, McManus and Thomas (1986).

Some personal examples

I was standing in a glasshouse at Kew Gardens admiring a very beautiful orchid when I overhead a conversation that went something like this:

'That is an interesting flower isn't it? Why has it got that bit that looks like a tub under it?'

'That's where the insects fall down when they land on it. It digests them up and gets some of its food that way.'

The answer was given confidently and authoritatively, and puzzled me greatly, until I noticed that the specimen stood just outside the entry to a side house that was labelled 'Insectivorous Plants'. Apparently the young man had put the observations together, made an interpretation that was consistent with these pieces of information and some knowledge that he already had, and helped his companion make sense of her original puzzle. The labellum in this orchid did look like a pitfall trap that could be found in several species in the other house, and the error is understandable.

In 1985 I was present at the first preview of the Janus-2 exhibition at the temporary site of the new Musée National des Sciences, de Techniques et des

Industries being constructed at the Parc de la Villette in Paris. One of the exhibits concerned the role of plastics in everyday life. There was a very colourful display of an incredible range of plastic goods, along with a brief history of the development of plastics from Bakelite to the present day. In a very prominent position was a large console with a set of four video-screens, a large handle as in a poker machine, and a simple statement of the properties that molecules must have to allow a polymer to be formed. Pulling the handle started a display on the screen with a series of compounds passing across it. The question above the display asked something like 'Can your substance make a polymer? If it can, you will get a token that you can use to make a plastic ball in the moulding machine around the corner'. I started it off, saw a compound that I thought would polymerize appear on the screen, and tried to stop the display at that point by pulling, pushing and then pressing the control lever. It could not stop, and finally a compound appeared on the screen with a message telling me that my luck was bad because the compound would not polymerize. Everyone else that I saw using the display appeared to have the same reaction, so it was not a function of my French being too poor to understand the instructions. Eventually my companions and I worked out that it was really a poker machine, and the outcome, whether I could get a token or not, was purely a chance event. There was no control over the machine, so I could not learn whether I understood the structures that would polymerize.

For our purposes these are instructive episodes. They illustrate pieces of learning taking place outside the confines of a school, without the presence of a person whose job it is to instruct, and, in the first case, probably without prior intent on the part of the 'learner' or the 'teacher'. It is with the consequences of such real-life events that theorists must be concerned when they discuss the origins and implications of 'mis-conceptions', 'pre-conceptions' and 'alternative frameworks' that children and adults hold. We will return to these examples later.

A heuristic typology

To help think about accounts of learning from informal sources it is useful to use a heuristic typology which considers both the 'learner' and the 'source'. There is no necessary theoretical interpretation built into it. Consider the couple in the orchid house. Neither of them is likely to have gone there with the intent to learn about insectivorous plants; most visitors to Kew Gardens go for an outing, for aesthetic enjoyment. But there are some who go with a deliberate intent to learn some botany, perhaps economic botany by visiting the museums in the grounds.

Thus the first dimension of the typology concerns the intentions of the learners. They may deliberately seek knowledge, or they may learn from an episode they encounter accidentally.

The other dimension of the typology can also be illustrated by reference to Kew Gardens. Much of the landscaped park is designed for the aesthetic effects of massed specimens, skilfully contrasted with tall trees providing backdrop to the seasonal colour. Other parts of the grounds, however, are planted in a very different style. The redesigned grass plots, for example, show the story of wheat evolution, the different types of grass mixtures used for different sporting surfaces, and the major cereal crops of the world, as well as containing specimens of the grasses of Europe. These new plots are planned with the intent of conveying information other than the name of the specimen and where it grows in the wild. That is, the newer beds deliberately provided structured knowledge. Yet it is possible to learn some concepts from the ornamental plantings. I might seek out in the gardens a series of plants in the same genus, or the same family, so that I can try to understand the criteria that taxonomists use to delimit species, genera and high taxons.

The second dimension, then, concerns the providers of information. They may deliberately seek to inform, or their information may be provided unintentionally.

EXAMPLES OF INFORMAL SOURCES

Television science

British television is rich in examples of scientific documentaries, especially the various aspects of natural history. Clearly these are intended to convey information, about a location, about a group of organisms, or about some pervasive concept, where examples may be drawn from many places and many species. I suspect that the audience for these series and single films is composed both of some who tune in deliberately to learn about the particular topic being treated, and some who use the films as pleasant diversions from the cares of the human dramas around them.

Compare the two series *The Body in Question* and *Life on Earth*. Jonathan Miller's imaginative treatment of the human body requires much more intense concentration on the part of the viewer than Attenborough's delightfully filmed animals and plants. Miller presents a tightly argued, highly sequenced lecture with dramatic images replacing each other quickly; Attenborough has many examples of one or two basic ideas per programme. One can let the attention wander in the latter, and still pick up the thread. You are lost if you are distracted from Miller. Perhaps it is the subject matter that produced the different style, perhaps the different experience of the presenters. It is possible that Attenborough will catch some unintentional learners, but less likely that Miller will teach any but the fairly dedicated viewer/learner. Unfortunately, these predictions are speculations. I know of no systematic analysis of the ways that viewers approach the two series.

But even this superficial analysis of the series themselves suggests that it is misleading to lump 'TV documentaries' together as a source of learning. They have different styles, different assumptions about the knowledge that a viewer already has, and different idiosyncratic presenters.

It is also important to remember that the apparent authenticity of the documentary may not always be accepted by the viewer. My own pre-teenage children, for example, when they saw the more recent Attenborough production *The Living Planet*, would not accept the reality of the ocean floor volcanic sequences, until they saw a meta-documentary about the making of the series. They had believed the film was shot in the same way that such sequences are created when fictional films are produced, by using models in the studio. Buss (1984), reviewing the same series, suggests that it insulates the viewers from their world, since the difficulties of access to such phenomena are not made clear. Buss contrasts such series with the Durrell's *Amateur Naturalist* which 'without making it seem easy . . . did show how it was done.'

There have been some studies of adolescent learning from a TV sequence that they are unlikely to have sought out. Ryder (1982) reports a detailed study of adolescent children watching a 4-minute news item from the BBC 'Nine O'clock News' of 2 April 1979. The item concerned the nuclear power plant accident at Three Mile Island in Pennsylvania. The children were not studied as they viewed it live, so we do not know what their spontaneous reactions would have been, but the way in which they reacted to it under a variety of situations during participation in a research project at least lets us see the realm of possibility. In one phase of the study Ryder had his subjects write down their ideas about the 'energy problem'. He then showed them the first 45 seconds of the news item, stopped the tape, and asked them to recall as much as possible of what they had seen. None of the seven subjects recalled any of the information. He comments, 'I am sure that had they been warned they would be tested, they could have done better, but then few of us watch the News with notebook in hand in everyday life' (p. 226). Yet a context had been provided by the preliminary activity, and they were in a setting where they knew research was being undertaken. These pupils were most unlikely to have gained information from this source, which had been deliberately created to convey specific information, had they encountered it in a normal way, more or less accidentally as far as this topic is concerned.

However, other subjects in Ryder's study showed clearly in their conversations that they had been attending to information from other sources. The conversation of three boys who had viewed the tape of the news item was monitored as they described it to a classmate who had not seen it. As they described what they had seen and what it meant to them they used references to other sources: the feature film *The China Syndrome*; news items on testing nuclear waste containers and on previous nuclear reactor incidents; solar furnaces and solar panels; modern windmills and wave power; and the hazards of nuclear war. (The boys were from classes considered insufficiently able to present any science for examination at age 16.) These boys were unlikely to have sought out the information on nuclear incidents, and at least some of the material they drew upon had information-giving as a secondary motive. However, much of the information that they recall in the conversation is partially incorrect, garbled, or mis-remembered. Perhaps this is the fate of most information accidentally encountered by viewers?

O'Connell (1975) provided an example of viewers who did act on information that they obtained from a source where information giving was a secondary concern. He describes the production of the TV series *Marcus Welby MD*, which was designed as prime-time entertainment. It was carefully produced so that the medical details were accurate and in one episode the plot revolved around the diagnosis of autism in a young patient. O'Connell reports the case of a couple who realized after watching the episode that the same problem probably afflicted their son.

It is difficult to find instances of someone deliberately seeking knowledge from a television production that does not set out to be a documentary, but it is conceivable that someone might look to biographical series, whose main interest is in the development of character, for information about the relevant science. The attention to detail in the biography of Marie Curie might have helped someone interested in the development of radioactivity theories, but if they were really interested then they are far more likely to have sought a print source.

Television and the press

There are studies of the use of media in the United States that suggest that 'information to be learned from television is more closely related to events, more likely to capitalise on the present moment, than is the information to be obtained from newspapers and magazines, which can afford to offer more perspective' (Wade and Schramm 1969). But do these users of the printed media deliberately seek out information on specific issues, or do they tend to read any science material that happens to be offered? Grunig (1980) reviews the literature of the readership of science news and concludes that newspaper science is read because it is there and arouses curiosity. Deliberate seekers of information are more likely to choose specialized magazines. These deliberate seekers will be included in the 18 per cent of the United States of America adult population that Miller (1983) counts among the 'attentive public' for science, those whose active interest includes subscription to magazines equivalent to *New Scientist* in Britain. However, as in our orchid example, there is no guarantee that attention produces a 'correct' understanding. Only 30 per cent of the attentive public for science met Miller's very minimal criterion of scientific literacy.

Museum science

One of the more potent sources of informal learning of science is the museum. It deliberately sets out to provide information for the visitors whether they go specifically to look at a particular exhibit, or whether like Louis MacNeice they see museums as places that

> Offer us, running from among the buses,
> A centrally heated refuge, parquet floors and sarcophaguses.

from which, after a time spent warming among the cases, the visitor

> Returns to the street, his mind an arena where sprawls
> Any number of consumptive Keatses and dying Gauls.
>
> (MacNeice 1979)

Whether, in Falk's (1982) terms, the visitor comes as a buyer or as a window shopper the museum must assume that the task is to provide some information. There are some studies, reviewed in Lucas (1983) and Falk and Dierking (1992), that suggest that orientation devices can help visitors structure their visit, that what visitors learn is affected by what they knew before they came, that physical interaction with objects can help learning, and that there may be important affective effects from visits even if they do not produce much cognitive change in the direction that the designers intended. Most studies are evaluative in style, or assess learning by tracking visitors and interviewing them about the exhibits that they have seen. They do not produce evidence of what happens during learning events.

Observing visitors   Our group is collecting data that provide a great number of instances of people interacting with exhibits. In the British Museum (Natural History) Paulette McManus (1987, 1988) listened to the conversations that take place between the members of groups as they examine an exhibit. She placed a microphone in the exhibit, with an appropriate warning sign, and later transcribed the tapes and associated them with the relevant visual observations of group composition and basic behaviour. Some examples of the transcripts are given below to illustrate the type of data she collected. The exhibits are first described so that the context in which the recordings were made can be understood.

The first exhibit has some physical manipulations possible. It is a game within the *Origin of Species* exhibition. The game is in the section of the exhibition entitled 'How do we recognise species', and comes before an account of the techniques taxonomists use to sort organisms into species, using examples of plant and animal genera. The game requires the visitor to sort ten discs, each with an illustration of a pond organism, into three groups. A number of suggestions is made in the accompanying text to help players decide on the criteria that they might use to make their groups, but there is no indication of whether any solution produced was an acceptable solution. The first group reported here consisted of an adult couple, who first briefly read the text of the display. The man initially moved the discs, but the woman took over. (In the following records the words and spaces in parentheses are uncertain transcriptions. Details of pauses and inflections are omitted here. Statements are numbered for ease of reference later. The woman is identified as F and the man by M.)

Transcript A

1   *F.*   [Laugh] (divide this) up to make three groups. A group in each dish. Ooh, plants, things with hard exoskeletons, things.
2   *M.*   ( )
3   *F.*   How many groups? You gotta have three.
4   *M.*   Mmm.
5   *F.*   Um.
6   *M.*   You can make it.
7   *F.*   No, no, no, you've got to have that one up there and that in the middle. I don't know. It depends which things go together. You've got things with hard exoskeletons. Mmm. Now here's a plant.
8   *M.*   ( )
9   *F.*   That's something that ( )
10 *M.*   ( )
11 *F.*   Something; a larvae or worm or caterpillar. No, that's some- thing like that. Um, not really ( ) Um. They've all got hard exoskeletons. You see that one? Now, if that's a larva that would go in that one and that would go in that group. That's got an endoskeleton. I want to know if this is right.

[Board clears automatically]

12 *M.*   (Laugh) Doesn't it tell you?
13 *F.*   It's coming back again.
        How do you know if it's right or not? That's going to bother me, that is. Is it right or not?

The complete visit lasted 2 minutes 26 seconds, of which the above dialogue occupied 2 minutes 17 seconds. After the game had been completed the couple moved on and read the text describing the classification techniques of biologists.

Not all of the groups that stayed at the exhibition for a reasonable length of time spoke a great deal, so little was revealed about the way in which they were thinking. Consider this second adult couple who stayed at the game for 1 minute 45 seconds. The complete transcript is:

Transcript B

1 *M.* (cough) Perhaps we take the crab.

[41 seconds pause]

2 *F.* The shell.

The importance of previous experience is shown in some groups who immediately attempt to produce a solution based upon the classification scheme that they know. The following extract from an interaction between two teenage boys is an example. (Some transcript is omitted, mainly reading aloud the instructions.)

Transcript C

2 *B1.* Ah molluscs. I'm not sure actually.
3 *B2.* May be supposed to be in each.
4 *B1.* Make three groups one group in each dish.
5 *B2.* Are you sure. Functionally they're ( ).
6 *B1.* Amphibian.
7 *B2.* Doesn't seem right. Move them.
8 *B1.* What about these claws?
9 *B2.* That is that's up there, that's mmm. Molluscs, right. That's arthropoda.
10 *B1.* Oh, arthropoda he, he's alright.
11 *B2.* That's arthropoda yeah, that's, that's arthropoda.

The interaction continued for a total of 4 minutes 26 seconds, including a return visit after reading the next set of information panels.

The second set of transcripts was collected at a much more traditional exhibit. The glass case of *Insect Pests* in the old Insect Gallery has no interactive game or other device. The extract below is taken from a group consisting of two elderly couples. One of the men did not speak for the 1 minute 23 seconds that the group was at the case. The exhibit is near a spectacular case of butterflies and the first part of the conversation (1–5) seems to be related to that case.

Transcript D

1 *M.* There's a (place) at (Syon) house. It's about as big as this room. Oh! if you walk around there's butterflies flying all around you, hundreds of them.
2 *F.* ( )
3 *M.* They fly them over, er, um, from Manila and places like that.
4 *F.* ( )

5 *M.* Some of them die pretty quick, but others, you see them on television catching them.

6 *F1.* Mmm. Ah! A bacon beetle.

7 *F2.* Is it?

8 *F1.* I remember there was a pub in (Peters Marland). We got (sickness) of people once. And it had a big old fashioned kitchen with a big black range and we came back from a dance at about two in the morning and went to the (fridge), moved the carpet back a bit and *beetles* just came out everywhere. We got one girl that came from London, a rather posh girl as it happened, and she *jumped* on the *table* and *screamed!* We had long skirts on you see.

9 *F2.* (Ah) ( )

10 *F1.* They weren't nice, I don't like the thought of beetles in the small hours.

Our final example comes from the Salles de Découvertes of the Musée de la Villette in Paris, where Gillian Thomas has collected similar data during the development phases of some exhibits aimed directly at young children. It was possible to observe the children using different forms of the same exhibit, and to compare the observations with the judgements of an evaluation team.

One of the exhibits being tested used coloured lights arranged so that the images being projected overlapped. Each projector was provided with a switch so that it was possible for visitors to systematically switch off one or more of the three light sources to explore the effects of mixing lights and different colours. Observations were made of the behaviour of groups of visitors as they interacted with the exhibit, each other, and with the assistants. Audio records were not made, but the observer was able to note the behaviour of the members of the group and to write down the conversations of some members as they occurred. The example is part of a record made when a group of 8 and 9 year olds visited the display with a teacher and another adult helper. The record illustrates that children can learn by systematic observation of phenomena, but that the ideas investigated are not necessarily those intended by the designers of the material, even when the context is one that puts the learner into a deliberately learning mode.

Transcript E

29 Looks at projects.

30 Argues with friend about which switch should be used.

31 Talks. 'Qu'est-ce que ça fait? Ça fait mal?'

32 Sticks finger in hole where indicator light shows colour of projector.

33 Burns finger.

34 Discusses with friend whether the light would burn finger when switches off. ('Si on appuie . . . Quand c'est éteint, ça fait mal?')

35 Switches off by pushing each button in turn.
36 Burns finger three times by trying each light while off.
37 ...

The work in the museums that is reported here does not allow us to say what has been learned as a result of the visitor's interaction with the exhibits. It is concerned with the process, not the product of learning. But in that process we have instances of visitors recalling past episodes (Transcript D–8), using previous knowledge (D–5, C–2, C–9 to C–11, A–1), working co-operatively (C–2 to C–11) and trying to make some sense of the cues given by the structure of the exhibit (A–12 to A–13). We have also seen an instance of a long independent interaction with the exhibit (B). The final example (E) shows children working in a systematic and unbiased way.

But are the examples I have used instances of marginal learning? That is, learning that is not directed toward the important aspects of life, personal survival in a comfortable way. Were the children in example E merely playing some form of joke, knowing full well that what they were doing was a parody of a school investigation? (We do have instances of overt joking in the transcripts from McManus' study in the Natural History Museum.) The adult group in transcript D are clearly using the presence of insect pests to provide a focus for their conversation about previous experiences, which may be most important as a means of social cohesion, not biological learning of an applied kind. The couple playing the sorting game (Transcript A) are working at the task set, and the dominant player is clearly anxious to know whether she got the 'right' answer. She was sufficiently motivated to work at the task for nearly two and a half minutes. The question that concerns us here, however, is whether the visitors' experience can form the basis of a more coherent learning set at a later stage. Can they fit this experience/knowledge together with other material and use it? Does this material help create a 'concept', alternate to or coincident with the one that scientists would use to describe and operate on the phenomena in question?

EMERGING THEMES

Despite the investigational difficulties, there are some themes which begin to emerge in this work on informal sources.

Potency of accidental sources

There are now sufficient anecdotes and personal experiences to convince us that connections *are* made between accidentally encountered ideas, objects and events. Ryder's pupils, who related feature films to the TV news broadcast, are one example. Another is given by student teachers who were asked to interview a small number of children before they began to teach a new topic. The intent was to help the student teachers understand what types of ideas their pupils had about the subject to be taught. The students also asked their pupils about the source of their knowledge. In one discussion with 12–13 year olds about the structure and function of skeletal muscle, three pupils in a group claimed to have learned about ligaments, tendons and muscles from watching television sports programmes (an instance also reported by Wright 1980), especially when there is an injury to an athlete and slow motion replays and commentators provide an explanation. In another group a pupil explained about 'cuts going septic from bacteria that get in'. He said that these terms had been learned from a sticking-plaster advertisement on TV.

I was personally surprised when walking in the Science Museum with my children, then aged 7 and 9, to be told that 'that is the model of the stuff that genes are made of'. 'How did you know that?', I asked, and was told that 'There was a bit about genes and making new ones on John Craven's *Newsround* on the television. He showed this model.' As far as I know this had not been a very recent programme, and apparently the connection had been sufficiently well made for the model to be picked out of a large number of molecular models, and sufficient of the context to be recalled. In none of these cases is it likely that the viewers were attending to the programmes from the point of view of seeking to remember these 'scientific ideas'.

Incidents like those reported here represent, I believe, the type of events that are relevant to those who are interested in the origins of knowledge held by pupils when they encounter topics at school. Similar phenomena are seen in museums, which deliberately set out their exhibits in an attempt to provide knowledge, whether the visitors come to learn or whether they encounter the ideas accidentally. Similarly, the accidental encounters with sources that are not intended to instruct, TV sports programmes for example, have produced some ideas of biology.

Authenticity and the rules of the game

The problem of achieving appropriate knowledge is related to knowing how to judge whether a piece of information received from a source is accurate, especially something from a source that does not intend to be educative. Emma Lathen's detective story *Green Grow the Dollars* contains many apparently authentic details of plant breeding techniques used by modern genetic laboratories. Yet the final product around which the plot revolves sounds fantastic. How am I to know which pieces of information are authentic and which to disregard as artistic licence?

The problem is often resolved by some sense of 'authority'. Consider the child that I overheard leaving the building where the London Zoo houses its invertebrate collection: insects, spiders, millipedes, snails and scorpions are all displayed. The child was saying that the teacher at school was wrong about insects, and the conversation developed something like this:

'How do you know she was wrong?' asks the adult in the group.

'She said that insects have got six legs, and lots of those things had *hundreds* of legs!'

'Perhaps they were not all insects.'

'Of course they are. There is a big label up there saying INSECT HOUSE. And the Zoo must be right.'

[The Zoo has since re-labelled the building as 'Invertebrate House'!]

Constructivist notions of building upon what one already knows appear to fit the data discussed in this chapter. Past experience and background *is* drawn upon in some of the transcripts and anecdotes. But it is clearly not just knowledge of 'facts'. The incident at the Insect House illustrates this: the prime piece of background knowledge was 'knowledge' of the authority of the Zoo. The 'statement' made by the Zoo was perceived as having greater authenticity than the pronouncement by the teacher. Similarly, the automatic movement of the discs in the game at the Origin of Species exhibit (Transcript A, p. 141) was interpreted as a cue that the game has ended, but it was not clear to the user what this cue meant. In one sense, this interpretation is a result of previous experience of games: the women 'knew' that some signal is given on completion of a game, but her experience was not sufficient for her to be able to interpret the movement, so she was 'bothered' by the message. The Plastics exhibit in the Janus-2 exhibition at La Villette provides another example of users mis-perceiving the intent of the designer. We all assumed that our success would not depend upon chance. We must have been expecting such devices to provide us with feedback on our interpretation of the message given us; that is, to be rewarding us when we get the answer right. Here we were mistakenly using our 'knowledge' of how exhibits are supposed to work, and I at least felt cheated when I didn't get a token after recognizing a correct formula, but others whose luck was in got a reward just by chance, even though they might not recognize a compound that could react in the correct way.

NEXT STEPS?

Any theoretical account of learning from informal sources must take into account a number of related issues. It must account for the traditional notions of motivation, learning style and previous 'factual and conceptual knowledge', and in addition pay attention to a number of features: the learner's perception of the intention of the other persons or the intention behind the programme, exhibit, or article; the learner's perception of the role of the provider of the learning event; and the learner's estimation of authority and authenticity. (These issues apply to schools as well, but they do not loom so large in accounts of school learning since the pupils and the teachers quickly become expert in establishing the rules of their game: they are common features and are not noticed as things to be explained.)

Are we at the stage where we have enough descriptions of the processes that go on in learning from informal sources outside the context of schooling? If so, what sort of research do we now need? My guess is that we will benefit from more examples of interactions in a number of new contexts. It turns out that it is much easier to collect data from museums, where there is a clear intention to instruct and it is at least reasonable to expect that people come with the intention of 'learning' something, than it is to study accidental encounters with learning contexts that may not have been deliberately created. How can one systematically study science learning that takes place over the dinner table or by conversations with fellow tourists (see examples in Lucas 1981)? A richer supply of well documented anecdote will be necessary.

But for the easier case of museums, it is probably time to begin to pay attention to the features, of the exhibit and of the learner, listed above. Is it the case that people who accurately perceive the intention of the designer learn more, or differently, from those whose perceptions are mismatched? How do visitors attribute 'authenticity' to an exhibit or 'authority' to an exhibitor? Are some features of an exhibition more helpful than others in creating the awareness of the rules of the game, and does this matter? Tulley (1990) provides evidence of the effect of the name of the exhibit in provoking different styles of thinking: an abstract caption – 'Energy Store' – provoking abstract accounts of the exhibit from those who can give an account, with a more concrete name – Water-powered Generator – encouraging more people to give an account, but with fewer of the accounts being 'conceptual'.

We have a long way to go to develop a theory that will enable us to explain what happens in encounters with learning possibilities outside school, and even further to go to produce a predictive account. But what we already know – fragmentary, messy, and inconclusive as it is – will enable us to ask questions about the role of prior knowledge that treat 'knowledge' much more broadly than has been done to date in constructivist accounts of learning science.

Acknowledgements

Paulette McManus, some of whose work is reported here, was supported by a postgraduate research award from the Economic and Social Research Council under a CASS award to King's College London, University of London and the British Museum (Natural History). Aubrey Tulley was supported by a grant from the Gatsby Charitable Foundation for studies in the Science Museum.

REFERENCES

Buss, R. 1984. 'Where there's life' (Review of BBC TV's *The Living Planet*), *Times Educational Supplement*, 20 January, p. 46.

Falk, J. H. 1982. 'The use of time as a measure of visitor behaviour and exhibit effectiveness.' *Museum Roundtable Reports: The Journal of Museum Education.* 7(4): 22–8.

Falk, J. H. and Dierking, L. D. 1992. *The museum experience.* Whalesback Books, Washington, DC.

Grunig, J. E. 1980. 'Communication of scientific information to non-scientists.' In Dervin, B. and Voigt, M. J. (eds) *Progress in Communication Sciences*, Vol. 2. Ablex Publishing, Norwood, NJ, pp. 167–214.

Lucas, A. M. 1981. 'The informal and the eclectic: some issues in science education practice and research.' Inaugural Lecture, Chelsea College, University of London.

Lucas, A. M. 1983. 'Scientific literacy and informal learning,' *Studies in Science Education*, 10: 1–36.

Lucas, A. M. 1991. ' "Info-tainment" and informal sources for learning science.' *International Journal of Science Education*, 13: 495–504.

Lucas, A. M., McManus, P. and Thomas, G. 1986. 'Investigating learning from informal sources: listening to conversations and observing play in science museums.' *European Journal of Science Education*, 8: 341–52.

McManus, P. M. 1987. 'Communication with and between visitors to a science museum.' PhD thesis, King's College London, University of London.

McManus, P. M. 1988. 'Do you get my meaning? Perception, ambiguity and the museum visitor.' *ILVS Review*, 1: 62–75.

MacNeice, L. 1979. 'Museums.' *Collected Poems*. Faber & Faber, London, pp. 20–1.

Miller, J. D. 1983. 'Scientific literacy: a conceptual and empirical review.' *Daedalus*, 112(2): 29–48.

O'Connell, D. J. 1975. ' "Marcus Welby MD" as medical communication.' In Day, S. B. (ed.) *Communication of scientific information*, Kargel, Basel, pp. 165–73.

Ryder, N. 1982. *Science, television and the adolescent: a case study and a theoretical model.* Independent Broadcasting Authority, London.

Tulley, A. 1990. 'Seeing through the name.' *International Journal of Museum Management and Curatorship*, 9: 53–62.

Wade, S. & Schramm, W. 1969. 'The mass media as sources of public affairs, science and health knowledge.' *Public Opinion Quarterly*, 34: 197–209.

Wright, T. J. 1980. 'The effect of non-schools television on learning school biology.' MSc dissertation, North East London Polytechnic.

Chapter 9

Vernacular science: something to rely on in your actions?

Neil Ryder

'Science pervades our society.' Few will argue with the starting point for Bodmer's report on the public understanding of science (Royal Society 1985). But just how far does science pervade our lives? The technology we use about the house is witness to the science in our lives, but how far do laymen use scientific ideas? The stronger claims imply that we can hardly survive a day without a large body of scientific knowledge and process skills (Department of Education and Science 1985). Such is the rhetoric behind the changes in the school curriculum. Yet ask any group of science educators what science they have used so far today and you will leave them groping for examples. Thermodynamics is pressed into action to choose between one garment and another. Polymer chemistry is used to decide what to spread on their toast. Occasionally the Principle of Least Action is used to deal with correspondence. It is hard to suppress the subversive thought that they plan their day with MacStars™, the astrology application for their microcomputer. At best these examples seem to float over the surface of everyday life. At worst they sustain a magical image of science as some unexplained force, like Leach's (1976) spell analogy for using a light switch. It should be possible to offer more authentic, even urgent, evidence.

Although science pervades our society and technology creates our physical environment, perhaps our minds are very little troubled by either. If we have such difficulty finding convincing examples of science in the experience of everyday life, perhaps it will help to think in more theoretical terms? We may be looking in the wrong place for the wrong kind of science. Remember Kelly's (1963) use of the model of 'man the scientist' in psychotherapy and Rom Harré's (1979) development of the idea of 'ethogeny' to explain social life. Harré's (1976) focus on the search for generating mechanisms to explain patterns of behaviour of both physical systems and social systems brings out surprising resonances between theories of science and theories of everyday life.

This chapter assumes that most people do indeed have scientific thoughts about situations which matter to them. In it I present an account of an episode from everyday life which had critical consequences for the actors concerned. I use it to illustrate theories of science, everyday life and of narrative that bridge the gap between the rhetoric and lived experience. I propose a model of man that will generate the patterns of behaviour in the account. But its significance could be far greater. It is a model against which we can test attempts to explain science to the layman to see whether they will work; and if not, to see why not. In doing so I introduce the concept 'Vernacular Science', a way of thinking that operates in everyday life and, in this case, has distinct survival advantages.

A PERSONAL ACCOUNT

Monique works part-time in a supermarket store where she stacks shelves. The store has frequently asked her to work full-time and tried to tempt her with supervisor status. She would probably be a very good manager, but it conflicts with her sense of herself, apart from making demands on her commitment that she would not be prepared to give. This commitment is focused upon her family, in particular her two sons, Dan aged ten and Peter, aged eighteen. To the extent that one can sum up anybody's life, Monique's is a question of nursing and motivating Dan and Peter through their various delights and crises by mobilizing the grandparents and provoking, shaming or cajoling Ed, her husband, into fruitful activity. It was the death of one of the grandparents, her father, that occasioned our conversation. Our family had suffered in exactly the same way. She was puzzled as well as sad. Her father had died looking a very fit man. Although he was seventy-one he was very 'active'. He had worked through his retirement, doing odd jobs, mowing the local tennis courts. In particular he had helped bring up another daughter's two children after their father had been killed in an accident. On reflection she described his life as sedentary in spite of this activity. He took no special exercise. He smoked. He drank. Nearly all his food was pre-packaged and processed. His short temper was a source of stress. He suffered a heart attack a fortnight before he died and there had been warning signs before that. After the attack his doctor advised him to cut three things from his diet; salt, fat, and fries. 'It's like a car engine when the hydraulics fur up', Monique explained. 'Cholesterol clogs up your arteries. He was a classic case.'

Their grandfather's death had more than the anticipated impact of grief on the two boys and their father. With the sadness and the change in social routines came a change in diet. The advice the doctor had given their grandfather was now being employed at their own meal times. When Monique went round the shelves for the weekly shop, she became much more discriminating. She found some references to fats and salts which she could avoid, but most of the names meant little to her, 'after all, we are all made of chemicals, aren't we?' She began to use health food shops for flour and sugar. 'The kids even got to accept Health Food crisps!'

In all of this she was slightly surprised to discover she had the tacit support of Ed. Their normal relationship was one of bantering, half-serious dispute, usually resolved by Monique giving way. Monique would be given to enthusiasms and Ed would respond with sceptical demands for reason, demonstrations of proof. Her indoor house-plant book told her that a particular plant was sensitive to direct sunlight, so she moved it away from a south-facing window of their tenth floor flat. Ed, without discussion, would move it back. When she broached the issue with him he demanded that she explain in her words. 'How does he know?' he asked of the author.

The forceful, egotistical side of Ed's character had an equally important counterpart in his self-reliance. He thinks of himself as 'travelling light', able to work things out for himself. He is particularly dismissive of experts on TV: 'What do they really know?' It may also explain something about his relationship to employers and their authority.

However, the reason for Ed's support was his recollection of a TV programme seen a year earlier that had impressed him – an unusual event. Even stranger, Monique was to see a repeat showing, and this produced even more changes in the diet. Homemade soups appeared in place of tinned varieties. They stopped sprinkling monosodium glutamate on their Chinese meals. No more banana or raspberry flavour on their Miracle Whip – 'they include the "same" chemical as rat poison'. The few chips she did allow were now bigger so that the total surface area of potato in contact with the fat is much less. No more fish fingers. 'All that processed goodness,' she smiled.

After the immediate events Monique's project lapsed. A diet consisting entirely of health foods was too bland: 'Why do we look for so much excitement in our flavours?' Several factors conspired to thwart this culinary revolution – the inaccessibility of the ingredient suppliers, the extra effort in the kitchen for a working mother. Health and convenience compete, in moderation.

THEMES IN THE SEARCH FOR THEORY

A specific situation like Monique's permits us to recast in a much more useful form the general problems with which I began. How far do reasons account for actions in everyday life? Can science change those reasons?

One kind of answer, which is seldom acted upon, is that scientific arguments must first of all be integrated into everyday arguments about everyday projects if they are not to be 'magical' in Leach's sense. We might go further and note that the factors which clinch an argument in the everyday world are something which increases immediate reward or decreases immediate effort. Anyone who wishes to change everyday life into something more scientific has first to accommodate to the nature of this effort, to these rewards and to the qualities of everyday argument. Unless they do, science will fail to engage with it; it will merely skate over the surface of everyday life.

Let me now explore a number of themes that thread through Monique's account, keeping this broad argument in mind. The ultimate task is not to answer a set of tightly defined questions, rather it is to learn from Monique what *her* questions are and explore how science can help. For the moment, I ask readers to put on the back burner their assumptions about the nature of everyday life and the nature of science. We will need to take these concepts apart before we can re-assemble them as a unity.

Everyday life

At first glance the account seems transparent. No clear problem, either social or scientific, stands out. Even the death of the father seems relatively unsurprising to the outsider; he was, after all, over seventy. Since we are all expert in managing an everyday life of our own it can even appear that there is no problem at all. The idea of 'common sense' explains all the thinking that takes place, until we reflect how Monique, Ed and the boys employ conflicting *uncommon senses*. We need a theoretical approach that throws problems into relief.

There are other issues below the surface that call for attention: conflict between short-term and long-term goals; offering reasons for actions, the last lines in personal arguments for acting one way rather than another; shifting allegiances and conflicts; the personal interpretation of new ideas; the credence given to others' ideas; how hopes turn into plans. Above all, although it seems tautological to say so, the approach we choose must limit itself to the skills and operations that Monique can perform within her own culture. These determine her range of actions, and that includes anything about her life that we might want to call 'scientific'.

Narrative

The account itself resembles a story, but one with no clear ending. It seems to be about survival, not now, but in some distant future. There is a set of events with a chronological order and a set of roles or characters. How do these characters see their own stories developing into the future?

Belief

How do these characters select between one future and the other? Clearly they have to do the best with the intellectual resources they have to hand. What are these resources? We might imagine that in everyday life beliefs will exist in systems, or webs, and that the systems are likely to be conservative. The refutation of a single proposition will meet resistance from a supporting framework of beliefs by shifting attention to weaknesses in the process of refutation. Just what do individuals like Monique believe? How do their actions and decisions incorporate their beliefs? How is the conflict between social pressure and reason resolved? Remember that Monique's social position as mother and daughter requires that she master a set of beliefs about diet, and that it is a part of her culture to pass on, to teach, explicit beliefs – at least to her family.

Science

If there is science in Monique's account it doesn't look like the science that we know and love. It is essential therefore to make clear what we mean by 'being scientific', and to do so in a way that allows science to interact with the account by embracing the elements and operations of vernacular culture.

What is the role of experts within that culture? Is it to supply new beliefs that work? Or simply to specify actions for which no corresponding belief is offered? Are experts best thought of as teachers from an external culture? How does one culture translate ideas into another? Should we conceive of it as a power relationship? And how should we deal with the conflicts between experts? After all, one set of experts put the additives into food; another set tells us to avoid them.

Communication

In speaking of science, we have also, unavoidably, been talking about communication; 'supply', 'specify', 'teach', 'translate'. Within Monique's account different attempts at communication met with different degrees of success. Let us apply to the account the most common model of communication, the 'Conduit Theory', used in everyday life (Reddy 1979), the social sciences (Miller 1970) or in engineering (Shannon and Weaver 1946):

We may then evaluate performance as follows:

Sender	Message	Receiver	Result
Doctor	diet	Monique	success
Monique	diet	boys	failure
Monique	diet	Ed	success
Monique	plants	Ed	failure
TV	diet	Monique and Ed	success

What are the conditions for success? Are other models and strategies available that would turn the failure with the boys into success? Would they also apply to other media, such as education, TV, or research?

What kind of theory will help?

The plan of this chapter derives from Harré's development of a social science from his philosophy of science. In the latter the description of nature in terms of laws and patterns is only a part of the scientist's work. The main task is to understand how the patterns are generated.

For example, given a recurring pattern of observed results, like the Gas Laws, it may be explained as the behaviour of some invisible clockwork or 'generating mechanism' (GM). Clearly explaining is an imaginative act. We can only guess at this mechanism. One method of guessing is to identify some object whose behaviour is analogous to the behaviour observed. The structure of this object then suggests features the generating mechanism may possess. Figure 9.1 illustrates how the analogy between behaviours may lead to analogies between structures.

Harré argues that Social Science has an analogous task. For us, Monique's account is the Pattern Observed. The task is to specify a Generating Mechanism.

A successful theoretical survey must identify models of individuals and their exchanges in such a way that a construction based upon them could plausibly make the decisions and exchanges Monique has described. It must also help us decide whether there is anything about the life that lies behind this pattern that we could justifiably call 'scientific' apart from the ideas, concepts, theories and so on that enter it from the world of formal science. My ultimate purpose is to make alternative patterns explicit to actors like Monique and to those who wish to help her, health professionals, writers, TV producers.

To this end I shall use Brémond's (1970) method of describing narrative, Harré and Secord's (1972) view of social life as a sequence of acts and actions

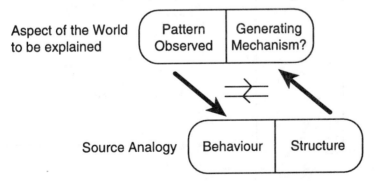

Figure 9.1 How the analogy between behaviours may lead to analogies between structures

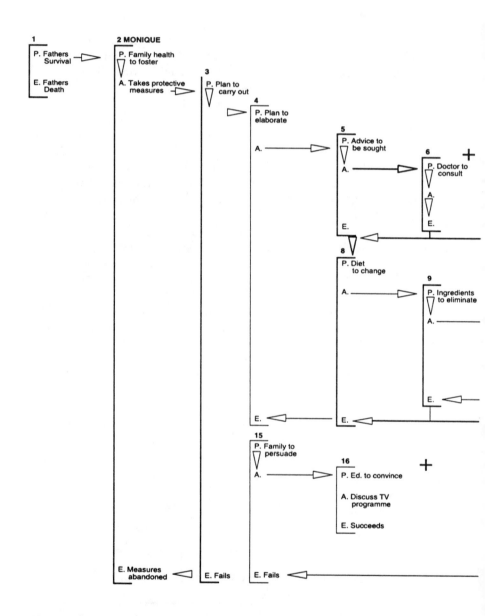

Figure 9.2 Schematization of Monique's account using Brémond's method of representing narrative

7
P. TV programme to view
A.
E.

+

10
P. Ingredients to identify
A.
E.

11
P. Labels to find, read & understand
A.
E.

12
P. Ingredients to introduce
A.
E.

13
P. Ingredients to locate
A.
E.

14
P. Resources to buy & use to be found (Time, money, energy, skill)
E.

17
P. Boys to convince
A.
E.

18
P. Argue explanation vs. rewards of palate
A.
E. Fails

19
P. Argue authority vs. rewards of palate
A.
E. Fails

20
P. Expression of Authority to be Managed
A. Argues over houseplant
E. Loses

DJP 88

within some metaphorical drama. I shall then identify the elements they hold in common with a specific (Popperian) view of science. This common set of elements, vernacular in nature, scientific in its dynamic, is what I shall call Vernacular Science.

THE STRUCTURE OF MONIQUE'S ACCOUNT AS NARRATIVE

The aspect of narrative that I concentrate on concerns the plot or the sequence of events. For the moment I set aside the more interesting problems that emerge when we can see these events as a product of interacting characters.

The immediate value of Brémond's work lies in its useful notation. It offers theory only in a weak sense, providing a clearer way of seeing the pattern in an episode from a person's life. The idea behind the notation is that of 'function'. A function is a 'task-to-be-accomplished'. It comprises three stages. The first stage is the creation of an aim or possibility; the second describes whether any action is taken or not; the final stage evaluates success in achieving the aim. Figure 9.2 is a representation of Monique's account in terms of functions. The symbol for a function includes a reference to a character, the name of the function and the following shorthand: P (Possibility, Aim); A (Action); E (Evaluation, Result). I have condensed Monique's account into twenty functions, for example:

2   *Family health to foster*
11   *Labels to find, read and understand*

In any interesting story the actual sequence of events interrupts the neat P, A, E sequence for a single function and follows a path that jumps from function to function and character to character. For example, Monique doesn't pass directly from stage {2 *Family health to foster*, P} to {2, E}; {3 *Plan to carry out*, P} intervenes. More complicated situations arise when two new P stages intervene. For example, the progress from {8 *Diet to change*, A} to {9, *Ingredients to eliminate*, P}, and {12, *Ingredients to introduce*, P.}

Often this disruption is caused when an actor applies some means to achieve ends, for example;

End: {5, *Advice to be sought*}
Means: {6, *Doctor to consult*}

It may also arise from a conflict between ends:

{16, *Ed to convince* } and {20, *Authority to express*}. In the diagram, Figure 9.2, pp. 156–7, the 'means' seem to be nested within the 'end'. An over-arching end nests a sequence of specific means.

The driving force behind a story is the tension created either by the failure of an attempt to achieve some end, P, or, given some P, by the undetermined

A and E spaces. Part of the interest in drama arises from the manner in which the resolution of tension surrounding overarching functions depends upon the E stage of specific ones.

If science and everyday life are to engage we might expect to find outcomes of overarching everyday functions hanging on the evaluations of intermediate, scientific ones. In Monique's account, her project to protect the family's health is an overarching function, but one she does not achieve.

Brémond's notation allows us to formalize Monique's account. Before we can decide whether anything within it deserves to be called 'scientific' we need theories both of science and of everyday life.

THEORIES ABOUT EVERYDAY LIFE

There is no shortage of theories to relate individuals to the culture in which they find themselves. The most useful of these theories will offer ideas we can convert into empirical questions; the most interesting will overlap with theories of science in some significant way. Harré's way of conceiving the relationship between people and their culture is both striking and useful:

> The fundamental human reality is a conversation, effectively without beginning or end, to which, from time to time, individuals make contributions. All that is personal in our lives is individually appropriated from the conversation going on around us, and perhaps idiosyncratically transformed.
>
> (Harré 1983)

Suppose we take the idea of conversation as a model for a culture. Immediately certain features of the appropriate model of a person follow. The central feature is the use of language, since the model person has to be able to generate the model conversation and vice versa. Let's look more closely at what happens in an encounter between two people, in order to make the model person more explicit.

Each participant is working with the impressions they take of the other on the basis of expressions, some conscious, some unconscious that each manifests. Both seek to reserve as much control as possible over future events by defining the present situation on their own terms. Ideally, according to Goffman (1971) each person P_1 will seek to 'express himself in such a way as to give [P_2 – the other] the kind of impression that leads them [P_2] to act voluntarily in accordance with his [P_1's] own plan'.

At the same time, from whatever clues are presented, each has to guess the other's intentions – whether these are to be highly thought of, to convey what they think highly of, to confuse, to dismiss, or simply to maintain enough harmony to keep the encounter going. By application of their stereotypes and theories each tries to determine the nature of the other – how trustworthy is he? how competent? what attitudes does she extend to different categories of people?

How can we turn these insights into a model? Many different models of the individual have been used in different fields. Metaphors based on a clock, a slate, a digestive system or a computer have all been used. They have varying degrees of success in different situations. Yet they lack the fundamental qualities which would generate the behaviour Goffman describes. In an odd, but telling, phrase, Harré and Secord (1972) insist that only the 'anthropomorphic' model of man is a valid one.

There is a number of determining features of the 'anthropomorphic' model. The first, easily neglected, is that the individual is indeed active and we need to have some concept of what form this activity takes. The second is that the individual generates intentions; third, that intentions are fundamentally linguistic in nature. In everyday life, men act because they have, simultaneously, a given intention and a belief that a particular action will realize it. Alongside intention, therefore, lies another basis for activity, anticipation, which may be thought of as inference based on the implicit theories that underpin the use of language.

Later, I shall present a question-asking, inference-making model of the individual which embodies these features. One purpose of empirical work, collecting more accounts like Monique's, is to list and classify the sorts of questions and inferences that different kinds of people ask and make. How does this analysis bear upon different sorts of conversation? Central to Harré's account are intentions, which he refers to as 'acts', and the forms by which they are accomplished, called 'actions'. The act–action relationship is seen in Figure 9.2, for example:

Act: 19 *Argue authority versus rewards of the palate*
Action: 20 *Expression of authority to be managed*

The sequences of events (or *episodes*) that concern us are sequences of acts and actions and they exist in different forms. They may be formal, like entering and leaving university through ceremonies of matriculation and graduation, or informal, like the routines of a family quarrel. Episodes can be classified by comparison with the models which together constitute Goffman's 'dramaturgical analogy' for social life. Sometimes it is best to think of them as rituals, sometimes as games, sometimes as drama. They all have something in common. Whether it is the sequence of actions for a ritual, which may be written down, or may be preserved in the initiation process for acolytes; or a drama, where conventionally there is a script, or a game, where there is a strategy, in each case there is an implicit plan of events in a sequence.

These plans, with their chronological or cause-and-effect sequences, are the products of intentions and of beliefs. Their structures appear to have much in common with the structure of narratives. I will proceed on the assumption that individuals form for themselves a structure analogous to the diagram of Monique's account and that they try to determine the most advantageous way through the various options that their model presents. The better their structures, the better their future.

BELIEF

I suggested that Figure 9.2 shows a pattern of life that is the product of beliefs; what it does not show are the rejected alternatives or the beliefs that led to the choice that was made. For example, the sequence in the diagram that moves from function 7 to function 8 does not say why Monique acted in that way. Can we find out?

A tangle of problems emerges. If we ask Monique why, we could get different answers at different times; then again different questioners might get different answers; or the study of her behaviour might suggest to the researcher more plausible reasons for her actions than those she is prepared to acknowledge. These are all different dramas and they call for different lines, even from the same character.

From all of this we need to disentangle intention from belief. How can we construe this belief? First, suppose we think of it as an explicit formal proposition in everyday language bound to others like the strands of a web (Quine and Ullian 1970). We can find explicit examples in Monique's account. But some beliefs are implicit, unstated 'beliefs-in-use', or 'theories-in-use' in the phrase of Argyris and Schon (1974). Any given 'theory-in-use' may simply be one among many, each tied to specific contexts, or to use Kelly's (1963) term, 'ranges of convenience'. Many beliefs are transient. Even if they are bound to a specific context where a need for advice arises, they are just as likely to be transformed, even into their logical *negation* (Maranda and Maranda 1971). It is only when beliefs-in-use are reflected upon and shared that they take a propositional form. If they are written down they can be systematized and a sense of coherence can be required of them.

All cultures are rich in sets of sayings, songs and stories people tell each other, which comment on the world or give advice about how to deal with it. Their range can make them a valuable cultural resource which closely informs language itself. They can also be a serious hazard. They are most important constituents of the 'conversation'.

In many folk there exist beliefs which compete with formal science. Beliefs about health survive (Foster and Anderson 1978) which jostle with professional medical advice (Simons 1977). Beliefs about the weather (Duff 1970) and the daily stream of claims about the influence of the stars provide more clashes. Alternative conceptions research has excavated many more (Viennot 1979). Californian creationists try to refute basic scientific beliefs head on and proceed to draw practical implications far beyond the issue of evolution and creation (Nelkin 1982). And there is no reason to assume that the cosmology of other cultures could not demonstrate other sets of beliefs-in-use relating myth and, for example, farming or child-bearing practices (Foster and Anderson 1978).

In everyday life, vernacular man and woman consciously search for new relevant beliefs just as the formal scientist does. They enrich their system of beliefs with transient experiences; conversation, newspaper reading, radio and TV to view and to forget.

The forms they find are not restricted to pithy sayings or explanations of peculiar scientific phenomena; often they are embedded in stories which circulate like rumours or children's games (Brunvand 1981). Attempts to find a sense of coherence among them sometimes have simple practical forms (Dundes 1961); some seem gratuitously elaborate. The danger with all of these approaches is that they take only belief into account and ignore beliefs-in-use.

One of the worries educators sometimes express is the fear that implicit beliefs spread by a process analogous to contagion. Watch violent TV stories and you will believe that violent behaviour is acceptable. Read advertisements for drink which exploit the female form and you take on a belief that sexual restraint can be abandoned. How can we explore this process? The conduit theory suggest that tangible beliefs pass into minds as if they took part in a physical transport system (de Saussure 1974). What happens when belief is implicit – or with beliefs-in-use? They have to be constructed anew by each user. Is a 'transport' system the only possibility? Earlier, Goffman hinted at a much less direct process. The parallel is with language-in-use rather than language which is 'idling' (Wittgenstein 1958). Could this suggest an alternative communication strategy to the conduit theory?

The role given to belief in Figure 9.2 is quite fundamental. Belief is a tool-kit for getting from one story to another or even to indicate the very existence of other stories. Even in our innocence we know that in acting on a belief we are acting in hope and not certainty. But some of these beliefs are given a different status. They are referred to as knowledge. They are, apparently, validated (Ziman 1968). That requires that they are validated by someone in particular. Harré makes the point that a claim to know something is a moral claim (Harré 1983). It carries with it a promise: you can rely on this in your actions.

Science is a subset of this knowledge. Is it true then that we can rely on it in our actions? Does it make sense to ask 'what are the act–action sequences or stories characteristic of science'? If there are such acts and stories we may look at an account like Monique's and find that it is at least in part already scientific.

We are now approaching a resolution to the major issue underlying the problems we began with: what *is* the relationship between science and everyday life? If it is the relationship between vernacular knowledge and scientific knowledge, expressed in terms of the structures of everyday life, what does this mean in detail?

Knowledge

The matter is confused by the existence of two *sorts* of theories of knowledge. 'Resource theories' emphasize the idea of knowledge as content, the *true* beliefs in the set we have just investigated. 'Action theories' emphasize the skill of the person who acquires or uses the knowledge. Other philosophers and educationists have developed this distinction. Ryle distinguished between 'knowledge that' and 'knowledge how' (Ryle 1949). If, like Olson and Bruner (1974), we distinguish our knowledge of chairs from our knowledge of sitting, we might begin to relate the two kinds of knowledge in an analogous way to that between structure and behaviour in Figure 9.1.

Another factor is the way that, within a given social order, access to knowledge is socially differentiated. Harré draws attention to 'men's knowledge' (Harré 1983). A striking example of social differentiation emerges when one considers the different responses people working in different roles receive to a specific request for knowledge. An academic rival, a PhD student, a television producer, a school teacher and a pub acquaintance will all be told distinctly different stories in response to the same enquiry. Filkin (1984) describes how the same TV producer was first ignored by a particular academic when he made enquiries on behalf of *Tomorrow's World* but was welcomed when he transferred to *Horizon* soon after.

The social distribution of knowledge doesn't only affect the way projects are implemented, however. It plays a part in identifying them in the first place. This raises the question 'whose projects receive attention?' The implications of this, taken alongside the moral dimension of knowledge claims, highlight the serious social consequences of being forced to withdraw. Vernacular knowledge then, has to do with identifying projects in everyday life and avoiding having to withdraw one's agenda along with one's claims.

Scientific knowledge, too, has both resource and action aspects. The information that a particular item of food contains a specific chemical additive is scientific knowledge as resource. It may be used by vernacular persons, but it lies in the vernacular culture undigested. If we are to find an aspect of vernacular culture that is also scientific it will have to be an action theory. In this case we will want to ask 'Are there act-action sequences or stories that are characteristic of science?' If there are, then when we look at an account like Monique's we may find that it too possesses some of these sequences: that it is, at least in part, already scientific.

But there is another constraint governing our approach to scientific knowledge. In choosing an approach that will safeguard the vernacular individual, especially when experts disagree, we need to keep in the foreground the question 'Can we rely on it in our actions?' The fallibility of scientific knowledge claims should be built into our perception of them. Fallibility is something we should take for granted from the start, and then try to limit it. The question is now inescapable: what do we mean by science?

SCIENCE

The approach to science that combines all these features most economically is expressed in Popper's (1963) schema:

$$\Rightarrow \quad P \quad \Rightarrow TT \Rightarrow EE \Rightarrow P' \Rightarrow$$

In this schema, TT is a 'tentative theory', raised in the face of some problem, P. EE is 'error elimination'. P' is a new problem that the activity of testing and argument will reveal. The significant thing from the point of view of our current project is that the definition of problems, guessing at solutions, attempting to find all their weaknesses, and taking a new, revised perspective on the problem are all processes that can be described and carried out one way or another using only ordinary language.

It won't use the same concepts and techniques as science and it will reach cruder conclusions, but it is a strategic sequence of linguistic moves and actions in the real world that will improve on conclusions reached in any other way apart from formal science. That is Vernacular Science.

In principle there is no difference between the result of EE in the everyday world or in the formal world, except that the penalty for failure of EE in the everyday world can be more serious than an editor's rejection slip. People stake their lives, not just their reputations, on their beliefs or on the beliefs of the experts that they call upon. It follows from this that some revision of Harré's remarks about moral claims is necessary. It seems to be fundamentally rash either to assert, or to believe, the statement 'You can rely upon Q in your actions'. The most we can hope for is: 'Q is the best advice I can give you at the present time'.

To make the schema work, an additional feature, 'argument', is required. 'Argument' will be interpreted in what follows simply as the skill of putting all Popper's stages together in such a way that, to the best of the participant's ability, no contrary propositions can undermine the conclusion.

What we have is clearly an action theory. The actions it generates are clearly subject to criteria, not only about the survival of the tentative theories under test, but also about the significance of the problems, P, chosen for attention. Just what is to count as a problem? And how are theories arrived at?

Problems

In *Scientific Knowledge and its Social Problems* Ravetz (1971) carefully distinguishes between 'problem-situations' and 'problems' by using the analogy of science as craftwork. And, using Aristotle's analysis, the production of a theory becomes the production of a tangible artefact, a sentence, whose production is governed by four distinct categories of cause. In order of increasing importance these causes are: material causes, the substance, language, which is worked upon; efficient causes, the scientist and his activity; formal cause, the argument which generates the shape of the final product; and final causes, the purpose for which the artefact is constructed. A problem only exists when the whole set of causes is present. Final causes without feasible, practical means of solution simply contribute to a problem-situation. Using this analysis, Monique's campaign may be seen as an attempt to convert what, for her, is a worrying 'problem-situation' into concrete solvable problems.

To adapt Ravetz's scheme to the vernacular context there are two main considerations. First, we check that it is constructed out of vernacular materials, that is, from ideas expressed in ordinary language. It is even inappropriate to expect an artefact like a written sentence as a solution. Then we have to take vigorous steps to ensure that what we are talking about is a vernacular problem.

The problems in Monique's account

So let us draw up a list of the problems that describe Monique's situation in the account. Notice how they correspond to the 'aim' component of the functions in Figure 9.2, whose numbers are given in parentheses.

1 Her father's recovery. (1)
2 Protecting the health of her family. (2)
3 Eliminating harmful components of diet. (9)
4 Finding substitutes. (12)
5 Getting practical support from Ed. (16)
6 Persuading her sons to accept the new regime. (16)
7 Protecting condition of house-plants. (17)
8 Finding arguments that satisfy Ed. (16)

Some of these problems can even be identified with those that a formal scientist would recognize.

Our next step is prompted by the observation that Monique's attempts to solve her problems become, in turn, problems for others. At first the consumption of Health Food crisps was not a problem for the boys. But their eventual refusal compounded Monique's original problem. So a complete picture of what is going on requires a delicate correlation of problem and solution, possibilities and actions for a number of actors as well as a sequencing of P's following the Ps. This is what the Brémond notation allows us to visualize.

The decomposition of Monique's account into problems throws new light on the search for science in her life. Without it we would have been satisfied to say that the doctor, the TV programme and the house-plant book brought it in as a resource via the 'conduit' from the world of formal science. Now we can see a complex patchwork of problems, some acknowledged, some abandoned; of theories, some well understood, some magical because Monique's inability to build them herself renders her vulnerable; of tests, from which she cannot escape.

There are parts of this picture of Vernacular Science to admire; there are gaps. One can admire the teamwork, the integration of a pattern of performance wherein one partner makes a successful contribution to one stage of argument, to be followed by the other succeeding at the next. At other points partners appear to work actively against each other.

Theories and explanations

In the foregoing account, theories and beliefs seem to share a simple propositional structure. However, a modern 'sophisticated fallibilism' deals with networks of theories. Some have a 'core' status; if they are successfully challenged the whole network fails. Others, easier to discard, are 'peripheral'. Any single theory under attack draws strength from others in its network.

Central to most networks is a model, which is likely to be a generating mechanism. The scientist and social scientist feel uneasy faced with a pattern which they cannot explain. Similarly in everyday life, without a generating mechanism how can we tell the difference between a prediction based on good reasons and one with concealed reasons? Between science and magic? Explanation is an important criterion for Vernacular Science.

But is it expecting too much to require explanations from vernacular man? It is worth reflecting that when scientists seek 'generating mechanisms' for their own patterns it is to everyday ideas and familiar technologies that they often turn: flow of liquid to explain electric current; pumps to explain the heart; computers to explain the working of the brain. It is easy to see that the raw materials for generating mechanisms exist in everyday life. Are they used?

In Monique's account the ability of the actors to generate or use explanations is not pronounced, in spite of Ed's insistent demands. The problem was explicit. The 'findings' were clear. Although Monique could explain the threat of a heart attack from cholesterol, the only weapons the parents used were commands based on 'authority', not reasons or explanations. Perhaps the boys knew too little about cars.

The need for the picture of the relationship between science and everyday life that I present here hardly needs emphasizing. There is a danger that formal science feels to Vernacular Man like a foreign, hostile invader of everyday life. The alternative is to develop Popper's problem-spiral sequence within vernacular culture. We can do this, not by uttering unexplained mysteries, but by empowering individuals to make better understood choices about their own futures.

A MODEL OF VERNACULAR MAN

On the basis of the theories discussed so far I can now develop a model of Vernacular Man based on the questions he asks. The idea is to create an entity that could survive in the situations that everyday culture presents by asking questions, interpreting and acting on the answers. Think of this model as the 'generating mechanism' which, when it is allowed to run, produces the pattern described in Figure 9.2.

Questions can be organized into three overlapping categories:

> *Commitment.* How do I relate to individuals? to groups? How do groups relate?
>
> *Story.*   What is going to happen, next, later, ultimately?
>
> *Criticism.* What ideas can I rely on? What is the problem?

Fully developed, the model of Vernacular Man begins to look like this:

Commitment
(a) What is he driving at? What is he hoping to achieve?
(b) What problem is he trying to solve? What position is he trying to gain?
(c) How can I achieve . . . ?
(d) What next? What happened?
(e) How do I begin to . . . ? What is the next stage in achieving . . . ? Will he successfully complete . . . ?
(f) How do people in her capacity respond to people in mine? What kind of person will want to get involved?
(g) What rules, plans, theories do people use in situations like this? What justification could I give for . . . ? Why did you . . . ?
(h) What rules do I prefer? What will he choose to do within his constraints?

Story
(a) Who are the characters?
(b) What are the teams?
(c) What is the outcome?

(d) What is the plot?
(e) Who is the audience?
(f) How are they persuaded?
(g) What are my lines?

Criticism
(a) What's the purpose, problem?
(b) What's the puzzle? What's the surprising pattern?
(c) What's the answer, solution, theory, guess?
(d) What could produce, explain a pattern like that?
(e) So what?
(f) What can we use to solve this?
(g) What do I know that works in a similar way?
(h) How do you arrive at the answer?
(i) How do you know? How do you justify that? Why?
(j) Where does that land us? Will it work? What surprises are there in store?

Thrust 'Vernacular Man' into a new situation and he will spontaneously produce a series of questions like these to generate his contribution to Harré's 'conversation'. The questions are always there. He continually needs reassurance about answers. He continually needs to practise his systems. When his questions meet with no answer at all, or with unwelcome answers, he will dissociate himself from the situation.

Goffman (1972) talks about the 'entrancement' people find in games which takes them out of the 'real' world and into the world of the game that is being played. Perhaps it is like the concentration that is needed to learn formal science. In our attempts to explain science to the layman we shouldn't take readiness to step into a scientific world for granted. We need to deal first with our learner-viewer's actual social world.

VERNACULAR SCIENCE OR MAGIC?

So parts of everyday life, and parts of science can be represented on the same model. We also know where to relate the remaining parts of science to the model. It remains to show that parts of Figure 9.2 represent both everyday thinking and scientific thinking, or that the different parts of the story engage in a meaningful way rather than simply lie, inert, side-by-side. Otherwise it seems that the two different aspects of life they represent will also fall apart. What kinds of model for closer contact are there? Do they adhere? Spontaneously? Or do they need glue? Do they attach like pieces in a jigsaw puzzle? Does one flow through the other? Is it even more fundamental: an organic shading off of one kind of structure into another? In this organic model some elements belong to and play an important role in two adjacent structures. Monique's account illustrates this model.

Vernacular Science is a way of thinking and acting which addresses itself to everyday problems. Vernacular Man, like Levi-Strauss' 'bricoleur' will take hypotheses from anywhere, but will re-interpret them in vernacular language and action. Hypotheses of Vernacular Science are frequently converted into actions rather than words. While I think of expert advice in this respect as a hypothesis, even when it is expressed in the form of a conclusion, in vernacular life the abstract statement of fact turns into an imperative, although its logical status remains tentative. 'Diet X, Y, Z is recommended in cases like yours Mr. Jones', becomes 'Steve, eat X, Y, Z.'

The testing of these 'hypotheses' employs only the resources of the vernacular world. Features of formal scientific activity like analysis of concepts, arguments and explanations are all to be found there, but they are restricted by the fact that they are all expressed in everyday language. Analogy, experiment, even ideal experiment, are used; but the degrees of precision, the decontextualization, the patience to collect statistically valid samples, are all vastly different. The key difference between vernacular and formal science is the way in which vernacular man is committed to his results. When a scientist's theories fail in test, it is his ideas, mainly, that suffer. When Vernacular Man's theories fail, his stories, his social existence, and even his physical existence, are at risk. We have seen how explanation is a critical concept. The search for explanation, and the mistrust of advice that omits it, is clear in Ed's impatience with the media expert. His insistence on belief-in-use undermined Monique's acceptance of expert authority because she acted upon a belief she could not explain.

I can now specify what I mean by 'magical'. The use of ideas in the vernacular world which are not understood there is either the exercise of magic or of formal science. The magical includes elements like 'problem', 'hypotheses', even 'test'. What it conceals is 'explanation'. Situations where no explanation exists can be distinguished from those where, although the explanation exists, it is not offered. That constitutes a straightforward exercise of power. I can see no difference between this and the practice of magic.

We may speculate that Vernacular Science is that part of the vernacular culture out of which Formal Science grows. Less mature maybe, less powerful certainly. Made out of the raw materials of vernacular life, it nevertheless shares with science many, if not all, of the patterns and strategies that science itself uses. Its vernacular qualities recommend it as a rooting point for the conversation about specific scientific issues. Its scientific qualities make it a feature of everyday culture, already living within its members, that they can develop into a more formal science when the occasion demands.

Using the idea of Vernacular Science

This chapter offers only working ideas. It contains a story which explores the kind of science that might inform the life of an everyday person. There is a visualization of the story. There is a model of such a person. There is the concept of Vernacular Science. These elements are backed by a sketch of an argument to show how a view of science, taken analytically, can be seen to have structures analogous to those of story and of episodes in everyday life. I have suggested that the search for science in everyday life should focus on the way vernacular problems are attacked in stages comparable to those in scientific thinking, rather than on the results of science floating undigested in vernacular culture.

I will close by trying to suggest how these ideas might be turned into practice and the main directions in which improvements might be sought.

There are two ways in which these ideas may help practice. The first concerns the way educators or communicators construe their clients. The second concerns their strategies for communicating with them.

Science educators, whether their medium is television, the classroom or the museum exhibition, already work with models of their target audiences. Many of them already have a stock of anecdotes about the use of science in the everyday life they experience themselves. They might use Monique's account then to try to elaborate their own anecdotes: to make explicit the stories of the characters there, their acts and their expressions, their explanations and arguments. Given such accounts, educators may then ask themselves where their own work fits into the story, the act, or the argument. If they can find a place, they should then try to make clear to themselves *how* it fits in.

Or educators may look at their own attempts to relate science to the layman and ask: is it formal or is it vernacular? If it is formal they should ask: is it more important that a scientist will not dismiss it than have vernacular man pick it up and improve his arguments from it?

Alternatively, they may take the model of Vernacular Man and try to answer the questions the model puts to a particular programme, lesson, text or display. It should reveal quickly where a failure to meet a social or a narrative imagination creates a barrier to an understanding of the science.

The model of Vernacular Man helps us conceive alternative communication strategies to the conduit theory. For example, a strategy of 'communication by sympathetic provocation' can be envisaged. The sender can ask what thoughts are likely to be provoked by various disturbances in the receiver's environment. Communication of the particular idea is achieved by devising a string of disturbances through which the receiver may be helped to a useful insight. These disturbances may be a mixture of statements, images and actions; they may demand attention to the topic or they may work through switches in roles and social settings. Moves like these provoke vernacular man to thought on occasions when the transmission of explicit statements fails.

Let me make this hypothesis concrete. Consider a formal scientific statement uttered in the vernacular world. It may lack any reference to actors, yet it is precisely actors who provoke the first set of vernacular questions. Finding no material to work on, vernacular man assumes that this odd behaviour can only be explained by cold, even sinister, intentions, as would be the case in his everyday world.

Now consider a statement about characters from the vernacular world, like Monique, who run into trouble. Identification with her provokes questions designed to resolve her plight. These are questions about science.

How can this theoretical sketch be improved? One striking omission is the lack of development of the characters who people the vernacular world. Silverstone (1981) presents the modern counterparts of the mythical world of heroes, villains and magicians. Some account of 'character' to go alongside the notion of 'team' and role' is called for, but there are real problems in avoiding triviality. I have set them aside for the moment.

The attempt to use the philosophy of science analytically is an important feature of this work. Too many writers give an account of their views of science and then ignore the concepts and arguments that arise when it comes to looking for and looking at data. My treatment of Popper, Ravetz and Harré could be thought of as intellectual bricolage. I offer it as a prototype and a challenge.

The most fruitful area for further development, however, is easy to specify. In Monique's case we can see some prototype scientific thinking at work over a practical, possibly a survival, problem. More accounts are needed. Ethnographers have methods for finding them at hand. There are many issues in personal health and in practical politics where it seems essential to know what people understand before massive campaigns begin to teach them anything new. AIDS and nuclear power are obvious examples.

But the most interesting areas may turn out not to be practical. I would like to know how Vernacular Man copes with the task of explaining the world 'just because it is there'. We may expect to find at least two approaches. In the first he takes on board concepts like 'mollycuells' as part of a world view which will help to brush aside old institutions as well as old ideas, just as O'Casey's Covey dreamed (O'Casey 1974).

The second area is concerned with origins. Vernacular Man has just as powerful a need to exercise his imagination over questions about the origins of stars as he has to design a better plough (Ryder 1982). I want to watch that imagination at work.

Acknowledgement

I gratefully acknowledge the opportunity to discuss the ideas in this paper at the 1985 Rencontre Internationale, Pensée Scientifique et Technique et Savoirs Naturels dans le Champ Social Contemporain held in Paris at L'Ecole des Hautes Etudes en Sciences Sociales.

REFERENCES

Argyris, C. and Schon, D. 1974. *Theory in practice.* Jossey Bass, San Francisco.
Brémond, C. 1970. 'Morphology of the French folktale.' *Semiotica,* 7(3): 247–76.
Brunvand, J. H. 1981. *The vanishing hitchhiker.* Norton, New York.
Department of Education and Science. 1985. *Science 5–16: A statement of policy.* HMSO, London.
de Saussure, F. 1974. *Course in general linguistics.* Fontana, London.
Duff, G. 1970. *Country wisdom.* Pan, London.
Dundes, A. 1961. 'Brown County superstitions.' *Midwest Folklore,* 11(1): 25–56.
Filkin, D. 1984. 'Presenting science on television.' A paper presented to the Republic of Science seminar, Department of External Studies, The University, Oxford.
Foster, G. M. and Anderson, B. G. 1978. *Medical anthropology.* Wiley, New York.
Goffman, E. 1971. *The presentation of self in everyday life.* Penguin, London.
Goffman, E. 1972. *Encounters.* Penguin, London.
Harré, R. 1976. 'The constructive role of models.' In Collins, L. (ed.) *The use of models in the social sciences.* Tavistock, London.
Harré, R. 1979. *Social being.* Blackwell, Oxford.
Harré, R. 1983. *Personal being.* Blackwell, Oxford.
Harré, R. and Secord, P. F. 1972. *The explanation of social behaviour,* Blackwell, Oxford.
Kelly, G. 1963. *A theory of personality.* Norton, New York.
Leach, E. 1976. *Culture and communication.* Cambridge University Press, Cambridge.
Maranda, E. K. and Maranda, P. 1971. *Structural models in folklore and transformational essays.* Mouton, The Hague.
Miller, G. A., 1970. *The psychology of communication.* Penguin, London.
Nelkin, D. 1982. *The creation controversy.* Norton, New York.
O'Casey, S. 1974. *'The plough and the stars.* Macmillan, London.
Olson, D. and Bruner, J. 1974. 'Learning by direct action and learning by media.' In Olson, D. (ed.) *Media and symbols.* Yearbook 73 (part 1) of the National Society for the Study of Education. University of Chicago Press, Chicago.
Popper, K. R. 1963. *Conjectures and refutations.* Routledge & Kegan Paul, London.
Popper, K. R. 1972. *Objective knowledge.* Oxford University Press, Oxford.
Quine, W. V. and Ullian, J. S. 1970. *The web of belief.* Random House, New York.
Ravetz, J. 1971. *Scientific knowledge and its social problems.* Penguin, London.
Reddy, M. J. 1979. 'The conduit metaphor.' In Ortony, A. (ed.) *Metaphor and thought.* Cambridge University Press, Cambridge.
Royal Society, 1985. *The public understanding of science.* The Royal Society, London.
Ryder, N. 1982. *Science, television and the adolescent.* Independent Broadcasting Authority, London.
Ryle, G. 1949. *The concept of mind.* Hutchinson, London.
Shannon, C. E. and Weaver, W. 1946. *The mathematical theory of communication.* University of Illinois Press, Urbana, Ill.
Silverstone, R. 1981. *The message of television,* Heinemann, London.

Simons, J. 1977. 'Measuring the meaning of fertility control.' In Slater, J. (ed.) *Explorations in intra-personal space.* Wiley, New York.

Viennot, L. 1979. 'Spontaneous reasoning in elementary dynamics.' *European Journal of Science Education,* 1: 205–21.

Wittgenstein, L. 1958. *Philosophical investigations,* second edition, Blackwell, Oxford.

Ziman, J. 1968. *Public knowledge.* Cambridge University Press, Cambridge.

Chapter 10

Schematic representation in optics

Jayashree Ramadas and Michael Shayer

RATIONALE

Perhaps the interest in content-centred issues in science education started with the curriculum reform movement of the 1960s, which brought into the field of education scientists who became interested in the nature of learning in their own subject areas. However, the result of the focus on content has been that this research has followed a clearly Baconian approach. Data related to thinking and learning in particular subject areas are collected, and then patterns and perhaps generalizations are looked for. The data collection and analysis are only rarely, or not at all, driven by any explicit theory about cognition.

The approach to research is often the result of a deliberately flexible methodology and a wish to record all data with the minimum of constraints. Sometimes this is seen in the use of ethnographic or naturalistic methods of data collection. The strength of these methods is that they avoid the danger in the uncritical use of an existing theory, which is that one may be adopting an unfalsifiable model, resulting in, for example, the reification of hypothesized constructs in the child's mind. Perhaps we have here a belief that the field is at present in an undeveloped, phenomenological stage in which theorization would be premature.

On the other hand, the content-dominated approach in research on children's ideas might derive from a certain belief about the nature of thought and learning, one which can best be explained with reference to the work of Jean Piaget. It was this work (Piaget 1929, 1930, 1974) which first revealed the enormous richness of children's ideas in different contexts. However, Piaget was interested in the structure of human knowledge and its development with age, not with the content of the knowledge. He argued and provided much support for the existence of context-independent, coherent structures of thought (e.g. Inhelder and Piaget 1958). A corollary of the existence of such structures would be that performance on any problem task would depend on the abstract logical structure of the task and not on its specific content.

However, later developments in cognitive psychology demonstrated that context does influence thought. For example, it was found that the expectations in terms of knowledge and attitudes which a person brings to a problem situation, and the human intentions perceived within that particular context, strongly affect performance (Wason and Johnson-Laird 1972; Donaldson 1978). Since then, there has been a move among cognitive scientists to consider intelligent behaviour not just in terms of abstract processes of thinking but very much in relation to the person's knowledge of specific situations (Larkin 1979; Resnick 1983). The focus, in the alternative conception movement, on studying children's ideas in specific topic areas draws its theoretical rationale from this work (Driver 1982). Perhaps we should also mention here the work of Pascual-Leone (1970), which described a new parameter to interpret the cognitive structure postulated by Piaget. This interpretation in terms of available processing space in short-term memory gave rise to the neo-Piagetian school of research, which has now provided evidence that the strategies used by the learner are also important in determining performance (Case 1978; Larkin 1979).

It is possible that these findings merely point to the need for more careful delineation of the domain of validity of the presumed content- and context-independent structures. A diametrically opposing interpretation would be that thinking and learning are so influenced by contextual factors that the abstracting-out of context-independent structures is impossible. Of course, the latter position, far from denying the possibility of a theory, forces us to search for such generalizations as would be consistent with the influence of context.

Two further points should be noted about the attempts to isolate context-independent cognitive processes. The first is that these perspectives, in their pre-Piagetian through to their neo-Piagetian forms, have viewed processes in a hierarchical way. Learners have been graded on some kind of a scale with an additional developmental interpretation. Secondly, the assessment tasks have been analysed for their structure and level of demands, with the result that the attributes of cognition are determined algorithmically, or even logically (e.g. Case 1978; Shayer and Adey 1981). In other words, these models of cognition have been more clearly articulated than the context-dependent ones.

The search for logically determined attributes on the one hand, and for modes of thinking specific to the given content area on the other, has given rise to two distinct schools of educational research. Though attempts to study both types of attributes simultaneously (Lunzer 1972) do exist, the two schools have remained distinct, not the least by virtue of their differing research methodologies. Perhaps it is not surprising that the research based on context-independent structures of thought, with its well defined models of cognitive behaviour, has involved rigorous experimental procedures and quantitative methods. The work on alternative conceptions, in contrast, has shunned models of development and has adopted an exploratory, qualitative, and perhaps more interpretative approach.

In this study we investigate, with reference to the above debate, the explanatory models used by children in situations relating to light. We start with a simple hierarchical model of the responses and see how well the data fit such a structure. Where the fit is not good, we look for a reason and can sometimes identify it in the influence of context.

CHILDREN'S CONCEPTIONS ABOUT LIGHT

Children's conceptions about the nature of light have been documented by a number of researchers. Piaget (1974) noted that young children do not concede the existence of light between a lamp and a patch of light it produces on a screen at some distance away. In a similar vein, Guesne (1985) concluded from her research and that of Tiberghien that most 10–11 year olds think of light as a source (an electric bulb), or a state (brightness), or an effect (a patch of light). They do not recognize light as a physical entity existing and propagating in space.

The connection made by learners between light and vision has been studied extensively. Piaget (1974) found that very young children imagine that there is no connection between the eye and the object, while at a slightly later age they think of vision as a passage from the eye to the object. These findings have been developed and modified to a great extent by Guesne (1985), Jung (1981) and Watts (1983), among others. It appears, for example, that although learners may interpret vision in terms of the eye being active, this notion may not involve the 'emanations' (Ronchi 1970) of the ancient Greeks (Guesne 1985). Also, a particular model of vision may be widespread without being consistently applied in different situations by the same child (Andersson and Karrqvist 1981).

In all of this work there has been some attempt to interpret the responses in terms of consistent patterns, but the results have not been very satisfactory. It has been difficult to do justice to the richness of the data deriving from children's responses. In Piaget's work the portion of the data presented to the reader is sketchy, while Andersson and Karrqvist's interpretation in terms of concrete and formal operational thinking deals with only selected aspects of their data. Watts (1983) and La Rosa et al. (1984) identify a set of interpretative frameworks used by children which are helpful, but they do not explore the rationale for the frameworks, in terms of any internal consistency criteria.

We can see, in work on children's conceptions about light, the beginning of a dialectic between structure and content of children's thought. Our interest is to explore this dialectic in order to develop a research methodology.

THE STUDY

We analyse, from the perspective of the above debate, the responses of a sample of 13–14 year old children to written tests and interviews relating to their conceptions about light, and their use of schematic representations of phenomena involving light. Four third-year classes were selected for the study, two in each of two schools in northern England. About ninety children were involved. They were given pre-tests before they had any formal instruction in optics. They were then followed through their teaching unit and given post-tests at the end of the unit. The pre- and post-tests were practically identical. The tests consisted of open-ended questions on light as well as problems to be solved using schematic diagrams. It is the latter which form the subject of analysis in this paper. Nine of the children were interviewed on their responses to this test; five were interviewed both pre-and post-teaching and the other four post-teaching only. The interviews, of about half-an-hour duration, explored the children's conceptions in further detail by getting them to talk about their responses. The complete study is described in Ramadas and Driver (1989).

The test was administered in three versions to three different groups of children in each class. Children who were judged by their teacher to be of 'high', 'medium', and 'low' ability were represented in equal proportions in the three groups. The same (or almost the same) problem situations were presented in each of these three versions and the children were asked to predict, describe and explain whatever happened in each situation. In the 'verbal' version (given to 36 children in the pre-test, and 39 in the post-test), the situations were presented via purely verbal descriptions. In the 'diagram' version, (used with 37 pre-test, 34 post-test), they were presented with the help of schematic diagrams which the children had to complete in order to answer the questions. In the third, the 'real situation' version, (9 pre-test, 12 post-test), the presentation was again with the help of schematic diagrams, but the children had an opportunity to set up a model, showing the geometry of the situation, before making their prediction. They then saw the model working before giving an explanation of the phenomenon.

The test items elicited children's ideas related to the geometry of the propagation of light, including ideas about vision, line of sight, and regular reflections. The four problems in their 'verbal' version are shown in the appendix to this chapter (see p. 186). The other versions had equivalents of the same problems, except that in the 'real situation' version, the 'moors vision' problem was omitted.

The children to be interviewed were selected from the group that had done the 'verbal' version of the test (one of the nine happened to have done the 'diagram' version) to avoid prejudice owing to previous exposure to the diagrams or models.

THE ANALYSIS

Our structured approach, while dealing with a hierarchy in the children's responses, derived this hierarchy purely empirically, and not from any stage theory of cognition. The basic structuring of the problems into the stages of 'situation', 'predictions', 'description' and 'explanation' may be thought to parallel Piagetian methodology, but since that paradigm is inherent to science itself, and since it is now so prevalent in work on children's conceptions, it can hardly be linked with any one theory of cognition.

A preliminary examination of the responses showed that some were at the level of observation or prediction, while others used explanatory models which subsumed some kind of an observation-type response. The hierarchy was therefore developed around this descriptive-explanatory dimension.

Construction of a hierarchy

Piaget (1930), in analysing responses to questions about natural phenomena, noted that the youngest children gave purely descriptive responses while in the higher age groups the responses included predictions about phenomena, and finally, explanations of some kind. Peel (1971) studied maturity of judgement in adolescents by classifying their written responses in a scale going from simple descriptive to explanatory. His three basic categories of increasing sophistication in responses were 'restricted', 'circumstantial', and 'imaginative'. He found evidence which led him to a developmental interpretation of these classes of responses. On this issue our own stand can only be that, since this is a phenomenological study, we simply aim to arrive at a classificatory system that will describe most of the data, and further, to study the nature of that data which does not fit into the system. This position is close to that of Biggs and Collis (1982), who have explored and classified the structure of student responses without assuming an underlying generalizable cognitive structure. We do look for generalizability by studying consistency in response levels across situations, but the result can be only a first approximation to any explanatory scheme. The question of development is much more problematic than that of generalizability. Though at times we draw upon the results of developmental studies, we do not here have sufficient longitudinal or cross-sectional data to examine a developmental interpretation of the responses.

The observed hierarchy of responses to each of the four problems in the test was found to fit into an overall hierarchy with ten levels as shown in Table 10.1. The full range of levels was applicable only for the 'verbal' version. Some modifications were necessary to describe responses in the other versions.

The levels of solution shown here for each problem were in most cases logically consistent in the sense that performance on a higher level implied

Table 10.1 Hierarchy of responses

		TEST ITEM		
	Moor-vision	Lamp-hole	Eye-hole	Lamp-mirror
	Question 1	Question 2	Question 3	Question 4
Descriptive (no explicit model) — Non-predictive: A = Listing components of situation diagram	Lamp, person	Bulb, board, screen		Bulb, mirror, eye
Predictive (phenomenological): X = Partially correct prediction			You see less	
B = Correct prediction	Lighted areas	Spot on screen	How much you see	Brightness, dazzle
C = Non-interpretative model	Rays of variation in shading			Rays
D = Interpretative, inaccurate model	No connection with eyes or vision start from eyes			
Explanatory (with model) — Non-geometrical: E = Interpretative, accurate model	Object-eye connection			Object mirror-eye connection
L = Model; no measurement		Spatial arrangement	Spatial arrangement	
Geometrical & interpretative: M = Model; elements of measurement		Some factors for size	Some factors for size	
N = Model; accurate measurement		All factors for size	All factors for size	
Descriptive — Predictive: F = Prediction of image				Prediction of image

acquisition of the lower. However, at some points this connection did not exist. Examples of these are discussed in detail here, because they illustrate a potential source of conflict between logical and causal reasoning which lies at the root of the debate on context dependence and independence. Piaget (1974) has argued that logico-mathematical operations and the understanding of causality develop together by mutual interaction. Wason and Johnson-Laird (1972), on the other hand, take the position that, since it is possible to construct tasks where causal and logical reasoning come into conflict, the generality of logical structure (as postulated for the formal operational stage) must be questioned.

In the construction of the hierarchy of Table 10.1, where logical criteria were found inadequate two other kinds of criteria were called upon. The first was empirical evidence. If one kind of response was empirically subsumed by another, then it was put on a lower level. Consider the case of levels E and F in question 4 (see Table 10.1). It was found that of the 26 cases of children (out of the total of 150 doing the pre-and post-tests in the verbal and diagram versions) who predicted that an image would be seen in the mirror, all but one showed light rays going from object to mirror to eye (a response judged to be at explanatory level E). The latter response was also much more common than the 'prediction' of image (F) response, thus F was placed higher than E even though it was nominally designated 'descriptive-predictive'. Since the levels in a single question were in most cases determined either logically or empirically (the one exception is discussed in the next paragraph), no scalogram-type analysis was found necessary.

The second kind of criterion comes from developmental studies. In question 1, levels D and E were logically both at the level of interpretative models. The rightness or wrongness of the response was irrelevant for determining levels. However, Guesne (1985) has found evidence that a response showing a movement (of light or sight) from the eye to the object (level D) comes at an earlier stage than that showing light going from the object to the eye (level E). Piaget (1974) made a similar observation with children who had probably not had any formal instruction in science. On this basis, level E was placed higher than level D.

The use of non-logical criteria meant there were a few responses (less than 3 per cent) which did not fit into the hierarchy. These occurred mainly in the 'lamp-hole' question, where a schematic representation of the situation, sometimes with the path of the light shown (response at an explanatory level), was sometimes not accompanied by a correct prediction. Two children in the pre-test and four in the post-test predicted instead that an upside down image would be seen. This was a clear case of a causal relationship learnt in one context interfering with logical analysis in a related context. In the few remaining cases the source of the discrepancies could not be identified.

Three versions of the test (total score analysis)

The children were scored for their attainment of each level of each question so that a total score for each child could be calculated. The summation of scores is justified since the scores were assigned on a single (descriptive-explanatory) dimension. Since each of the four questions was scored on five levels, the maximum score on the verbal version was 20. (The three versions are henceforth called V, D, and R; pre and post refer to scores on the pre-teaching and post-teaching tests). In the D and R versions, some of the above levels were missed out for the reason that they already existed in the presentation of the problems. In comparing the scores on the three versions, therefore, only those levels common to all were counted. As a result, for comparisons between the V and D versions, the maximum score was 16, while for the V, D and R comparison, the maximum score was 9. The analysis which follows assumes a continuous distribution underlying the discrete scores. Table 10.2 shows the significance of difference between the mean scores on these versions with maximum score 9. With maximum scores 16 and 20, the t values and therefore the effect sizes (a parameter which estimates the difference in success rates corresponding to the observed differences in scores: see Rosenthal and Rubin 1982) were higher than those in Table 10.2, but the significance of the results at the 1 per cent level remained unchanged.

The order of increasing facility on the tests was V pre; R pre, D pre, V post; D post, R post. The post-test scores were significantly higher than the pre-test scores, which is encouraging. Our main interest here, however, is in the differences between the three versions. These show that presenting the problem situation in the form of a diagram makes the test significantly easier, but providing the opportunity to set up the situation in laboratory does not seem to give additional help.

The result on diagrams needs to be reconciled with the results of other researchers which show that students find it difficult to use schematic representations. Gott (1985) found that 15 year olds had equal difficulty setting up an electric circuit, given a verbal description, as they had starting from a circuit diagram. A considerably larger proportion could set up the circuit correctly from a photograph. In our optics problems, on the other hand, diagrams were an intermediate step in the solution, so giving the diagrams rather than verbal description helped problem solving. However, this explanation does not account for the fact that the diagrams in optics posed less difficulty than the circuit diagrams in Gott's study. We might guess that the symbols used in the former were closer to the real situation. A Piagetian interpretation is that these diagrams, by ordering the elements of the situation, facilitated the use of the concrete operational strategies of classification and seriation.

Table 10.2 Significance of differences between mean scores

	V post n = 39	D pre n = 37	D post n = 38	R pre n = 9	R post n = 12
V pre n = 36	5.2 (73) * 0.52	3.5 (71) * 0.38	8.6 (72) * 0.71	1.4 (43) * 0.20	6.9 (46) * 0.71
V post n = 39		1.1 (74) ns 0.13	4.3 (75) * 0.44	1.4 (46) ns 0.20	3.8 (49) * 0.47
D pre n = 37			4.8 (73) * 0.49	0.73 (44) ns 0.11	4.3 (47) * 0.53
D post n = 38				3.7 (45) * 0.48	0.9 (48) ns 0.13
R pre n = 9					3.8 (19) * 0.65

In each cell the entries represent, from the top, the t-value, the degrees of freedom (in parentheses); the statistical significance of the t-value (*: $p = 0.01$); and the effect size, r, given by $r = (t^2/(t^2+df))/2$. V: verbal form of the test; D: diagram form; R: real situation form; pre and post refer to the position of the test in relation to the instruction children received.

Consistency in response levels

To some extent, the hierarchy on response levels was imposed within each question. Our aim was then to study the consistency of the levels across the questions. The method of analysis was one developed by Shayer (1980) to test the scalability of group Piagetian tests (Shayer, Adey and Wylam 1981). The detailed analysis was done with the verbal version, with pre- and post-test combined.

For this analysis, the children were ranked by their total scores (maximum score, 20) into four groups 1, 2, 3, 4, of increasing scores. The number of children in each group were as shown in Table 10.3.

Table 10.3 Sample size for discrimination level diagrams

Rank number	Total score	Number of children
1	1–5	11
2	6–10	24
3	11–15	35
4	16–20	5

For each level in the hierarchy, the percentage of children in each group attaining that level was plotted against the rank of the group to give the graphs of Figures 10.1(i) to 10.1(x).

Although some positive correlation between attainment of each level and the total score is predetermined by the hierarchies, Figure 10.1 shows that there is a consistency between individual hierarchies and the test as a whole. The steeply rising curves are characteristic of levels which discriminate sharply between groups and which therefore have a high correlation with the whole test. In general, the explanatory levels seem to be more sharply discriminating than the descriptive ones.

The unidimensionality of the test was further examined, representing the discrimination ranges by means of curves, showing the difference in rank order between the groups with 25 per cent and 75 per cent attainment of the levels, adding half a rank as a correction for continuity, on a graph of overall facility of the level versus group rank. In Figure 10.2, the broken lines show the descriptive levels and the solid lines show the explanatory levels. For unidimensionality the plot should lie along a line from top left to bottom right, which is roughly seen to be the case. However, some items, such as MV(B) (moors-vision, glow around lamp) and EH(X) (eye-hole, you see less) have too broad a discrimination range to fit into a unidimensional construct. The most striking feature of the plot is, however, the clear division of the groups of levels and of the children scoring on these levels into the descriptives and the explanatories. Thus at least a gross division along this dimension seems to have some validity.

Effect of context

We have shown that the hierarchy is valid across the four contexts considered here. Considering the similarity between the situations (all to do with schematic representations in the context of light), this observation may not be too surprising. However, the method of analysis has not only allowed us to extract a general construct from the variety of responses, it has helped us examine the differences between the problem situations in a more informed way.

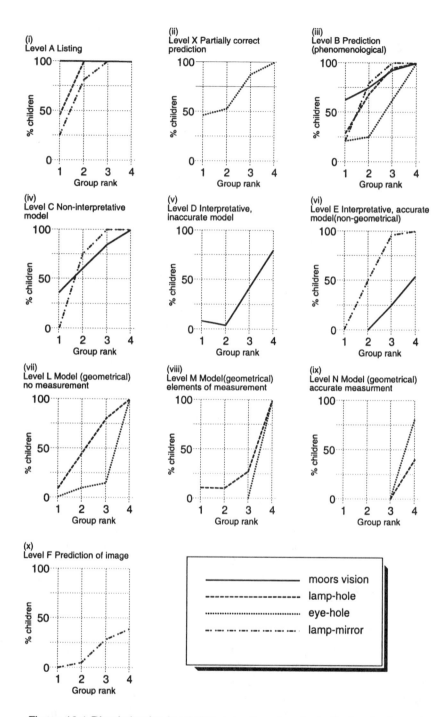

Figure 10.1 Discrimination level diagrams. (Levels refer to the levels shown in the hierarchy in Table 10.1)

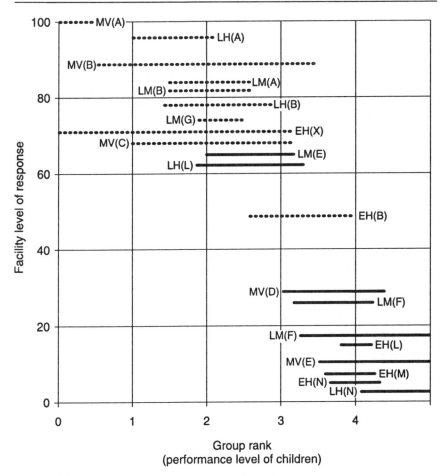

Figure 10.2 Discrimination ranges of the levels of responses
Key
MV: Moors vision   LH: Lamp-hole

LM: Lamp-mirror   EH: Eye-hole

A–N: Levels of response – for details see Table 10.1.

Solid lines represent explanatory levels; broken lines represent descriptive levels

Figure 10.1(vi) shows that children in all ranks find it easier to show the lamp–mirror–eye path than the direct lamp–eye path. In the first case the path of light from the source to the eye is shorter, also the physiological (i.e. dazzling) effect of the light on the eye is more obvious. The connection between vision and light entering the eye is probably established more easily in this context. It is interesting to recall that Alhazen in the tenth century hit upon the idea of light entering the eyes producing vision, by considering the lamp–mirror and similar situations, and then extrapolating to ordinary objects (Ronchi 1970).

The lamp–hole and eye–hole situation can be compared similarly (Figs 10.1(iii), (vii), (viii), (ix)). The first is comparatively the easier situation, starting from the 'phenomenological' level up to 'interpretative models'. This observation does not apply to the Group 4 children, who have a perfect score up to 'model with some measurement' (Fig. 10.1(viii)) in both situations. It is difficult to explain the apparent reversal of the trend for the Group 4 children in Fig. 10.1(ix). It may be due to their small number, and hence percentages. The difference in facility levels between the two situations is thus quite systematic. Children were more likely to show the lamp–hole situation in terms of its components (lamp, hole, screen) in their relative positions. On the other hand, they showed the eye–hole situation most often as the view through the key hole. We hesitate to enter the problem-ridden area of egocentrics at this point. In fact, a simpler explanation in terms of the children's understanding of the requirements of the problem seems more plausible to us.

Interestingly, it was quite common for children also to show the lamp–hole situation in a front-on rather than a side-on view, even though the former involved showing a superposition of the map, board and screen. This may have a bearing on learning to use ray diagrams in optics. Probably the convention of showing optical systems in a side sectional view is a learnt one, arising from the need to show the path of light beams. That this is what counts as an explanation in optics may be a fact not appreciated spontaneously. Perhaps we could find many more situations in school science where it is necessary to demonstrate to children what it is that counts as valid answers to 'how' and 'why' questions.

Another interpretation of the hierarchy

The analysis of each level in the hierarchy with respect to the total score revealed some of the structure in the responses. Here the total score was expected to be a reliable measure of performance on the test. If we assume that children's performance is unimodal, then this score is a uniquely meaningful measure. However, it is possible to work with the empirical hierarchy without making that restrictive assumption.

Further motivation for this analysis comes from the differences in facility levels across contexts seen in the previous section. These differences could be the result of there existing not a simple correlation, but an asymmetric relationship between performance on the questions. That is, attaining a certain level on the easier question might be a prerequisite for doing so on the more difficult one. Of course, it is conceivable that relationships of this kind might be found which are statistically significant but educationally hard to make sense of. In this case we might at least have exposed a set of possible connections in the data. As it turned out, the results here were not statistically significant. Nevertheless, the patterns found are interesting enough to merit discussion.

Only the gross descriptive vs. explanatory (and interpretative) division, as seen in Fig. 10.2 was considered. Responses on each question were cross-tabulated against each of the others. The test for asymmetric relationship was one used by Qualter (1984) who has followed Hildebrand *et al.* (1977). The rationale behind this test is as follows. In a 2×2 cross-tabulation of questions with differing facility levels, one of the off-diagonal cells (here a descriptive level on the easy item and explanatory level on the difficult item) would be expected to have a very low cell frequency. Under the stronger condition that the easy item is a prerequisite for the harder one, this particular cell should have zero cell frequency. This hypothesis can be tested using the statistic of Hildebrand *et al.*

The low off-diagonal cell frequencies were found in four of the six cross-tabulations. They indicated the possibility of an internally consistent scheme in which an explanatory response on 'lamp–mirror', could possibly be a prerequisite for an explanatory response on 'eye–hole' and 'moors-vision'. The small sample size meant that the frequencies in these cells, though low (1 or 2) were not significantly close to zero. However, the existence of a pattern permits us to speculate. Perhaps functioning at the explanatory level for the former two situations, which are of the school science type, might be a prerequisite for doing so in the everyday situations typified by the latter two.

CONCLUSION

We have illustrated here an approach to the analysis of data on children's conceptions. The aim has been to identify generalizable features of the responses, and then to connect these responses to their roots in the specific context. In the language of the response hierarchy discussed here, we hope that the paper is a modest step along the descriptive-explanatory dimension.

Acknowledgements

The work described here was undertaken during a period that Jayashree Ramadas spent with the Children's Learning in Science Project, University of Leeds, supported by the British Council. The help of Professor Rosalind Driver in the design, data collection and analysis is gratefully acknowledged. The work could not have been completed without the help of the teachers concerned: Keith Lawes, Jane Liptrot, Stewart Liles.

APPENDIX

Items used in the verbal version of the test

The questions formed part of the data gathering for the Children's Learning in Science Project, University of Leeds and are reproduced here by permission of the Director of that Project, Professor Rosalind Driver.
    Students were told:

These questions are to find out how you think about problems.
Your ideas are important to us, so try all questions.
Only simple drawings are needed here, so have a go at them, even if you think you are no artist.
Use a pencil and ruler for drawing.
Label your drawings.

    Space was left on the questionnaire for drawings and for written responses. The questions used are reproduced here without these spaces.

Question 1. Moors-vision (MV)

You are lost on the moors on a dark moonless night, miles away from any roads or houses. Suddenly, far away, you see a small lamp shining.

    *Make a simple drawing which shows you and the lamp.

    *Show where there is light in the drawing.

    *On this drawing, explain how you are able to see this small lamp shining.

[Space for Drawing]

    *In the space below, write several sentences to explain why you think there is light in the places where you have shown it.

[Space for Response]

Question 2. Lamp–Hole (LH)

A large, thin board with a hole as big as a 1p piece in it stands upright in a dark room. A light-bulb, which is switched on, is placed near the hole on one side of the board. A white screen stands on the other side of the board and close to it.

    *What can be seen on the screen?

[Space for Response]

    *Make a drawing to show what can be seen on the screen.

[Space for Drawing]

*In the space below, make another drawing which shows the bulb, board and screen.

*Show where there is light in the drawing.

[Space for Drawing]

*Using this drawing, answer these two questions:

1 What happens to the light from the bulb?
2 Why is it that the thing shown in your first drawing is seen on the screen?

[Space for Response]

Question 3. Eye–hole (EH)

You are looking into this classroom through a round keyhole in the door.
a) First, you keep your eye as close to the hole as possible.

*How much of the room do you imagine you will see?

*Give examples of things that you will see and things that you will not see.

[Space for Response]

b) Next, you move your eye about 5 cm back from the hole.

*How much of the room will you see now?

*Give examples of things that you will see and things that you will not see.

[Space for Response]

*Make a drawing to show situation (a).

*Use this drawing to explain why you see whatever you see in situation (a).

[Space for Drawing]
[Space for Response]

*Make a drawing to show situation (b).

*Use this drawing to explain why you see whatever you see in situation (b).

[Space for Drawing]
[Space for Response]

Question 4. Lamp–mirror (LM)

*You use a mirror to reflect light from a bulb into your friend's eye.

*Make a drawing which shows the mirror, the light-bulb and your friend's eye.

*Show where there is light in the drawing.

[Space for Drawing]

*Explain what happens between the mirror, the bulb, and your friend's eye.

[Space for Response]

*Do you think your friend can see anything in the mirror? If so, explain *what* he or she can see and *why*.

[Space for Response]

*If you think your friend sees something in the mirror, try to show it in the drawing above.

REFERENCES

Andersson, B. and Karrqvist, C. 1981. 'Light and its properties,' EKNA Report No. 8, Institute for Praktisk Pedagogik, Göteborg Univiersitet.

Biggs, J. B. and Collis, K. F. 1982. *Evaluating the quality of learning: the SOLO taxonomy.* Academic Press, London.

Case, R. 1978. 'A developmentally based theory and technology of instruction.' *Review of Educational Research*, 48: 439–69.

Donaldson, M. 1978. *Children's minds.* Fontana Paperbacks, London.

Driver, R. 1982. 'Children's learning in science.' *Analysis*, 4(2): 69–79.

Gott, R. 1985. *Electricity at age 15.* APU report for teachers, No. 7. Great Britain, Department of Education and Science.

Guesne, E. 1985. 'Light.' In Driver, R., Guesne, E., and Tiberghien, A. (eds) *Children's ideas in science.* Open University Press, Milton Keynes, pp. 10–32.

Hildebrand, D. K., Lainig, J. D. and Rosenthal, H. 1977. *Prediction analysis of cross classification.* John Wiley, New York.

Inhelder, B. and Piaget, J. 1958. *The growth of logical thinking from childhood to adolescence.* Basic Books, New York.

Jung, W. 1981. 'Conceptual frameworks in elementary optics.' In Jung, W., Pfundt, H. and Rhöneck, C., von (eds) *Proceedings of the International Workshop on 'Problems concerning Students' Representations of Physics and Chemistry Knowledge.'* Ludwigsburg Pädagogische Hochschule, Ludwigsburg, West Germany.

La Rosa, C., Mayer, M., Patrizi, P. and Vincentini, M. 1984. 'Commonsense knowledge in optics: preliminary results of an investigation on the properties of light.' *European Journal of Science Education*, 6: 387–97.

Larkin, J. 1979. 'Understanding and teaching problem-solving in physics,' *European Journal of Science Education*, 1: 191–203.

Lunzer, E. A. 1972. 'The development of formal reasoning: some recent experiments and their implications.' In Frey, K. and Long, M. (eds) *Cognitive processes and science instruction*. Verlag Hans Huber, Bern.

Pascual-Leone, J. 1970. 'A mathematical model for the transition rule in Piaget's development stages.' *Acta Psychologica*, 32: 301–45.

Peel, E. A. 1971. *The nature of adolescent judgement*, Staples Press, London.

Piaget, J. 1929. *The child's conception of the world*. Routledge and Kegan Paul, London.

Piaget, J. 1930. *The child's conception of physical causality*. Routledge and Kegan Paul, London.

Piaget, J. 1974. *Understanding causality*. W. W. Norton, New York.

Qualter, A. 1984. 'APS practical investigations: a study of some problems of measuring practical scientific performance of children.' PhD thesis, Chelsea College, University of London.

Ramadas, J. and Driver, R. 1989. 'Aspects of secondary students' ideas about light.' Centre for Studies in Science and Mathematics Education, University of Leeds.

Resnick, L. B. 1983. 'Mathematics and science learning: a new conception.' *Science*, 220: 477–8.

Ronchi, V. 1970. *The nature of light: an historical survey*. Heinemann, London.

Rosenthal, R. and Rubin, D. B. 1982. 'A simple general purpose display of magnitude and experimental effect.' *Journal of Educational Psychology*, 74: 166–9.

Shayer, M. 1980. 'A new approach to data analysis for the construction of Piagetian tasks.' Paper delivered at AERA annual conference, Boston, Mass., 1980. Available as ERIC Report, ED 194 629.

Shayer, M. and Adey, P. 1981. *Towards a science of science teaching*. Heinemann, London.'

Shayer, M., Adey, P. and Wylam, H. 1981. 'Group test of cognitive development: ideals and a realisation.' *Journal of Research in Science Teaching*, 18: 157–68.

Wason, P. C. and Johnson-Laird, P. N. 1972. *Psychology of reasoning: structure and content*. Batsford, London.

Watts, D. M. 1983. 'A study of alternative frameworks in school science.' PhD thesis, University of Surrey.

Chapter 11

The interplay of values and research in science education

Guy Claxton

> If you want to make sense, I've learned, you should never use the words *should* or *ought* until after you've used the word *if*.
>
> (Barth 1967)

The extent to which the recent work on children's intuitive ideas about the natural world has paid off in terms of improved classroom practice is so far disappointing. This chapter is an attempt to draw out, from the realization that schoolchildren enter science lessons already possessing scientific knowledge and scientific skills, some implications for teaching. These implications emerge not as prescriptions but as choices. Specifically *the way a science teacher responds to his or her students' prior conceptions is crucially dependent on the outcomes that he or she wishes to achieve.* In order to draw conclusions about how to teach on the basis of 'Alternative Frameworks' research, we have first to clarify our aims. We need to specify what it is we want our students to possess, in the way of knowledge, competence, perceptiveness, interest or intellect, as a result of spending time in our lessons, more precisely than has normally been done (see, for example, the Association for Science Education 1981). Particularly, we need to specify these objectives in more psychologically sophisticated terms than has been done heretofore. What kind of learning do we wish to produce? Are we aiming for deep understanding, fluency of symbolic manipulation, accurate recall, or everyday competence, for example?

Thus this chapter seeks to blend together the educational research on children's informal understandings of science topics with both psychological and philosophical ingredients in order to produce, in the end, some practical suggestions. It is neither possible nor desirable to attempt a Teacher's Manual. Rather, I hope, having spelt out some of the options that are available, to indicate in a down-to-earth way what is involved in their achievement and thereby to enhance teachers' ability to go about their job with insight and sensitivity. Some of the aims of science teaching, as practising teachers know, are inherently difficult to achieve. Only by understanding the nature of the difficulties can a teacher respond in ways that alleviate rather than compound the problems. And some combinations of aims, for good psychological reasons, cannot be pursued simultaneously with the same pedagogy and attitude. This conclusion also arises from empirical studies such as that on Plant Nutrition by the Children's Learning in Science Project (Bell, Barron and Stephenson 1985). Only by seeing clearly which options and combinations are, and which are not, on offer can a teacher avoid falling between different stools, or trying to achieve the impossible.

The chapter first describes some recent psychological research that has relevance for learning in schools. In particular this work shows that the way something is learnt (and therefore the way it should be taught) depends on the anticipated circumstances of its retrieval. In the light of this, our concern has to shift from 'teaching for acquisition' where the focus is solely on the learning event, to 'teaching for use', where we must be concerned with the degree of congruence between the contexts of learning and recapitulation. This follows from the realization that things are not stored cognitively in such a way that, once learnt, they become automatically available when subsequently needed. Rather a description of *when* to retrieve them is built in right from the start. This section in effect provides an empirical rationale for the minitheoretic approach to learning I described in Chapter 3.

This discussion leads directly to the next section: an annotated catalogue of some of the purposes for which school science might be being taught. If we have to teach for use, we need to know exactly what that eventual use is – what the aim is. Thus we are driven by the psychology to a clarification of the philosophy. What emerges from this section is that the more clearly specified the different aims of science education are, the more different they become. In many cases they are seen to require quite different – and incompatible – pedagogical approaches. It is for this reason that we are forced to make the choices of value and method which I mentioned above.

Finally, I shall spell out some of the implications, and end with a few more untidy speculations concerning the teacher's role in teaching for transfer.

THE LOCALIZATION OF LEARNING

One of the most important shifts in cognitive psychology over the last ten years has been towards the realization that learning is localized. What we know, the 'knowledge' and 'skill' that we acquire, remain in general tied to a more or less precise specification of when, where, why and how we acquired it. And these sorts of 'adverbial' tags serve to indicate the new situation within which the 'nouns' and 'verbs' of content and process will be retrieved and reactivated. Even content and process, so-called 'declarative' and 'procedural' knowledge (Anderson 1976) cannot be dissociated: our know-how is associated with a sense of what to apply it to: our know-that comes back to use with its own packages of processes and operations for using and expressing it.

Obviously we do transfer, as old knowledge is applied to new situations, and the extent to which we can do so is a matter of degree. But this extent is determined largely by the sphere of relevance that was taught or intuited at the time of learning. We as teachers have no psychological right to assume that transfer of a skill from task A to task B should, or will, occur. And this in turn means that we must be very careful about using performance in one situation (an examination, say) as an index or predictor of performance in another (solving a real-life problem). The well-known and frequent lack of transfer between an academic's skill as a researcher and as a teacher is a case in point.

Generalization – sometimes very broad generalization – occurs, as we learn to abstract the relevant, trans-situational triggers from the optional or incidental ones. And experience and language have complex and complementary roles to play in determining the rate and extent of generalization. But as a general principle we must now see our knowledge as situationally embedded, and much of our learning as a movement towards dis-embeddedness (Donaldson 1978). The rest of this section reviews some of the evidence for this position.

Research from developmental and cross-cultural sources, as well as laboratory studies of cognition, has shown irrefutably that the processing operations 'called' by a task are determined by the content of the tasks as well as its form. The work of Donaldson (1978) and others shows that Piagetian logic of using a single task as a 'dipstick' to test whether children do or do not 'possess' a certain 'operation' is invalid, because it ignores the retrieval problem. For someone to manifest an ability, it is a necessary *but not a sufficient* condition that they 'possess' that ability. It must in addition be addressed, accessed and reactivated by the task; and whether that happens depends in general on the similarity between the total situation with which the child is faced and the range of situations within which the ability was acquired and developed. (This conclusion is again supported empirically by the CLISP work, e.g. Bell and Brook 1984). Relevance is not given; it is learnt. Thus when superficial, apparently incidental, details of a task are altered, the recognition that previously dormant processes are in fact relevant and useful may occur. The introduction of 'Naughty Teddy' (McGarrigle and Donaldson 1974) enables a child to re-construe the conversation situation so that the operation of reversibility magically appears. Shifting the content of a sorting task from pictures to leaves (Cole *et al.* 1971) enables Kpelle tribesmen to demonstrate their ability to use categorization as a mnemonic strategy. And so on.

Changing details of the physical, physiological or psychological *context* also affect what is retrieved. Godden and Baddeley (1975) gave divers a list of words to learn either on the beach or submerged, and showed a large decrement in recall when they were tested in the alternative environment. Smith, Glenberg and Bjork (1978) showed the same 'loss of memory' could be produced simply by changing the room between learning and recall. Furthermore, this context-dependency of memory records applies to the total state of a learner, which includes physiological and emotional components as well as perceptual ones. Eich (1980) and Lowe (1980) have shown that lists of words, or a route on a map, which were learnt in a mild state of intoxication are recalled better when that state is reproduced than when sober. Bower (1981) has shown the same effect for mood: things learnt sad are better recalled sad; things learnt happy are better recalled happy. Even the type of test or mode that is anticipated at the time of learning gets written into the record. Words learnt for recall are better recalled; words learnt for recognition are better recognized (Schmidt 1983). On the basis of much evidence of a similar nature authors such as Allport (1980), Baddeley (1982) and Fodor (1983) have proposed that we view our knowledge as fundamentally modularized. Content-, context- and task-dependence are the rule, and independence only appears (in rare cases) as the limits of generalizability or disembeddedness are approached. More detailed summaries of this position are available in Claxton (1977) for psychological audiences and Claxton (1980) for educational audiences.

Examples of the same dependencies are common in the literature of science education. The apparent 'ability' that a student displays depends on the details of the task or the phrasing of the question. For example, research by Terry Russell (1985) for the Assessment of Performance in Science project invited children to solve two homologous problems that involved deducing which of a number of possible agents were responsible for the sickness of a subset of a group of children, given a chart of information about who had come into contact with what. In one case the possible agents were types of food, in the other they were other (hypothetical) children. The results showed that the Food form of the problem was better solved than the Children form (46 per cent of maximum possible score as opposed to 35 per cent). But more interestingly, when asked to justify their answer, 27 per cent of the answers to the Food problem imported beliefs and information that were additional to the presented information, while for the Children problem only 2 per cent of the answers showed such gratuitous imports. Why? Because the 'characters' in the Children problem – Simon, Jill, Karen, Tasmin and their friends – are unknown to the problem-solvers, whereas they have extensive first-hand experience of the sickness-making properties of the 'characters' in the Food problem – ice cream, hot dogs, chips, toffee apples, and so on. We cannot assume, therefore, that any problem can induce children to act as pure (albeit flawed) logicians. Rather the way they solve the problem (the 'abilities' they reveal and the 'success' they achieve) depends on their psycho-logic – their experience and beliefs – and this may serve to short-circuit the logic in a way which is either appropriate (in that it gives the 'right answer') or which leads the logic astray. Similar effects in adult problem-solving are well known (Lefford 1946; Wason and Johnson-Laird 1972).

example, from Strauss and Stavy (1983), shows the crucial
ology. Children were told that two equal lots of water were
, and asked to say what the temperature of the mixture was.
re the contributions were described as 'two lots of cold
lren rightly responded that the temperature of the mixture
would be the same'. But when the problem was about 'two lots of water at
10°C', there was a marked tendency to say that the temperature of the
mixture would be 20°C. The mere presence of numbers caused the children
to call inappropriate mathematical operations ('minitheories') that over-rode
or displaced the theory based on their own experience. Interestingly some
children, when confronted with the apparent conflict between their two
answers, continued to side with the number theory, and changed their
(correct) answer to the first problem, saying 'Oh it must be *twice* as cold.'
But note that the formula 'twice X', applied where X = cold and where X =
10°C, gives contradictory answers. The 'cold' water gets colder; the '10°C'
water gets hotter. Yet this is not spotted by the children because they are
operating with a mental programme that is designed to generate numerical
answers to problems, not real predictions about the physical world. This is
analogous to the common situation in maths where children seem happy to
produce answers that are not 'sensible'. If the particular minitheory being
used does not itself contain a 'check-for-reasonableness' sub-routine, then
while that programme is running, common sense is simply not available.

WHAT ARE WE TEACHING SCIENCE FOR?

Many attempts have been made to specify the aims of science teaching in
schools, with varying degrees of clarity and refinement. Often the terms in
which they are couched are vague and rhetorical, offering little assistance to
the teacher who has to ask: 'Yes ... but how?' They are too much pious hope
and not enough job specification. I wish here to outline a variety of aims in
such a way that the problems, practical and psychological, involved in their
implementation are more, rather than less, apparent. The literature on
children's intuitive ideas and on the modularity of knowledge will prove to
be of considerable value in this exercise.

To improve people's everyday competence with matter and machines

'If children come to school with all kinds of intuitive ideas about how things
work, many of which are wrong, one of our jobs at least ought to be to help
straighten them out.'

Despite the fact that, as the philosophical adage puts it 'You cannot
deduce an Ought from an Is', there is a tendency to jump from the discovery
of children's' alternative conceptions to the conclusion that school science is
the appropriate vehicle for improving them. It may indeed be, but we need

to think carefully about whether and how it could be done. One particularly dubious assumption is that all we have to do is to confront their intuitive expectations or ideas with a better theory, or an empirical demonstration, and they will, or anyway ought, to see sense. Yet there are good reasons why people should not surrender their informal understandings so easily.

First, 'better' in formal scientific terms usually means 'neater and tidier' in the sense of more mathematically tractable, more all-embracing and more parsimonious. Such considerations often lead scientists to focus on ideal stylized cases that may exist only *ex hypothesi*, or as a specially created laboratory scenario. The 'real world' is then construed as a particularly messy and complicated variant of this ideal, full of uncontrolled and ill-understood perturbations that annoyingly obscure its essential simplicity and elegance. From the research scientist's point of view, where theories are judged by their coherence and their 'explanatory and predictive power', such an attitude is most fruitful. But from the point of view of getting by in the real world, incoherence and domain-specificity are not a problem, and there is no reason why they should be seen as such. If our rules-of-thumb about force and electricity enable us to get about, and rewire the house, what more do we need? We meet a Newtonian, frictionless world only rarely, on skates perhaps, or playing certain video games. Yet even here it seems unlikely that a good pass in O-level physics will help us very much, because the understanding we have gained is designed for, and limited to, generating computations and explanations, not twists of a knob or thrusts of the feet. School science *is* concerned with understanding the world, but it is concerned with understandings that are embedded within a very strict protocol of canon and style, and which has no *a priori* claims to acceptance in areas where that protocol does not apply.

Of course it would be going much too far completely to deny the everyday value of coherent articulate systems of understanding. Such systems, while they are not yet written into the minitheories that control spontaneous reaction, perception and intuition, nevertheless can serve important roles in the development of these minitheories, and in providing checks on impulses that might be dangerous or inappropriate. We can call maxims to mind that may serve to guide the exploration and practice that will generate intuitive confirmation (see Claxton 1984, for a fuller discussion). And when there is time we can use an intellectual frame to 'work things out from the first principles'. But such conscious systems of thought may on occasion equally well be irrelevant to the task in hand, and may hamper, confuse or undermine us by providing a source of advice, or ways of construing, that conflict with (quite successful) intuitive or tacit minitheories. (The avid reading of 'How to Bring up Baby' books by anxious parents may, as Dr. Spock himself declared a few years ago, be a good example.)

Secondly, as described in Chapter 3, there are costs involved in replacing old understandings with new, as well as benefits, and these are instinctively weighed up by a learner when confronted with the invitation to change. In performing this intuitive 'cost–benefit analysis', learners ask themselves these questions. First, what are the benefits? Is there a perceived *need* to change? Why should I? Do I experience my current understanding to be inadequate? Have I been sold the new product in such a way that I am convinced of, or at least optimistic about, its merits? Then there are the perceived costs. How much effort is going to be involved in assimilating the new theory? Are there risks of looking foolish or incompetent while I am doing so? If I do take the new idea seriously, are there going to be knock-on effects; is it going to cause a major upheaval in my cognition (or even, in some cases, in my life-style)? Is it going to make my way of thinking or talking or acting out of line with my family or friends? And how much do I care if it does? Finally, into the equation goes an estimate of the likelihood of achieving successfully mastery. Do I have the necessary skills, strategies, support, time and room for manoeuvre that might be required to learn it?

Out of all this comes a rescindable decision about how to respond to the learning invitation, which is in a real sense rational, though usually not articulated. If the costs outweigh the benefits it makes sense to turn the invitation down – to ignore it, or, if pressed, to belittle it ('It's stupid', 'This is boring') or to denigrate the whole situation ('I hate chemistry') or the invitation-giver ('I hate Mr. Wilkins'). At the other extreme, where the learning on offer seems valuable and attainable, and where the situation seems safe enough for the transitional floundering and apprehension to be tolerable, the invitation is fully taken up. In the middle, there may be equally good reasons why the prior, intuitive theory should not be given up. In this case the invitation is accepted, but the *conflict* is denied, so that the learning is relocated to a bit of virgin territory (labelled 'physics', perhaps), while the pre-existing culture (called 'How I deal with moving objects') is left undisturbed – and therefore unimproved.

If we use these learning options to look at the way children tackle science we might identify four sub-groups. There are those, the outstanding few, who successfully aim for full integration. There are those, the regular 'bright ones', who successfully implement the segregation strategy. There are those, untroublesome but unsuccessful, who aim for segregation, but are unable to achieve full apartheid, so that lay meanings keep intruding into the school context, causing confusion, ambiguity and forgetting. For such children new bits and pieces arrive too quickly for them to build a stable and separate picture of school science. Instead their knowledge is fragmentary and the boundaries of the fragments are diffuse and permeable, so that no substantial, structured understanding emerges. Their concentration is therefore weak: having established no point of view, no coherent story-line, and no specialist vocabulary, associations and images keep breaking through from out-of-school contexts. Such a child's experience is one of fleeting trains of thought, ephemeral interests, and confusing or entertaining puns. They grab at the gas tap or the double entendre, like bits of flotsam, because they have not been able to lash together a raft of their own.

And finally, there are those whose cost–benefit analysis clearly says it's not worth the bother at all, and they either retreat into invisibility or advance into defamation, denigration and disruption.

To dissolve science into common sense

This aim seems similar to the last one, but deserves consideration on its own, having been powerfully expressed by Churchland (1979). His argument is this. Common sense, by which he means the way people ordinarily think about and perceive the world, is theory-laden. This theory derives in part from our attempt to make sense of our first-hand dealings with the world. But it is also based in large measure on the way people talk, the way they use the terms and expressions of their language. To an extent these meanings derive from the slow diffusion into the common culture of the findings and formulations of research scientists. Because this diffusion is relatively slow, our common sense is largely built on an out-of-date science. A legitimate aim of science education, therefore, is to speed up the rate of diffusion, so that our ways of talking and perceiving incorporate more up-to-date, more sophisticated and more accurate scientific insights. It is worth quoting Churchland himself at some length here:

> Our current modes of conceptual exploitation are rooted, in substantial measure, not in the nature of our perceptual environment, nor in the innate features of our psychology, but rather in the structure and content of our common language, and in the process by which each child acquires the normal use of that language. By this process each of us grows into a conformity with the current conceptual template. In large measure we *learn*, from others, to perceive the world as everyone else perceives it. But if this is so, then we might have learnt, and may yet learn, to conceive/ perceive the world in ways other than those supplied by our present culture. After all, our current conceptual framework is just the latest stage in the long evolutionary process that produced it, and we may examine with profit the possibility that perception might take place within the matrix of a different and more powerful conceptual framework.
>
> The obvious candidate here is the conceptual framework of modern physical theory – of physics, chemistry and their many satellite sciences. That the conceptual framework of these sciences is immensely powerful is beyond argument, and its credentials as a systematic representation of reality are unparalleled. It must be a dull man indeed whose appetite will not be whet by the possibility of perceiving the world directly in its terms ... (p. 13)

If our perceptual judgements must be laden with theory in any case, then why not have them laden with the best theory available? . . . [T]he resulting expansion of our perceptual consciousness would be profound. Should we ever succeed in making the shift, we shall be properly at home in our physical universe for the very first time (p. 35).

(Churchland 1979)

It will be obvious that Churchland's agenda for science education goes way beyond a piecemeal upgrading of localized domains of understanding and competence. The perceptual world we inhabit is a Newtonian one: it comprises a three-dimensional space, an independent and unidirectional time, and interactions between independently existing bodies. Churchland's implicit assumption is that we have learnt, we have been socialized into seeing, the world that way. And his challenge is: if relativity and quantum theory are more accurate descriptions of reality, could we not learn to see it in *those* ways – and how would it look if we did?

It must be said that, though I find this argument thought-provoking, exciting and plausible, I have but the sketchiest of notions as to what we can do about it. Certainly – and here we shall have to leave it – there seems little possibility of schools as they currently exist being capable of, or even interested in, taking up the challenge.

To teach science as a worthwhile body of knowledge

'Children should "know some science" because science constitutes an important part of our culture. A person cannot be considered to be educated unless they "know some science".'

This aim is a perfectly legitimate confluence of C. P. Snow and R. S. Peters, but it is incompletely specified. Aside from the impossible question of deciding (as the examination boards must do every year), which bits of science are worthwhile enough to be included in the syllabus, and which are not, it does not tell us what we expect people to be able to *do* with their knowledge. And unless we begin to spell out – behaviouristic though it may sound – what kinds of products or performances we expect, there is no way of knowing whether the aim has been achieved. Embedded in this goal is a variety of process and content possibilities, to be considered below. But until this is clear, then this goal is reduced by default to that of passing examinations – a performance that, as we saw above, cannot be assumed to be accurately predictive of a person's ability to converse intelligently about topical science over dinner, nor of the likelihood of their becoming a lifetime subscriber to *New Scientist*. The examination assesses skills not of conversation or subscription but of retention, justification, recapitulation and symbolic manipulation.

To pass exams

'In order to get a job in science and technology, and/or to gain access to further education in these subjects, a person must pass public examinations. So while these exams continue to be based largely on the recapitulation and manipulation of non-negotiable subject-matter, we must teach our students in like fashion.'

This is a perfectly lucid and sensible aim of science teaching. Once we give up the fiction that public examinations (of whatever form) are a valid indicator of 'what someone knows', or 'how well they have understood X', that they are an accurate dipstick into the sump of someone's knowledge, then we are free to view them as assessing a particular package of content *and* process. To test someone is to demand that they *express* what they 'know', and thus unavoidably to conflate their facility with that mode of expression, and the extent to which that mode is connected with this domain of knowledge, with the acquisition and retention of the knowledge itself. Doing chemistry O-level is a performance as specific as doing a back-flip on the four-inch beam, and should be seen and trained as such. We should not hope to infer from someone's performance on the beam their ability as a fell-walker, nor even whether they can ride a bike. We must find out empirically whether the transfer happens or not.

The fact that we cannot *assume* the transfer of an ability from one context to another is highlighted by the demonstration that, despite the rhetoric of the curriculum, exams are less a preparation for a job or even for further study, than they are the price of admission. A-level results predict class of degree very poorly (Choppin 1979). For this reason, too, a teacher who is primarily concerned with exam success may need to abandon other, subsidiary goals entirely. He or she will serve the students best by teaching 'Science for Examinations', and not worrying about their understanding of its questionable epistemological status or its obsolescence.

The same caveats apply to the newer forms of examination that require students to integrate and use their acquired knowledge and skill to solve novel problems – perhaps even problems modelled on real-life technical or technological issues. On the one hand students are right to complain that such tests are unfair *if they have not been prepared for them* by systematic training of the requisite skills of integration, application and the perception of relevance. On the other, there is again no *a priori* reason to suppose that performance in a formal, written, stressed examination will be a reliable index of the ability to solve real problems, in real time, for an important purpose, in collaboration with others.

But when we say that passing exams is a legitimate goal for 'the students' surely we do not mean *all* of them? It is not defensible to insist that those who will fail these exams should follow the same regime. Some students would like to learn to fix their motorbikes; others, to worry away at the very idea of an 'element' or an 'electron'. For both these groups, and others as well, watered-down versions of the exam-passing pedagogy are inefficient and inappropriate. Manipulating knowledge in a mandatory way is not their game.

To be scientists

'As well as knowledge, real scientists need a bundle of skills and attitudes. We can prepare students for careers as scientists by laying their foundations in school.'

This is indeed a possible aim of school science teaching, certainly as far as the mastery of tried and tested techniques of experimentation is concerned. A chemist needs to be able to do a clean filtration, and to record the results in a clear, systematic and orthodox fashion. But he or she, like a good cook, needs to understand *why* certain procedures are necessary, and which short-cuts can safely be taken and which cannot. If one only repeats the measurement three times, and washes the apparatus thoroughly between each, because one has been told to, the risk is that the meticulousness will only appear in the presence of the supervisor. Often it appears that the *commitment* to carefulness only arises from the luxury of being able to explore for oneself the consequences of carelessness. And the pressure to 'cover the syllabus' may make these luxuries too costly.

Almost inevitably this pressure militates against the development of other abilities of the research scientist: the ability, for example, to decide which technique is appropriate for which problem, or to create and test new techniques when a suitable one cannot be bought off-the-peg. Or even, more basically, to decide how to formulate the problems; to sift and organize an ill-defined issue, making tentative guesses about what is relevant and what is not. Or to select one's topic in the first place, on the basis of an intuitive synthesis of the intriguing and the tractable. Or to choose a particular form and level for publication, and to learn to write appropriately. Most basically of all, the scientist needs attitudes of open-mindedness and creativity, of persistence and resilience, of fascination and wonder, whose cultivation may require a measure of patience and non-directive support that is quite precluded by the exam-oriented goals and methods of much traditional science teaching. Such a 'training' in independence and resourcefulness frequently does not appear until the doctoral level – and sometimes not even then.

To have a scientific attitude to life

'Science teaching helps to train the faculties of observation, hypothesis-generation and testing, logical thinking and analysis, and critical appraisal of empirical claims: faculties that will stand people in good stead in their daily lives.'

Were this to happen it would be a most useful function of science teaching. The questions are: does it, and can it? First, I know of no evidence that shows that science students are better real-life problem-solvers than others, or that such problem-solving ability is correlated with the duration of science teaching received. Wason and Johnson-Laird (1972) comment that science undergraduates are no better at solving a problem (the '246 problem') that requires hypothesis-testing than other students. Even within their specialist domain, Viennot (1980) has shown that physics undergraduates exhibit the same misconceptions about a fundamental notion like 'force' as do school-children.

Indeed it sometimes appears that the common practice of the science classroom serves to undermine rather than enhance these general abilities. A teacher, aiming to 'demonstrate the properties of metals' adds a piece of magnesium to dilute hydrochloric acid, collects the gas, and fails to produce the anticipated 'squeaky pop' when she inserts a lighted splint into the test tube. Undaunted, though mildly embarrassed, she tells the pupils what 'should have happened', and then invites them to assent to the conclusion that 'metals react with acid to give off hydrogen gas', thereby both invalidating their observation of what *did* occur, and seeking their collusion with an invalid (and false) over-generalization. Occurrences of this sort are commonplace in the science lab and serve to turn the enterprise, after a while, into a disembodied ritual of submission, in which the 'successful' student deploys and exercises retention (of what he was told) in defiance of the evidence of his senses and misgivings of his reason.

If the research on domain-specific and task-dependent learning is to be believed, then we may even have to give up the hope that a differently run lesson ever *could* produce a completely generalized enhancement of observational, intellectual and investigational skill – because any such enhancement will remain tied, at least to an extent, to the content, context and purpose within which and for which it was developed. Thus we must conclude that the presupposition of this aim is either unfounded, unproven or false. By the same token there is even no good reason to believe that, in the general case, 'enquiring minds' are fostered by science teaching, and some reason to believe that in fact they are not. While certain forms of teaching can enhance the generalizability of knowledge-modules by focusing on the discovery of the critical set of situational features that predict their appropriate applications, the process of 'disembedding' is always partial, tentative, and fallible. Science teaching of whatever sort may engage the enthusiasms and expand the competence of a sub-set of students within the scientific domain, but the claim to be making more successful human beings seems unwarranted.

202 Children's informal ideas in science

To make young people critical of science

'People need these days not to be scientific *literati* à la Snow but politically aware of the uses and abuses of scientific and technological power. They need to be able to spot scientism, to understand the falsity of the claim to The One True Knowledge that science makes for itself, and to possess some grasp of the issues involved in nuclear power, the dangerous ransacking of Nature by the multinationals, and soft technology.'

Whether we are talking about the minority of school children who wish to make a career as scientists, or the rest, such an aim seems to me laudable and important. If school science as it is commonly taught is guilty of criminal damage to children's trust in their own ability to perceive and question, it commits criminal negligence by ignoring the industrial and military manipulation of science.

The problem is that school science implicitly accepts the obsolete premises that science is value-free and that scientific theories are natural truths revealed by experiment. But naive realism is untenable. Science is a human activity undertaken by human beings for human purposes. And scientific ideas are provisional fabrications of human minds that render the world predictable and comprehensible within limits. In order to allow themselves the right (and responsibility) to discuss social and moral issues, science teachers would have to give up their tacit acceptance of the bogus split between scientists as the Good Guys, all honesty and objectivity, and the others, the wicked ones, who bung fiery chemicals into animals' eyes and cynically respond to nuclear accidents by changing the name of the plant. To make young people critical consumers of science requires teachers who themselves see science as provisional and problematic – and many of them do not. Those who do see the problem run the risk, if they begin to discuss these things with their students, of being dubbed political or subversive by others for whom questioning the taken-for-granted is destructive, dangerous and quite out of order in school. So the structure and assumptions of school militate against this aim being taken seriously.

IMPLICATIONS

Given these considerations, the laudable aim of teaching to enhance everyday competence, intuition, and sensitivity seems fraught with difficulties, certainly within schools as they are presently constituted. What is learnt in the arcane world of any school laboratory tends to remain tied to that world. Anything that is learnt in the context of the persistent (and frequently intrusive) presence of a teacher may remain bound to the context 'being taught'. Anything that is learnt in order to produce a performance that is evaluated with respect to criteria such as written fluency, verbal facility, factual retention, the logical manipulation of symbols, coherent argument and 'deduction from first principles' runs the risk of languishing untapped in everyday contexts that are characterized by different modes of discourse. In everyday contexts, success is an answer to the question: 'Does it work?', and not 'Does it follow?' or 'Is it accurate?' A basic premise of school – that young people can be 'prepared' for the job of living in a special context whose pervasive characteristic is that it is 'off the job' – is challenged by the psychology of domain specificity.

Thus science teachers face a basic choice. They can no longer hope that transfer will, or ought to, occur. And they can no longer vaguely hope that a variety of disparate aims will be achieved by the exercise, however earnest, of the same teaching strategy. The horses of instruction need very definitely to be horses for courses. The choice that remains is between identifying a specific context and performance of eventual use, and doing their best to train for it; and seeking to achieve as wide a sense of relevance, as much flexibility of usage as possible – in which case they have to train for that.

Much remains to be learnt about how to do the latter. Obviously if we wish an understanding to be held, cognitively, in such a way that it will be called by a wide range of situations then we need to teach it through a wide range of situations. Schematically, let us suppose that we wish people to retrieve understanding U or problem-solving strategy P in any situation that contains characteristic X. What we need to do is to train them to see X as a salient characteristic of (all, or some range of) situations. To do so, we need to present a variety of apparently disparate situations, involving different contents, contexts, task and demand features, and guide them towards discerning the omnipresent X, and towards seeing, through their own experience, the efficacy of deploying U or P. Unless X becomes, in George Kelly's (1955) terms, one of a person's 'personal constructs', part of the perceptual apparatus through which they filter and interpret the world, then U and P will be dormant. So, for example, we might help learners to see the presence, in otherwise disparate problems, of the words *ratio* or *force*, and to cue them into the conceptual operations that are likely to be helpful. Or in other cases the characteristic X will have to be defined disjunctively: 'When you see the words *times* or *multiply* or *by* (as in '4 *by* 6') or *of* (plus a fraction), then you use the multiplication program'. But note that it seems that these features will be more flexibly and intuitively registered if they are discovered from a range of examples, perhaps with guidance, by induction, rather than taught directly.

We can see the problem of domain-specificity re-emerging here, for there are very few perceptual features, probably only colour and some recurrent shapes, whose salience is ubiquitous. Rather, our perceptual parsing is contingent: we identify something as 'speech' or 'a person' or 'physics', and then select and run a domain-specific programme containing further perceptual distinctions, attributes, and points of view, and coping and learning strategies.

Another role for teachers in the acceleration of transfer, and the discovery of relevance, exists, though it is yet not well understood. It involves the hazy but widespread notion of 'getting them to think' in the same sense of encouraging and gently guiding students in their own personal exploration of relevance, i.e. in experimenting with the limits of applicability of what they know. In a famous variation of the classical experiments on 'functional fixedness' (Duncker 1945), in which people were prevented by their preconceptions from seeing a pair of pliers, say, as a potential pendulum bob, subjects' success rate was markedly improved by the experimenter simply saying, at an appropriate moment: 'Now, think! think!' What he was doing was interrupting a familiar and over-used programme that was running 'by default', and thereby creating the space within which to explore the relevance of other, less well-ingrained, more tentative programmes and points of view. The teacher can function in the same way: by disrupting the automaticity of children's intuitive ideas, so that the new, fragile modes of thought of formal science have a chance to become more integrated with other programmes, more tied to the salient characteristics of the situation, and more carefully mapped in terms of their limits of applicability. It is in the creation of a hiatus, the disruption of a habit, and the reminding of alternatives, that the science teacher, like the sports coach, assists the development of competence and understanding.

In fact there is evidence that children (and adults) naturally seek to consolidate, integrate, streamline and if necessary reorganize new understandings that they have been taught, or have worked out in the heat of the moment (Karmiloff-Smith, 1984). It seems to be a fairly general feature of learning that, given the time, opportunity and, if necessary, encouragement, we will indulge in this reflective exploration of the limitations and associations of what is already known. Ironically, the one place where these conditions for consolidation are systematically absent is the schoolroom. Children are required to be constantly 'on duty', always liable to be asked for an answer to a question that they have not properly understood. The successful students are those with a good, integrated, solid understanding of the subject, or those who are able to create a passable 'lash-up' of an answer, grabbing at bits and pieces of understanding and somehow cobbling them together to produce, transiently, an acceptable response. Yet the opportunity to go off-duty, to put into port and dismantle these leaky rafts, to mull over what one has, and put them back together in a more integrated and less perishable form, is missing. It is perhaps small wonder that the bane of the science or maths teacher's life is the class or the individual that 'seemed to have grasped it' on Friday, and who has lost it again on Monday.

The psychology we have been discussing here suggests that the teacher's frustration arises from misguided expectations. Once a learner seems to have mastered a concept or an operation, their job, and the teacher's, has only just begun. Its domain of relevance, its links with other concepts, both formal and informal, its appropriate connections with different forms of response all remain to be discovered. And the role of the teacher, if they choose to aim for this kind of broadening and deepening of understanding, is to provide opportunity and encouragement with one hand, and to prevent, with the other, the student falling back in to the old ruts of thought, so that the boundary between new and old can be investigated and redrawn.

CONCLUSIONS

In the space available it has been possible to make no more than a start on what I consider a vital task – developing a wide repertoire of teaching methods that are custom-built for different aims and different clienteles. The traditional teaching style of giving notes to be learnt, well-defined experiments to be done, tests and practical write-ups to be marked, was an appropriate and effective strategy for aiming students at public examinations. The comprehensive school teacher quite rightly sees this to be appropriate and effective for a minority, though even here its success is waning as the Examination Boards, out of an incoherent and misguided sense that 'proper' understanding will automatically generate transfer-ability, set trickier and trickier questions. But for younger and less academically inclined people this pedagogy is not what's wanted. There is no good reason to bombard eleven year olds with technical terms and text-book theories, many of which are ancient history compared with what they can watch on *Horizon*. Yet teachers, out of a mixture of habit and the inability to see what else could be done, continue to do so. Even many recent curriculum developments are merely dilutions and combinations of the traditional 'subjects', taught by teachers who know deep down that there are more important things for thirteen year olds to be thinking about than the extension of springs, the properties of bases, or even the names of the major blood vessels. They know that there are different things that science can and should be doing, and they know that to do them they will have to teach in different ways. But they don't know what they are.

It is, I say, only a beginning, but a vital one, to acknowledge loud and clear that the *modus operandi* that used to be good for helping pupils to pass exams is either ineffective, or actually counterproductive when it is applied by default to other, equally legitimate and increasingly pressing, aims. Having made this acknowledgement we can give up the vain hope that tinkering with teaching contents and methods will do, and begin to look for alternative pedagogies to deal with some new and different domains.

The major implications of research on the domain-specificity of learning for science education is easily stated: *we must be clear about the area of life within which we are aiming to raise people's competence, and in what way; we must design our teaching environment, teaching materials and teaching methods accordingly; and we must accept the probability that we will not be able to pursue all desirable aims simultaneously.*

Specifically, we must have in mind, as we teach, the 'context of eventual use' and we must create learning and testing environments and experiences that mimic or mirror this context as accurately as possible. If we wish people to be able to perform under stress, we should teach them under stress. If we wish them to pass exams, we should constantly set them 'mocks'. If we wish them to develop their own judgement we should encourage them to use it. If we wish them to trust their senses and observe accurately, we cannot at the same time tell them 'what they should have seen'. If we wish them to be interested in finding the answers to their own questions, we cannot hope to train them by working on *our* questions. If we wish them to be able to discuss the Sizewell Inquiry, we should have them discuss it. And so on. There is no reason to suppose that exercising their abilities in any one of these domains will transfer to their ability in any other. The psychological evidence is that if such transfer is sought, then it must be taught. The ability to see the relevance of something known to something new is not a matter of 'intelligence' or 'effort' or 'depth of understanding', but of experience, and of the specific strategies, born of experience, that a learner possesses for generalizing and extending their knowledge modules into unknown territory.

Acknowledgements

I am grateful to Beverly Bell, Arthur Lucas and Terry Russell for their detailed and very helpful comments on an earlier draft of this chapter.

REFERENCES

Allport, D. A. 1980. 'Patterns and actions: cognitive mechanisms are content-specific.' In Claxton, G. (ed.) *Cognitive psychology: new directions.* Routledge & Kegan Paul, London, pp. 26-64.

Anderson, J. R. 1976. *Language, memory and thought.* Erlbaum, Hillsdale, New Jersey.

Association for Science Education. 1981. *Education through science: a policy statement.* ASE, Hatfield.

Baddeley, A. D. 1982. 'Domains of recollection.' *Psychological Review,* 89: 708–29.

Barth, J. 1967. *The floating opera.* Doubleday, New York.

Bell, B. and Brook, A. 1984. *Aspects of secondary students' understanding of plant nutrition.* Children's Learning in Science Project Report, Centre for Studies in Science and Mathematics Education, University of Leeds.

Bell, B., Barron, J. and Stephenson, E. 1985. *The construction of meaning and conceptual change in classroom settings: case studies on plant nutrition.* Children's Learning in Science Project Report, Centre for Studies in Science and Mathematics Education, University of Leeds.

Bower, G. H. 1981. 'Mood and memory.' *American Psychologist,* 36: 129–48.

Choppin, B. 1979. 'Aptitude tests for admission to university: the British experience.' In Mitter, W. (ed.) *The use of tests and interviews for admission to higher education.* NFER, Windsor, pp. 121–34.

Churchland, P. M. 1979. *Scientific realism and the plasticity of mind.* Cambridge University Press, Cambridge.

Claxton, G. L. 1977. 'Content and discontent in psychology.' *Bulletin of the British Psychological Society,* 30: 97–101.

Claxton, G. L. 1980. 'Learning when.' *Journal of Curriculum Studies,* 13: 68–70.

Claxton, G. L. 1984. *Live and learn; an introduction to the psychology of growth and change in everyday life.* Harper and Row, London.

Cole, M., Gay, J., Glick, J. and Sharp, D. W. 1971. *The cultural context of learning and thinking.* Basic Books, New York.

Donaldson, M. 1978. *Children's minds.* Fontana, London.

Duncker, K. 1945. 'On problem-solving.' *Psychological Monographs,* 58: No. 270.

Eich, J. E. 1980. 'The cue-dependent nature of state dependent retrieval.' *Memory and Cognition,* 8: 157–73.

Fodor, J. A. 1983. *The modularity of mind.* MIT Press, Cambridge, Mass.

Godden, D. R. and Baddeley, A. D. 1975. 'Context-dependent memory in two natural environments: on land and underwater.' *British Journal of Psychology,* 66: 325–31.

Karmiloff-Smith, A. 1984. 'Children's problem-solving.' In Lamb, M. E., Brown, A. L. and Ragoff, B. (eds) *Advances in developmental psychology,* Vol. 3, Erlbaum, Hillsdale, New Jersey, pp. 39–90.

Kelly, G. A. 1955. *The psychology of personal constructs.* Norton, New York.

Lefford, A. 1946. 'The influence of emotional subject matter on logical reasoning.' *Journal of General Psychology,* 34: 127–51.

Lowe, G. 1980. 'State-dependent recall decrements with moderate doses of alcohol.' *Current Psychological Research,* 1: 3–8.

McGarrigle, J. and Donaldson, M. 1974. 'Conservation accidents.' *Cognition,* 3: 341–50.

Russell, T. 1985. 'Interpreting presented information.' In Harlen, W. (ed.) *Science in schools, age 11: Report No. 4.* Great Britain, Department of Education and Science, Assessment of Performance Unit, pp. 75–106.

Schmidt, S. R. 1983. 'The effects of recall and recognition test expectancy on the retention of prose.' *Memory and Cognition,* 11: 172–80.

Smith, S. M., Glenberg, A. M. and Bjork, R. A. 1978. 'Environmental context and human memory.' *Memory and Cognition,* 6: 342–53.

Strauss, S. and Stavy, R. 1983. 'Educational-developmental psychology and curriculum development: the case of heat and temperature.' In Helm, H. and Novak, J. D. (eds) *Proceedings of the international seminar on misconceptions in science and mathematics.* Cornell University, Ithaca, NY, pp. 310–21.

Viennot, L. 1979. 'Spontaneous reasoning in elementary dynamics.' *European Journal of Science Education,* 10: 205–21.

Wason, P. C. and Johnson-Laird, P. N. 1972. *Psychology of reasoning: structure and content.* Batsford, London.

Chapter 12

How can we specify concepts for primary science?

Paul Black and Wynne Harlen

INTRODUCTION

When the only science-related work in the primary curriculum emanated from the 'nature table' the aims of the work were modestly conceived in terms of skills of observation and classification and the naming of parts and species. Attempts to broaden the range of content to include the world of the physical sciences were made through documents produced by HMI (Ministry of Education 1961) and the Association for Science Education (1966) in the sixties. Apart from the Oxford Primary Science Project (Redman *et al.* 1969), which attempted to define the broad range of science concepts that should be introduced at the primary level, attention was almost wholly focused on science as a way of learning, on 'how' rather than 'what' young children should learn. This was in tune with the child-centred ethos of primary education in the post-Plowden era, which placed emphasis both on the child's own activity in raising and finding answers to his or her own questions and on the development of an enquiring mind.

While there was nothing theoretically incompatible in developing process skills and an enquiring mind at the same time as acquiring a given set of concepts, the belief that content was relatively unimportant and that attempts to cover certain concepts would invite a dangerous invasion by the secondary school ethos prevented any attempts in this direction. From the late 1970s, however, content and concepts began to reappear as respectable issues (Harlen 1978, Kerr and Engel 1980, Department of Education and Science 1983, for example). It was soon clear that attempts to specify content or concept areas raised a number of problems. Some statements, intended to be interpreted at a low level, could equally well be regarded as concepts that students are still struggling with at sixth form or undergraduate level. In some cases, there seemed to be no rationale for concept selection and no substantial arguments to relate concept selection to the processes of learning. The national science curriculum for England and Wales, as determined in 1989 and revised in 1991 (Department of Education and Science 1991), made clear and extensive specification of both content and process for primary science. However, we will argue below that it does not resolve the problem of concept specification.

The problem of specifying concepts appropriate for primary science is now seen to require more fundamental treatment. It is necessary to be clear about the intended meaning of concepts and about their role in a learning strategy that also aims to develop process skills. Ways of expressing different levels in grasping a concept have also to be found. Furthermore, recent research on children's informal learning shows that such learning also needs to be taken into account in the selection and interpretation of concepts.

In this chapter we sketch a rationale for the choice of concepts which faces these issues. The discussion is in two main sections. We first set out a view of the nature of concepts and of the distinctions and relationships between concepts and process skills. This leads to consideration of the way in which we use concepts and processes and to the need for some analysis of memory. The ways in which a learner's concepts might be changed and a rationale concerning 'level' of concepts are also explored.

We then apply that theory to meet the challenge in the chapter's title. General criteria are first set out and a specific example is then discussed. The approach followed in the discussion of this example is then outlined in a generalized form and is proposed as a general strategy which might be applied in other concept areas. The strategy leads directly to proposals for teaching programmes through which the ideas might be tested in school trials.

Assumptions about the nature of learning are not here set out or argued in broad terms. The general approach is in the constructivist tradition and is fully consistent with the generative learning model developed by Osborne and Wittrock (1985). However, although the correspondence with this model is quite close in some respects, the present argument differs by placing emphasis on the need to analyse the nature of the science concepts to be learnt. Osborne and Wittrock pay little attention to this aspect, but it has to be addressed if the selection of the menu of concepts is at issue.

CONCEPTS AND PROCESS SKILLS

What are concepts?

The first target here is to set out a view of the nature of concepts. This can start with the following quotation from a text on cognitive science – *Categories and Concepts* – by Smith and Medin (1981):

> Without concepts, mental life would be chaotic. If we perceived each entity as unique, we would be overwhelmed by the sheer diversity of what we experience and unable to remember more than a minute fraction of what we encounter. And if each individual entity needed a distinct name, our language would be staggeringly complex and communication

virtually impossible. Fortunately though, we do not perceive, remember and talk about each object and event as unique, but rather as an instance of a class or concept that we already know something about. When entering a new room, we experience one particular object as a member of the class of chairs, another as an instance of desks, and so on. Concepts thus give our world stability. They capture the notion that many objects or events are alike in some important respects, and hence can be thought about and responded to in ways we have already mastered. Concepts also allow us to go beyond the information given: for once we have assigned an entity to a class on the basis of its perceptible attributes, we can then infer some of its non-perceptible attributes. Having used perceptible properties like colour and shape to decide an object is an apple, we can infer an object has a core that is currently invisible but that will make its presence known as soon as we bite into it. In short, concepts are critical for perceiving, remembering, talking and thinking about objects and events in the world.

(Smith and Medin 1981: 1)

The argument applies directly when we consider particular object or experience concepts, such as 'table' and 'chair', 'trout' and 'salmon', or 'lifting' and 'kicking'. It still applies, but with differences of interpretation, if we are considering more general concepts, such as 'furniture', or 'fish' or 'pushes and pulls', or, to go even further, 'artefact', 'species', or 'force'. A concept need not be tied down to a single word. 'Light travels in straight lines' is a concept statement, although such a statement might, as in the case of the core known to be inside the apple, be setting out an attribute or relationship implied as part of a concept. It can also be added at this stage that the attributes and implications attached to a concept can relate it to others, perhaps in a complex network, and that these might form hierarchies if subordinate or superordinate relationships are involved. For example, 'charge' might be related to 'current' and both might be linked via a superordinate relationship between concepts concerning the atomic and electronic structure of matter and the concept of electric field.

Concepts and process skills

Bruner, Goodnow and Austin (1956) define a concept as 'the network of inferences that are or may be set into play by an act of categorization'. This is consistent with our discussion above but leads to the next step in the argument by its reference to categorization. When we try to understand phenomena or to solve problems we need to relate new information, about the phenomena or problems, to existing concepts. The outcome depends not only on the new data and on the existing ideas, but also on the way in which we actually make a relationship. This task involves a range of procedures and at least some of these, e.g. transformation of data or seeing patterns in observations, are generally regarded as the 'process skills' involved in learning science. The point to be stressed here is that such 'process skills' play a central role in concept development: They are the means by which the 'network of inferences' may be called into play, by which the power inherent in concepts may be put to use, and by which concepts may be modified or invented. The definition and specification of 'process skills' implied here cannot, without detailed analysis, be claimed to be identical with that used when curriculum planners (e.g. in *AAAS* 1975) or evaluators (e.g. the Assessment of Performance Unit in Science – see Harlen, Black and Johnson 1981) specify process skills. For the present purpose, it is only necessary to point to the evident overlap between the two approaches.

Categorization and transformation

For the present purpose, the interplay between process and concepts will be considered in terms of two main aspects:

Categorization is the means by which we see that a particular object or problem is a case of a particular concept, which is selected and brought into play. The selection might involve considering alternative candidates, and rejecting some (a teacup without handles in a Chinese restaurant may cause us to pause between 'cup' and 'bowl' before we decide how to regard and use it).

Transformation involves using the properties inherent in the selected concept in order to make predictions, to decide how to use or treat a new object, to invent procedures for solving a problem.

The term 'transformation' is used here to refer to the 'change' in form or 'nature' of the knowledge about the object or situation involved. For example, once we see an object in a room as a case of a chair, a particular set of sense data is circumscribed and then interpreted, as the quotation above from Smith and Medin explains, to infer non-perceptible attributes. Thus our knowledge, the set of sense data from the chair, is transformed into a wealth of expectations about the object and its structure, function and use. Similarly, experience of the onset of double vision and a rising headache can be transformed by the concept of migraine to develop predictions and ideas for action based on past experience.

These two aspects, categorization and transformation, are implied in Smith and Medin's example: the recognition that an object is an apple leads to the prediction that a core will be encountered when we bite into it. Although it could be argued that the separation of the two is artificial, the distinction between them is of central importance for the present argument. Much effort is expended, in the teaching of science, on the transformation aspect of concepts (using them as an algorithm), and too little is devoted to the categorization aspect (deciding which it is appropriate to use). Thus, a pupil may be able to transform data about an electric circuit by applying Ohm's Law to predict current given the resistance and potential difference involved, but may not think of using this particular concept network when trying to explain why a fuse has blown.

The weakness does not lie in any power to categorize – it is not possible to build a concept without some such power – but in the restriction of this power to the very narrow range of contexts within which the network was learnt. In the national monitoring exercises conducted in science for the Assessment of Performance Unit, it was found necessary to pay attention to the context within which a particular question locates a test of a pupil's ability, for it became clear that a pupil's performance on test items with the same logical or conceptual structure can vary with the context (Song and Black 1991, 1992). Children can have difficulty in understanding a concept such as 'animal' because they do not realize that this label is used for all objects sharing certain properties, so that it applies to humans and to worms as well as to horses; learning more about a concept can involve extending the range of categorization by which it can be evoked.

Studies of problem-solving with physics students by Larkin (1983) showed that they 'wandered around' their collection of concepts trying to use each in turn; by contrast, experts in the subject could go directly to the relevant concept. One main difficulty for the novices appeared to lie in the categorization step, for they could apply the transformations implied by the concepts quite competently once they had chosen the concepts correctly.

Memory

The text by Smith and Medin (1981) is devoted almost entirely to the problem of understanding how categorization can work in the case of object concepts. They discuss the difficulties that arise in discerning the rules by which we are able to decide marginal cases (e.g. is this concave impermeable object without handles a case of a cup or of a bowl?). The detail of this argument may be of importance for any future elaboration of the ideas in this present paper. However, for the present, it is important to note that the argument starts from and is conducted within an exploration of models of the ways in which we store and access our knowledge. This emphasis is central in other work in cognitive science. Consider the following quotation from Schank (1982):

> How we understand is affected by what is in our memories. That is, language understanding is different when there are different memory structures controlling the process. A coherent theory of the structures in memory must naturally precede a complete theory of language understanding.

> (Schank 1982: 4)

It is implicit in the theoretical approach developed by Schank that both of those aspects of cognition that are called 'concepts' and 'processes' in this paper are stored in memory structures, and that an understanding of these structures will be necessary if we are to understand how concepts and processes function and inter-relate. Just as arguments in preceding paragraphs indicate that it may make no sense to talk of a choice between concept learning and process learning because any analysis of ways in which concept learning occurs must involve process learning, so the argument here is that it makes no sense to be arguing against memory in favour of experience, or skills, or attitudes. The reaction against rote learning in school education is justifiable, but it is an argument against building inadequate memory structures: to argue against building memory structures at all is to argue against learning. Finally, it is not useful, in arguments about the balance between concept and process aspects of learning, to identify the concept aspect exclusively with memory and then to burden it with the pejoratives that attach to rote learning.

Changing concepts

If the informal concepts that children hold are effective and robust, the design of teaching has to use some strategy for changing concepts. Some of the issues involved here may be explored through an example. Consider the phenomenon of sugar dissolving in water. Starting from the (unstated) assumption that matter does not disappear, a teacher may ask children to solve the puzzle of sugar's apparent disappearance, by asking 'Where has it gone to?' To the children, this may appear to be a pointless question. There is no puzzle – it is common experience for stuff to disappear. Paper burns, pools evaporate, clothes wear out, sugar and salt disappear in water. The phenomenon is categorized by a concept of 'disappearing' and in that sense, is already understood. This view may be changed in several ways as follows:

> Different evidence may be taken into account: the water's sweet taste could be evidence, although it is not conclusive (the sugar left its taste behind when it disappeared).
> Alternative ideas may be applied: the idea that matter does not disappear and that when it appears to have done so it can usually be made to turn up again, would be relevant here. Perhaps other examples of disappearance have to be tackled.
> The same evidence could be categorized in a new way. In the present case this might involve recognition that the 'non-disappearance' idea, already held and used for lost property, was the appropriate category to which to refer the sugar–water situation.
> The new ideas, with or without re-interpreted evidence, may be used to make new predictions and so lead to new investigations.

New predictions may be used to re-interpret evidence, i.e. to categorize and transform it in a new way.

All of these possibilities imply the use of process skills. However, the processes imply critical reflection as well as practical activity and could hardly be effective without opportunities and stimulus for children to argue about their own ideas. The problem is to develop the critical powers exercised in process skills so that they can break the tendency to hold on to old ideas, and start the uncomfortable process of accommodating ideas to new evidence.

This argument suggests a possible strategy for effecting concept change. There are two features. The first is that such change involves critical use of process skills. The second is that it may be essential to understand children's informal ideas before one can start. 'Where has it gone to?' may be a good opening question, but teachers using it should not be under the illusion that children share their perception that there is a self-evident problem. Those for whom 'it's disappeared' is an adequate answer have to be exposed to other possibilities. Other ideas almost always exist in the views of a group of children and, if not, can be introduced by the teacher acting as a member of the group rather than as the authority figure with 'the right answer'. In general, where evidence about children's own ideas is not available, the exploration with children of these ideas may be an essential first step.

The argument does not constitute a developed theory of concept change. It implies, as a contribution to such a theory, that in some cases change will be a question of blocking a categorization to one concept (disappearing) and opening a new categorization to another (permanence of matter), so that one existing concept is curtailed and another is augmented.

Selecting concept level

It is proposed here that there is a spectrum of concept levels. At one end of this spectrum lie those object concepts and rules that are commonplace and readily acquired by all without formal education. At the opposite end lie abstract principles that emerge from years of study of related phenomena and of less general or subordinate principles. These two 'ends' of the spectrum differ from one another in respect of several features.

Table 12.1 sets out briefly three examples, and gives a schematic description of each in terms of four main features, two concerned with the categorization aspect and two with transformation. The three span the spectrum, with 'Overcoats' at the low-level end, 'Entropy' at the highly abstract end and 'Home Insulation' between the two.

These examples illustrate general properties associated with changes in level. At the low level, there are to be found very many concepts, each with a limited range of categorization, with act upon collections of instances, on common features and on links between phenomena which are unproblematic. At the high-level end are to be found few concepts, each with wide range of categorization; however, in these cases a rather sophisticated insight may often be needed to make the appropriate categorizations.

The transformations involved are also very different in character. There are many transformations at the low-level end: typically they may involve little more than recapitulation. Identification of any everyday object concept, such as a chair, is an example. At the high-level end, the transformations are fewer in number and both more subtle and more powerful. Those in the physical sciences particularly would involve relations between concepts where both the concepts themselves and the mathematical functions involved would be unintelligible to the layman.

Table 12.1 Example concepts

Feature	Overcoats	Home Insulation	Entropy
Aspects relevant to categorization	Knowledge of types of coats, their costs, and of patterns of weather	Areas and thicknesses of wall, wall coverings, floors, ceilings and windows	Changes, physical and chemical rates and energies involved under variety of temperatures pressures and compositions of components
Range of categorization	Personal experience of climate and of stock in local shops	Closed built spaces for human habitation	All natural phenomena
Nature of transformation	Expectation of coming season leads to prediction of type of coat to be bought	Data on walls, floors ceilings and on temperatures lead to prediction of energy input required, and to ideas to modify the walls, floors and ceilings	Mathematical – via various formulations equivalent to the principle of increase of entropy (Second Law of Thermodynamics)
Terms involved in the transformation	Warm, cool, freezing, thick, light, flimsy, foam-backed, lined	Joules, watts, U-values, temperatures	Entropy, free-energy, activity coefficients, chemical potentials

These notions about level have to be used in two ways. One is to analyse the conceptual structure of that which is to be learnt. In so far as the concepts form a hierarchical structure, which is usually the case in science, the assignment of a scheme of levels may follow naturally from a concept analysis. The second use is in relationship to the cognitive demands made on the learner. Here it would appear evident that the low-level concepts will be the easiest to learn. However, there is no guarantee that a hierarchy of learning difficulty will be identical to any hierarchy developed by a logical analysis of the subject. The distinguishing features set out above have been psychological and any structure derived from analysis of the subject should be mapped onto a psychological framework if it is to be a useful guide for learning. As we see later, such a framework is absent from the national curriculum for science in England and Wales.

CRITERIA AND STRATEGIES

General criteria

In order to specify concepts as learning targets, it is necessary both to make a selection and to define, for those selected, features such as level and range of categorization which are essential for unambiguous specification. In addition, the way in which children's learning is organized will have to be consistent with the learning model implied by the principles of selection.

Clarity of specification is particularly important for the primary curriculum: it may or may not be sensible to propose that a concept such as 'energy' be studied at the primary stage, but it certainly cannot be sensible if no distinction is made between the primary study envisaged and the study of 'energy' that might be appropriate in a course for a physics honours degree. In this present section, the discussion draws on the preceding section to set out criteria both for selection of concepts and for decisions about content and methods of teaching which are appropriate at the primary level. For the selection of concepts four main criteria are suggested which relate to different aspects of children's relationship with, and ability to learn with understanding about, the world around them:

> relevance to everyday events as seen by the child;
> potential for children to take part in the generation of concepts using process skills;
> consistency with the ways of thinking of young children;
> value in terms of a foundation for later learning
>
> (Harlen 1985: 54)

Each of these is now spelt out in a little more detail.

1 The concepts should help children's understanding of everyday events and of the world around them and should be applicable to their experience.

This criterion is partly justified because the understanding by pupils of the world around them is an aim, in its own right, for science education. It is also important because ideas which are not effectively linked to experience are unlikely to remain in children's minds. The criterion would rule out concepts, such as 'atom' or 'molecule', which deal with objects which are too small to see and so are not perceived in everyday experience, and concepts such as 'acid' or 'base' which are generalizations about generalizations (i.e. generalizations about substances which have in common certain generalizable sets of properties).

2 Children should be able to take part in the generation and testing of the concepts through the use of process skills.

This implies that in developing a concept children should have opportunities to collect evidence, to check its consistency with their ideas, and to make predictions. This criterion should not be interpreted as a rule to limit work to those concepts which can be 'discovered' by direct experience. Useful ideas can come from other sources, from teachers themselves and from books, television and radio.

3 Concepts should be at a level which children can learn with understanding, taking into account their limited experience and maturity.

It is clear that many concepts can be grasped at an abstract level only by older pupils. Since the same concept can often be presented at a low level or at a high level, this criterion can be interpreted as a requirement for the level to be specified and justified. Early exposure to concrete examples in a low-level treatment can be a useful first step towards the development of abstract appreciation. The difficulty here is in finding a theory which could give general guidance about appropriate levels – otherwise there is only empirical testing and the criterion reduces to saying that the intended learning should happen.

4 The concepts should provide a foundation for later learning in science.

The relationship implied to later science learning is part of the justification for including science in the primary curriculum. There is ample evidence (see, for example, Driver, Guesne and Tiberghien 1985) that children arrive in secondary school without the basic low-level science concepts which are well within their grasp and which could have been fostered in primary school work. In other words, secondary science needs primary science and although this dependence is only one of several reasons for science in the primary curriculum it is an important one to keep in mind when selecting concepts. However, this criterion must be operated in conjunction with the other three: if it were to have priority and to rule on its own, it would be a recipe for the 'top down' approach which is now so heavily criticized within secondary school science.

Implementation criteria

The four criteria just outlined relate to concept selection but their implementation depends on additional considerations. As we have seen, concepts are abstractions which are generated and changed through encounter with the specific content and contexts in which they are embedded. Attempts to teach concepts directly result at best in meaningless rote learning. There is an important difference between the consciousness of the teacher and of the child with respect to concept development, which is best illustrated by an example. A child who has succeeded in keeping an ice cube from melting for four hours, without a fridge or thermos flask, will be aware of having learnt something about the particular materials and conditions which were found most effective (expanded polystyrene was better than cotton wool or newspaper and having the material wrapped round the block better than insulating the container), rather than about the general principle about the heat insulating properties of materials in slowing down flow of heat rather than 'flow of cold'. The teacher, however, will see the learning as contributing to these more general ideas.

The existence of such differences in view between teacher and child has to be kept in mind in selecting the content and contexts in and through which selected concepts are to developed. This problem is a starting point for suggesting the four criteria to guide this selection.

1 The content should engage the interest of the children.

This criterion reiterates the point made above that it is the specific content and not the ideas embedded which engages the children. However, the criterion does not mean that content is selected by slavishly 'following children's interests'. Though well meant, this approach has distinct disadvantages in narrowing activities to those in which children have already shown interest. Instead, schools should aim to expand children's interests by introducing new things or new ways of looking at familiar ones. The criterion of 'interest' can be applied after children have had a chance to explore, question and find out what intrigues and puzzles them about the objects or phenomena that have been introduced.

2 The range of content should be such that emerging concepts are seen to have relevance and meaning to the children.

There has to be some consistency between separate encounters with things in the world around them for the children to begin to see that ideas from one activity can help in tackling another related one. The degree to which content should be simplified to help in the process of revealing these ideas and so expanding their categorization is something of a dilemma. If it is too 'cleaned up', the links between the real world and the content of activities becomes tenuous – what part does the study of a swinging pendulum play in understanding the world as seen by a child? If it is too confused by the complexity of real situations, on the other hand, the underlying ideas may never emerge. This criterion places emphasis on relevance *as seen by the children*, and acknowledges that this will vary with the children and with their past experience. Taking up the example quoted above, some children, who started with the problem of keeping the ice cube from melting, went on to study the insulating properties of materials by measuring the cooling of hot water in cans covered with layers of the materials in question. For these children this activity had considerable meaning and relevance, but for others not sharing the same starting point, the same activity could be meaningless with no relevance to understanding the world around.

More generally, the notion of range explored here is quite fundamental because it puts into practice the categorization aspect of the categorization–transformation model which underlies much of the argument in this paper.

3 The content should be so related to children's everyday experience that change in their everyday explanations is possible and can be planned.

This criterion refers to the teacher's view of the learning process, which has to penetrate beneath the specific to the underlying concepts and processes. If the content of activities is seen by children as relevant to their everyday lives, it is very likely that they have firmly held and frequently used ideas about it that might well have to be changed. Where the differences between the children's everyday ideas and more useful concepts are recognized by the teacher, it will be possible to design and test teaching which either challenges or expands the categorizations that children use and the transformations to which these are linked. Whether this is best done by a gradual change, aimed at successive modifications in children's ideas, or by presenting conflicting evidence which forces an abandonment of or radical restructuring of existing ideas is not clear: it may well vary from one topic to another. This is an area where some exploratory work has been done (Harlen 1992) although more is needed. Whatever the route, it is very likely that critical consideration of new evidence will play an important part. This leads to the last criterion.

4 The content should be presented so as to give opportunity for the development of science process skills.

Confronting children with new evidence to challenge their existing ideas will have little effect if the ways in which evidence is related to ideas are inadequate for revealing the need to change ideas. Everyday ideas are, after all, built up by the 'everyday' processes of thought which reinforce and do not challenge them. Recognizing the conflict between ideas and evidence requires skills and attitudes which everyday experiences do not necessarily foster and which demand particular attention in school experience.

The above discussions of selection and implementation criteria, while mainly focused on concepts, have led back to the recognition of the interdependence of concepts and process skills. Closely linked to any attempt to change concepts are such skills as concluding that a rule ought to be suspect if it only applies to a limited range of experiences or that one should not be satisfied with spotting only one common feature in a collection of objects assumed to be similar in several ways. More needs to be done to establish a firm theoretical ground, from empirical work that has already been done, for the notion of levels in relation to process skill development (e.g. Harlen *et al.* 1977, Russell and Harlen 1990). Moreover, further work has to consider process skill development in the context of concept development, just as we have seen that the reverse is also the case, for neither is independent of the other.

EXAMPLES OF THE APPROACH

The following examples are presented in the form in which they were analysed at the outset of a research and curriculum development project (SPACE – Science Processes and Concept Exploration, Black and Harlen 1990) which aimed to put into practice some of the ideas in this chapter. The aim here is to exemplify the programme outlined above, and not to describe the SPACE work: the advent of the National Curriculum during the course of its work altered that project by imposing constraints on its orientation. Brief references both to the SPACE work and to the National Curriculum are included below.

Electric circuits – an example

There is extensive research evidence of the difficulties and misunderstandings that even secondary school pupils have with this area (Osborne 1983, Shipstone 1984, Solomon *et al.* 1985). Our analysis starts with a brief summary of this evidence.

It seems natural to think a single lead takes electricity from the source, mains-socket or battery, to the device which consumes the electricity in order to work. Older primary children develop notions of the electricity being 'used up' ('switch off you're wasting it!') and of the dangers. The latter can come from the Electricity Board films about the dangers of climbing pylons and from family admonitions about electric shocks ('don't touch the plug' – or 'always pull it out'). Work on closed circuits seems to be irrelevant;

for dealing with torches, bicycle dynamos, motor car electrics and some devices at home, a unipolar source-to-consumer model seems to work adequately. When the concept of current is introduced, it is identified with 'the electricity' so that it is natural to believe that it comes from the source and gradually gets 'used up' as it goes round the circuit. In school circuits with dry cells, the positive side is usually identified as the source, so that there is little current left by the time it gets 'back' to the negative terminal. Some hold a more refined view in which the current is largest in wires close to either terminal and a minimal in the parts of the circuit remote from both terminals. Use of water circuits as an analogy may be unhelpful, since common experience of water supply is not concerned with closed circuits – the water from the tap is distributed all over the place and it is not natural to think of it as circulating in a conserved cycle. Small dry batteries and the AC mains are linked since both are electricity, so that some children approach laboratory work at under 6 volts with the fears and inhibitions implanted by warnings about mains and high-voltage transmission lines. These are not the beliefs and problems of a small minority of 'backward' children; the evidence is that they represent the views of the majority and that only a small fraction of the most able pupils at ages 15–16 escape from them. Given all this, it is idle to ask whether children can clearly distinguish such concepts as current, potential difference, energy and power in electric circuits.

It is not enough to brush aside these difficulties by pretending that children have simply failed to grasp some simple explanations. It is frequently the case that the simple ideas that can be extracted from scientific theory are not adequate to deal with more than a carefully selected set of everyday phenomena, since the latter tend to be complex. It is also common to find that the simplifications that are commonly used in elementary teaching have not been well chosen, and even where they have been, the optimum choice may be different when the aims are changed. So the second stage of the argument calls for a re-examination of the sophisticated theory of the phenomena so that more appropriate simplifications can be made.

Briefly, a physicist's view of electric circuits runs as follows. Charge does not pile up in conducting circuits, so current is conserved. Potential difference (p.d.), which is a measure of the field acting, is apportioned around items in a series circuit according to their resistance. Free energy is transformed at a rate determined by the product 'current times p.d.'. If one asks how the energy is transferred from (say) a dry cell to a small bulb, the best answer is that it is transferred through the electric and magnetic fields that surround the wire when a current flows: these fields are the means by which parts of the circuit wiring remote from the cell terminals 'know' that the current is to flow when the switch is closed: the effect of closing a switch is seen almost instantaneously (in fact it propagates with the speed of light) and does not travel around by means of shunting collisions of the electrons in the wires. The electrons travel quite slowly, and in an AC mains circuit they jiggle backwards and forwards with amplitudes of less than a millimetre. Thus no material substance enters one's house along the mains supply cable; the flux of surrounding fields delivers the energy.

The resistivities of different substances cover an enormous range – with ratios of order 10^{20} between the extremes. Because of this, a situation in which the terminals of a cell are connected by air can be regarded as qualitatively different from one where they are connected by copper – unless the air path is only a fraction of a millimetre wide, when sparks might start to occur. There need not be closed circuits for current to flow: in lightning, charges pile up between earth and cloud by a slow pumping process until the field across the air is too great, then they flow back in a flash; the 'source' has to be pumped up again before there can be a further discharge. Early nuclear accelerators used mains supply to charge up sets of capacitors to produce intermittent discharge in this way. However, such systems are rare, and we usually deal with closed circuits which cease to operate if the circuit is broken.

The above is not meant to impress or frighten. It provides the resource from which the selection, which is the third stage of the procedure, can be made. The account should make clear that an everyday reference to 'the electricity' does not map unambiguously onto either 'current' or any other single concept. It also follows that the concept of current does not on its own have useful transformations associated with it: such transformations only arise when the network of concepts linking current, potential difference, resistance, power and energy can be set up. To develop current on its own for later use may be creating puzzles to no good purpose.

A selection of concept treatment should be limited in the range of categorizations and in the level of concepts to be chosen. An appropriate limit here for the level might be that a circuit must be continuous and that some substances (conductors) can complete a circuit while others (insulators) cannot. A target list for the range of application of these ideas might be dry cells and bulbs in the laboratory, torches and bicycle circuits, and the plugs and leads of domestic mains devices. This choice meets the general criteria 1, 3 and 4 and also sets up conditions for meeting criterion 2. The implementation criteria can be met by a teaching sequence with three possible stages. The first of these would be work with cells, bulbs and wires. This would lead to examination of torches and bicycles and to fault-finding exercises to show the necessity and practical value of the concept of a closed circuit. This stage could end with examination of mains plugs and leads to establish that the 'closed-circuits' concept also applies in this context. A second stage might investigate the effect of pieces of different materials in closing a circuit, to build up a concept of conductors and insulators seen to be applied to a limited range of everyday conducting and insulating materials: this could include some study of the effects of being wet.

It might be possible to go further and work to an additional concept, that there is a range of sources which differ in their degree of danger. A particular reason for this addition is that research with secondary children has shown that at age 11 electricity is associated with fear and danger, derived from parental warnings about mains devices and Generating Board propaganda about dangers of pylons and overhead wires. Such cautions are not to be contradicted, but they do lead some children to be afraid of handling torch cells, and some way to reconcile the various ideas of danger may be necessary. The aim here, therefore, would be to establish a ranking of dry cell, battery of several cells, mains, pylon wires, perhaps lightning. This feature could be introduced as voltage, regarded simply at this stage as a measure of danger or strength.

The next stage of the analysis would be to work out in detail the teaching approaches which are sketched or implied in the above. This will not be pursued here. This stage should include proposals to evaluate the teaching in relationship to the criteria. It will be noted that little has been said about the third implementation criterion except that the general evidence about children's thinking on electricity has been used as a guide in constructing the scheme. It might be important to pursue this criterion by emphasizing that children's formulation and discussion of their own explanations should form part of the teaching strategy and that one test of the above design would be whether the teaching could proceed by building upon and modifying these explanations in ways that made sense to the children.

A general strategy

The above example shows how a particular topic area might be analysed to produce a teaching strategy. It is a specific example, and care has to be taken to not base generalizations upon its individual and specific features. However, it will serve, with reservations noted below, to illustrate four main stages which can now be stated in general terms:

1 Specify as clearly as possible what is known about children's own explanations and misconceptions.
2 Make a full analysis of the scientific concepts involved at a level adequate to deal with all of the messy everyday and complex phenomena that might possibly be used or evoked. This requirement raises the question of who would be qualified to do this across the board. It may be that advice has to be sought from several subject experts. This may seem a strange requirement for elementary science, but it is often the case that only an expert can see, or invent, simple and valid selections that make enough sense of common phenomena. It is also true that ordinary textbooks are often written by copying ideas from secondary sources and leave the inexpert reader incapable of radical reformulations of the subject.
3 Select the concepts to be established, specifying clearly the level, which involves the range of categorizations which the learners are to experience,

and the nature and sophistication of the transformations which will be implied through understanding of the concept.

4 In the light of the above, and of the selection and implementation criteria previously set out, select, identify and develop activities by which children might develop the use and meaning of the concepts within the categorizations planned. Any such plan would have to pay attention to the range of abilities and interests of the children involved. The plan would have to make clear what the children would actually do. The children's activities and responses would then have to be evaluated in order to determine whether the intended understandings were being achieved. Such evaluations might lead to re-consideration of all four stages.

It should be noted that these *rules* for construction are not the same as the criteria. The criteria are involved throughout. They would be used in the initial consideration of the concepts to be developed and the examples chosen to exhibit them, in the arguments about the four stages, and particularly in the evaluation of the results. It may not be possible to plan as neatly as the electricity example suggests: because this example involves a very specific 'technological' area of everyday experience, the first stage above is confined mainly to the effects of school teaching. Partly for this reason, the four stages can be seen as successive stages in a logical plan. In other areas, it may be necessary to learn from children, in stage four, before the first and third stages can be considered with any great confidence. However, the model of concept learning in terms of transformation and categorization, with the associated issues of process skills and the notion of level, should underlie the whole discussion; in particular, it provides the conceptual framework within which the outcomes of the first two stages are placed within a common rationale, so that the essential features of the selection for the third stage can be specified and justified.

Nutrition – a further example

Too much cannot be claimed for the strategy until a much broader range of examples has been studied. In particular, electricity is based on physics, where the background theory is sharply defined, if complex.

More diverse examples may or may not undermine confidence in the approach, but they would certainly modify it and bring out some implications and complications that are not apparent at this stage. For example, the topic of nutrition is an obvious candidate because of its relevance and importance, and it might here be argued that young children need to know something for immediate application to their everyday decisions rather than as a basis for some learning in the future (which may then be another basis for decision in an even more remote future). The research basis for nutrition is not as well established as for electricity, light and mechanics (see Chapter 1 for relevant references).

One generally acknowledged problem is that an analytic concept is frequently confused with its operational embodiment: in nutrition, confusion arises with the idea that food contains components and that we need some of each of four main types of component for a viable diet. Children may learn about four groups of particular foods: in Britain until recently the 'meat and fish', 'dairy', 'cereals' and 'fruit and vegetable' groups. These *foods*, commonly eaten by the dominant ethnic group, are in fact not necessary, although the *nutrients* that they contain are essential. It was not uncommon for members of a different ethnic group, who may be vegetarian, to show concern. Thus what may be needed is a more measured approach designed to establish the concept of components in food and the idea that these components can be assembled into four main clusters – proteins, fats and oils, carbohydrates, and vitamins and minerals – for the purpose of nutrition. The functional needs which each cluster serves could then lead to the idea of deficiency and its diagnosis.

A later stage may return to the functions of food to bring out that nutrition is only one function. This could lead to positive use of the topic to explore racial and cultural differences. Each of the concepts involved here – physiological function of food, components of food, clusters of components, specific nutritional function, deficiency, cultural differences – would need to be analysed in terms of a transformation–categorization dialogue in order to map out an approach in more careful detail. When this is done, it will be possible also to include issues of ritual, celebration, and social cohesion associated with the choice of food. Biological categorizations and transformations can lead to social ones.

The nutrition example is not developed here beyond a first sketch of stage 2 of the strategy with limited information about stage 1. It shows more clearly than electricity a case where delimitation of a single concept, or of a closely linked set, may not be possible if criteria concerned with relating to everyday needs and experience are to be met. A network of concepts may need to be addressed in a structured way.

The SPACE research and the English national curriculum

The SPACE Research reports (Osborne *et al.* 1990, 1991, in press; Russell *et al.* 1991, 1993; Watt and Russell 1990a, b, c) provide rich descriptions of data on children's own thinking obtained by a variety of elicitation techniques. The selection of concepts was influenced by National Curriculum require-ments, but largely implemented the principles explained above. Thus the work on electricity explored properties and uses of electricity, making circuits, conductors and insulators, and using more batteries, while that on light explored sources of light, representations of light, children's understanding of vision and context dependence of the last two of these. Intervention and post-test activities showed partial success in changing ideas in these areas, with more being achieved with upper juniors (ages 8 to 11) than with lower juniors (ages 5 to 7).

When this work, and the thinking outlined here on concept development, is compared with the National Curriculum for science in England and Wales (DES 1991), there is little correspondence. This is not because of disagreement, but because of the character of the learning expectations expressed in the National Curriculum Order. For example, the primary stages relate to levels 1 to 5 in the Attainment Targets: for light (AT4) there is one statement at each level. Each of the first four starts with 'know that', and the knowledge required is of 'simple properties' – transparent and opaque materials and shadows formed by the latter, that light can be reflected and that it travels faster than sound. The Programmes of Study discuss opportunities to observe relevant phenomena, and say they should be learnt about, and related to everyday effects. Representations, models, predictions, investigations are not mentioned. At level 5 (i.e. the above average child at age 11) the requirement is to 'understand how the reflection of light enables objects to be seen'. However, how this 'understand' is to be achieved is not clear – the only mention of any model or representation occurs in the Programme of Study: 'represent in drawings their ideas about how light varies in terms of brightness, colour and shade'. Understanding vision in terms of light entering the eye is discussed for the first time in Key Stage 3 (11 to 14 year olds). The ray model is nowhere mentioned, while the wave model and its use appear explicitly at level 7. The case of electricity is similar, there being several 'know that', 'be able to construct', 'know how' phrases, but nothing on 'understanding' until level 6. Activities with simple circuits, and knowledge derived from them, are outlined, but conceptual implications attached to such work are not discussed.

Thus for these topics the National Curriculum could be interpreted by many as stating that knowledge of specifics is all that is needed in primary science. More optimistically, the conceptual implications are latent but have not been spelt out. Indeed, some low-level concepts must be developed if (for example) the pupils' work with some circuits is to equip them to act on other circuits. A possible explanation is that because the language and rationale for low-level concepts has not been developed, those writing the curriculum were not able to express, for the primary level, the intentions lying behind their decisions to set out the 'know that' and 'know how' statements.

CONCLUSION

This chapter is essentially speculative and there is no body of empirical tests of the ideas against which their full potential for application may be evaluated (the SPACE research reports do not cover the full implementation stage, and the choice of concepts in that project was constrained by the specification of the national curriculum). What we have attempted is to provide a set of concepts and procedures, which may be better than those currently used, to meet the chapter's declared aim.

What may be claimed is that the approach meets certain criteria that any satisfactory method must meet. It does use an explicit model of concept learning that can be referred to the literature on cognition, and it does thereby have a way of making use of research results on children's own ideas. In addition, it does take seriously the conceptual structures of the science which is involved, without accepting that structure on its own can define what is to be learned and its sequence. Also, it does work with, but casts a critical light on, current concerns in science education, such as emphasis on processes and on the importance of relevance.

Finally, it should be noted that the approach offered has some similarities with that used by von Glasersfeld (1983) in discussing development of the concept of number. His constructivist approach starts from Dewey's assertion that 'Number is a rational process, not a sense fact'. A key notion is that of 'attentional patterns'. Referring to 'units' or 'singulars' and 'collections' or 'plurals', he says that these

> refer to conceptual structures that are dependent on material supplied by sensory experience. Insofar as these concepts involve sensory-motor signals, they do not belong to the realm of number. They enter that rarefied realm through the process of reflective abstraction, which extricates attentional patterns from instantiations in sensory-motor experience and thus produces numerical concepts that are stripped of all sensory properties.
>
> (von Glasersfeld 1983)

In terms of our discussion, this gives structure to the idea of categorization by emphasizing that 'attentional patterns' are driven by 'reflective abstraction'.

More generally, work in mathematics bears directly on the problem of analysing 'process skills' raised, but left unresolved, above. In considering the ontogenesis of the concept of number, all of ordering, counting, adding could be regarded as process skills, but they will only be used in a meaningful way, in unfamiliar contexts, if the higher level 'rational process', the concept of number, has been grasped by the user. It is possible that the notion of process–concept interaction might be more usefully analysed as an interaction between different concept structures, some (so-called science processes) being for very general concept functioning, others (so-called science concepts) being specific to the scientific or pre-scientific interaction with the natural world.

REFERENCES

AAAS. 1975. *Science. A process approach, II.* American Association for the Advancement of Science, in association with Ginn, New York.

Association for Science Education. 1966. *Science for primary schools 1. Children learning through science.* John Murray, London.

Black, P. J. and Harlen, W. 1990. 'Primary science in the National Curriculum. The SPACE approach.' *Links,* 15(3): 17–20.

Bruner, J. S., Goodnow, J. and Austin, G. 1956. *A study of thinking.* Wiley, New York.

Department of Education and Science. 1983. *Science in primary schools.* (A discussion paper produced by the HMI Science Committee). DES, London.

Department of Education and Science. 1991 *Science in the National Curriculum (1991).* HMSO, London.

Driver, R., Guesne, E. and Tiberghien, A. (eds) 1985. *Children's ideas in science.* Open University Press, Milton Keynes.

Glasersfeld, E. von. 1983. 'An attentional model for the conceptual construction of unit and number.' In Steffe, L. P., von Glasersfeld, E., Richards, J. and Cobb, P. *Children's counting types.* Praeger, New York, pp. 124–44.

Harlen, W. 1978. 'Does content matter in primary science?' *School Science Review,* 59: 614–25.

Harlen, W. 1985. *Teaching and learning primary science.* Paul Chapman Publishing, London.

Harlen, W. 1992. 'Research and development of science in the primary school.' *International Journal of Science Education,* 14: 491–503.

Harlen, W., Black, P. J. and Johnson, S. 1981. *Science in schools: age 11. Report No. 1.* HMSO, London.

Harlen, W., Darwin, S. A. and Murphy, M. C. 1977. *Match and mismatch.* Four volumes. Oliver and Boyd, Edinburgh.

Kerr, J. and Engel, E. 1980. 'Should science be taught in primary schools?' *Education,* 3: 4–8.

Larkin, J. H. 1983. 'The role of problem representation in physics.' In Gentner, D. & Stevens, A. L. (eds) *Mental models.* Lawrence Erlbaum Associates, Hillsdale, New Jersey, pp. 75–98.

Ministry of Education. 1961. *Science in the primary school.* HMSO, London.

Osborne, R. J. 1983. 'Towards modifying children's ideas about electric current.' *Journal of Research in Science and Technology Education,* 1: 73–82.

Osborne, J. F., Black, P. J., Smith, M. and Meadows, J. 1990. *Primary SPACE project research report: Light.* Liverpool University Press, Liverpool.

Osborne, J. F., Black, P. J., Smith, M. and Meadows, J. 1991. *Primary SPACE project research report: Electricity.* Liverpool University Press, Liverpool.

Osborne, J. F., Wadsworth, P. and Black, P. J. 1992. *Primary SPACE project research report: Processes of life.* Liverpool University Press, Liverpool.

Osborne, J. F., Wadsworth, P., Meadows, J. and Black, P. J. In press. *Primary SPACE project research report: Earth in space.* Liverpool University Press, Liverpool.

Osborne, R. J. and Wittrock, M. 1985. 'The generative learning model and its implications for science education.' *Studies in Science Education,* 12: 59–87.

Redman, S., Brereton, A. and Boyes, P. 1969. *An approach to primary science.* Macmillan Educational, London.

Russell, T. and Harlen, W. 1990. *Assessing science in the primary classroom. Practical tasks.* Paul Chapman Publishing, London.

Russell, T., Longden, K. and McGuigan, L. 1991. *Primary SPACE project research report: Materials.* Liverpool University Press, Liverpool.

Russell, T., Bell, D. and McGuigan, L. 1993. *Primary SPACE project research report: Rocks, soil and weather*. Liverpool University Press, Liverpool.

Schank, R. C. 1982. *Dynamic memory*. Cambridge University Press, London.

Shipstone, D. M. 1984. 'A study of children's understanding of electricity in simple d.c. circuits.' *European Journal of Science Education*, 6: 185–98.

Smith, E. E. and Medin, D. L. 1981. *Categories and concepts*. Harvard University Press, Cambridge, Mass.

Solomon, J., Black, P., Oldham, V. and Stuart, H. 1985. 'The pupil's view of electricity.' *European Journal of Science Education*, 7: 281–94.

Song, J. and Black, P. J. 1991. 'The effect of task contexts on pupils' performance in science process skills.' *International Journal of Science Education*, 13: 49–58.

Song, J. and Black, P. J. 1992. 'The effects of concept requirements and task contexts on pupils' responses to questions about control of variables. *International Journal of Science Education*, 14: 83–93.

Watt, D. and Russell, T. 1990a. *Primary SPACE project research report: Sound*. Liverpool University Press, Liverpool.

Watt, D. and Russell, T. 1990b. *Primary SPACE project research report: Growth*. Liverpool University Press, Liverpool.

Watt, D. and Russell, T. 1990c. *Primary SPACE project research report: Evaporation and condensation*. Liverpool University Press, Liverpool.

Chapter 13

Ways ahead?

Paul Black and Arthur Lucas

This book arose from a belief that this field of work has been strong in data and weak in theory. Any summary of the ideas offered cannot amount to more than 'notes towards a definition of theory'. The central concern of future work must be with a theory of learners and learning which might be adequate to interpret and guide research, and even a vague perception of this will have methodological implications. While these two issues are dealt with below, our summary must first draw attention to two related features that have arisen in several of the contributions. They concern respectively models of scientific knowledge and the importance of the context and purposes of people's knowledge.

SCIENCE – THE OBJECT OF THE KNOWLEDGE

While deep analysis of the science involved is an essential part of Black and Harlen's programme for action, the more basic need within research for an epistemology of the object of the research is emphasized by Bliss. The notion that there is a problem arising from a gap between how science is understood and how it ought to be understood, has received much attention, but without sufficient discussion of the beliefs that are held about how it ought to be understood. The nature of any gap will depend in part on the nature of the science topic involved; dyeing, nutrition, energy, relativity, each presents a very different cognitive challenge, so there is a spectrum of problems.

One could talk in this way even if one took the nature of science for granted. Even if educational aims were only directed towards a scientist's science, a philosophy of science might still be needed as a guide for discerning its essentials. However, the problem becomes more subtle if we accept, following Claxton, that the proper object of education in science has to be constructed by a transformation of scientist's knowledge and methods in the light of the aims of that education.

Such considerations affect the orientation of research in two ways. First, the choice of research topics and instruments is bound to be influenced by the view of the field of knowledge used in research. Secondly, a programme aimed at understanding how minitheories could be more effective would be rather different from one aimed at obliteration or coalition of them in order to establish the powerful macrotheories of high science: any theory to guide this field of research will have to be constructed in the context of a foreseen purpose and such different purposes as the strengthening of minitheories and the obliteration of them would steer rather different theoretical developments, if successfully pursued.

CONTEXTS AND PURPOSES

Many have pointed out that pupils' alternative frameworks arise from the culture, including particularly the specific language, of their everyday lives (see also Villalbi and Lucas 1991). The combination of Claxton's model of minitheories and Solomon's processes of social construction points to a system of beliefs and action that is profoundly different from that offered by school science, and yet strongly established. As accounts of origins, these leave at least one significant question unanswered. To what extent are we working with a constructivist child-as-scientist whose theories have been fashioned by encounters with reality, rather than with a socialized product of the culture, imbued with received wisdom? The answer may vary with age and 'treatment' and prognosis could differ accordingly.

However, these issues are given a different perspective in the contributions of Lucas and of Ryder. Everyday learning and everyday theories are not just different, perhaps inferior, forms of cognition. The everyday theories and concepts are embedded in the contexts and purposes for which they have been developed and, probably, frequently modified. They have to serve the individual's need to take decisions, often of (literally) vital importance. Here, decisions about whether to rely on magic or inscrutable authority, or on one's own capacity to understand or generate rational arguments, set limits and roles for cognition. These limits and roles must fashion the structure of everyday knowledge: when more of Ryder's everyday stories have been analysed we might understand this better.

Everyday understanding also has to conform to social exigencies; Solomon points out how children want a happy compromise of views, to the detriment of any objective aim of deciding who is right. In passing, it can be noted that outside his or her laboratory, the scientist is as limited as anyone else, and has to buy houses, or decide about marriage, or vote in elections, using an understanding of these problems which would appear as inadequate to appropriate experts as pupils' scientific theories appear to us.

Both Lucas and Ryder consider adult learners. While there seems good reason to suppose that similar considerations apply to young learners, their attention emphasizes also the issue of purpose. The everyday culture, language, experiences, decisions are not only the origin of pupils' ideas, they help define the arena within which they have to put to use anything that education can provide for them. Here Claxton's concern for interplay with values is relevant.

In summary, the everyday contexts are profoundly different from the research or the teaching laboratory, and yet are both the origin of what pupils bring to education and the destination for most of what most take away. Concerns with effects of 'context' and 'motivation' are essential, but treatment of them as marginal trivializes a central issue. The aims to which research is directed, the scope of what might be demanded if any theory or model is to be adequate, and the methodological requirements (e.g. on what counts as appropriate evaluation of effects of teaching) are all altered if the aim of learning is to help Ryder's Monique decide about her family's needs rather than to help her children pass written examinations.

MODELS AND THEORY

Continued accumulation of data on pupils' ideas without an explicit model of learning can only be justified by faith in Baconian induction. Few would think such faith justified. Collection of data needs to be informed by explicit assumptions and by sharply directed purposes, while the gap between any data and a working hypothesis or guide for teaching can only be crossed by way of a theory, albeit, but preferably not, an implicit one. Constructivism is the theoretical basis of much of recent work, but provides only the general conditions for a theory. For example, Piaget is certainly at home in the constructivist camp – but shares it with critics who reject any stage theory. There are, however, problems with versions of constructivism espoused in the literature that we have not touched on in this book, but which have been considered elsewhere, for example the detailed philosophical analysis by Suchting (1992) of von Glasersfeld (1989).

No model or theory emerges ready made from the chapters in this book. If it had done so, it would certainly, as Solomon points out, be a complex specimen. It would have to deal with learning in relation to such issues as context dependence, transfer and/or context aggregation, range of applicability, level of abstractions, meta-cognition, dynamics of renewal and change, concept-process interactions, parallel processing, effects of motive, and perceptions of adequacy and of the role of outside authority.

A brief summary here can go a little way beyond that mere list, by pointing out a few issues all of which occur in the arguments of several of the preceding chapters.

A useful start may be made by attempting to spell out the minimum requirements that any theory should meet. Ogborn's arguments could well be taken further by seeing whether, when applied to existing models of cognition, they illuminate potential limitations. The need he illustrates, for a dynamic renewal and for some form of meta-cognition, is echoed in other contributions. Russell's requirement about modes of representation of what is known should also be a candidate for incorporating in this minimum model.

A second general aspect is brought out in Claxton's arguments about minitheories. These are consistent with the stress on the context-bound nature of learning that occurs in most chapters. More is needed here on ways in which minitheories are packaged together or abstracted, and on how the range of applicability of each is constrained or altered (relevant to Black and Harlen's emphasis on categorization). The way in which inconsistencies may sometimes be accepted and at other times be reasons for reconstruction is an important puzzle, raised by Solomon.

This last point leads more generally to an interest in the dynamics of change. The Pask model builds in a basic mechanism, and shows why frozen structures could never be adequate to the purpose. However, change under pressure from new inputs may only be a flux whereby the details change but the overall pattern persists. For progression in learning, particularly towards generalizations and abstractions which would represent qualitative improvement, radical reconstructions, perhaps at a meta-level seem necessary. Russell's argument, that such changes may take time and may actually lower capability while in progress, shows how subtle the issues might become. Piaget's equilibration and accommodation will return to haunt us here – not surprisingly because, as Bliss points out, he was committed in general to produce the sort of model that the current state of research now needs.

A system, whether or not it works with minitheories combined with levels of operation able to reconstruct them, should have some form of structure. Most of the chapters, either implicitly or explicitly, look for or assume some guiding structure for cognition which determines the form, and potential for change, of particular aspects. Only in terms of such a model of overall structure can the many aspects of performance of any person, and their potential to change, be reconciled and understood. This need is perhaps concealed by researches in which any one individual is explored on only one topic and on only one occasion.

While much has been made in the past of the content–process dichotomy, the chapters in this book stress the relationship and similarity of these two. They must interact to describe any particular piece of learning, they may be inextricably packaged together in particular context binds, and both have to be remembered. Indeed the stress on memory, notably by Claxton, by Bliss, and by Black and Harlen, argues that a model of memory, and of the way it is accessed, updated and restructured, may be one way of representing what is needed.

Research in artificial intelligence will be a rich source for model construction, and such work has been quoted above in respect of memory. It is not clear, however, that the detailed explicit machinery that the AI programme has to set out is essential for the purposes addressed here. The interpretation of existing results, and the direction of new research and of hypotheses about teaching may be achieved with theories at a less explicit level.

Finally, any theory should have something to say about the significance of any means of collecting evidence. Research enquiry with children is not to be construed as a dip-stick or snapshot capturing a fixed state of the system. It is better seen as a piece of learning, and (*pace* Pask and Ogborn) as a conversation between researcher and pupil. Notions about dynamics of change and about the effect of perceptions, about the intent and authority of the enquirer, all apply: any theory has to collect and interpret its evidence within its own model. The 'collection' phase of research in this field may well, in retrospect, be seen to be gravely limited by the assumptions hidden inside its methodology.

RESEARCHERS: BE BOLD!

Discussion naturally follows here from the previous paragraph. Apart from that very general message, there are further issues to consider.

The issues of context and purpose indicate that understanding may develop through exploration of a wider range of topics and situations than those of school science, if only so that the latter can be both calibrated and put in context. Other school disciplines, or problems of understanding and decision which lie outside school contexts, may be helpful. Bliss and Ogborn, for example, deliberately chose an out-of-school context, but did not choose an area in which pupils have to make any decision of personal importance.

Their research with comics also illustrates another issue. That work aimed to produce a comprehensive description of pupil's theory and was not limited to a few instances or topics (it may of course be producing only comics/pictures minitheories). The breadth of issues explored in research may now need attention. There is little attention in published work to the interrelation of pupil's work across different tasks and problems, although some beginning steps have been taken (see Waheed and Lucas 1992 and Carvalho 1991). Most issues of consistency and structure require such work.

But real pupils are expected to develop greater understanding with more exposure to the curriculum. Study of development and progression further requires patient cohort studies, requiring commitment by researchers (and pupils!) to testing over several years: without such study hypotheses about dynamics of structures cannot be tested. A beginning has been made on the study of progression in understanding, and some of the specific difficulties have been explored in Black and Simon (1992). They point out that self-awareness (meta-cognition) – which has been emphasized in one way or another in many of the chapters in this book – may be a necessary condition, but not a sufficient one as pupils 'will still need to develop the scientific reasoning of which they might now be more clearly aware'. Black and Simon have thus taken seriously the issue of science as the object of knowledge, and have been looking for 'bridges' between the 'science country' (scientific knowledge) and the 'pupils' country' (their personal knowledge).

For Black and Simon,

> [t]he aim of describing progression raises first of all the problems of conceptual change. The approaches to this issue in research to date have been mainly pragmatic in nature (Scott, Asoko and Driver 1992) rather than linked to or derived from a theory of cognition. Some aim to create dissatisfaction of the pupils with their own country, an approach which risks doing more harm than good with the less able and less confident pupils. Others stress a search for continuity to achieve more gradual change. Clement, Brown and Zietsman (1989) have explored this approach, emphasising the value of seeking out 'anchoring conceptions' – ideas in the pupils' country which happen to be similar to those of the science country – and working by developing these as a base from which to lead the pupils into the new country.
>
> (Black and Simon 1992)

Black and Simon go on to point out that a few studies have

> set out to put pupils' ideas in a sequence of hypothesised transition from their own to the scientific ideas, but attempts to test these hypotheses by looking for correlations in the structure of pupils' ideas or by longitudinal study of the progress of a cohort of pupils are notably absent (see however Denvir and Brown 1986) . . . [Any] proposal to explore progression is hampered both by the lack of an effective theory of conceptual change and by the absence of substantial evidence about the changes in pupils' ideas with time. Ideally, data to strengthen the empirical base ought to be based in studies of several cohorts of pupils, each followed over several years, starting at different ages, and closely linked to studies of teaching programmes.
>
> (Black and Simon 1992)

The knowledge needed for confident, theory-led, curriculum development is unlikely to come from single research projects on progression using a small cohort over a short period: an extensive (and expensive!) research programme will be necessary before we have a thorough understanding of the way(s) in which pupils progressively build their understanding.

Finally, there is a case for replacing the rather open-ended 'fishing expeditions' of much of the published research with studies designed and analysed to explore ideas about structure. The chapter by Ramadas and Shayer is an example, in that analysis has been driven by assumptions about levels and, by implication, about progression. The programme set out by Black and Harlen has a theory sufficiently explicit that its inadequacies may be explored in the programme of action that they set out. There are, of course, other good examples already available in the literature.

CONCLUSION

Overall the message may be quite simple. The field of research has to be more clear about the object of its research and about the purposes that it is meant to serve. In the light of these, it needs to move to a more ambitious level in which theory, however naïve, guides research design and interpretation, and takes critical charge of the methodology. Such general nostrums do not need a collection of twelve papers to justify them, but their bare bones can have little attraction until clothed with the flesh that these papers provide.

REFERENCES

Black, P. and Simon, S. 1992. 'Progression in learning science.' *Research in Science Education* (in press).

Carvalho, P. 1991. 'Portuguese pupils and the water cycle: understanding inter-related scientific concepts.' PhD thesis, King's College London, University of London.

Clement, J., Brown, D. E. and Zietsman, A. 1989. 'Not all preconceptions are misconceptions: finding "anchoring conceptions" for grounding instruction on students' intuitions.' *International Journal of Science Education*, 11: 554–65.

Denvir, B. and Brown, M. 1986. 'Understanding of number concepts in low attaining 7–9 year olds: Part 2. The teaching studies.' *Educational Studies in Mathematics*, 17: 143–64.

Glasersfeld, E. von. 1989. 'Cognition, construction of knowledge and teaching.' *Synthese*, 80: 121–40.

Scott, P. H., Asoko, H. M. and Driver, R. 1992. 'Teaching for conceptual change: a review of strategies.' In Duit, R., Goldberg, F. and Niedderer, H. (eds). *Research in physics learning: theoretical issues and empirical studies.* IPN, Kiel.

Suchting, W. A. 1992. 'Constructivism deconstructed.' *Science and Education*, 1: 223–54.

Villalbi, R. M. and Lucas, A. M. 1991. 'When is an animal not an animal? When it speaks English!' *Journal of Biological Education*, 25: 184–6.

Waheed, T. and Lucas, A. M. 1992. 'Understanding interrelated topics: photosynthesis at age 14+.' *Journal of Biological Education*, 26: 193–9.

Name index

Subject index

accidental sources 143–4
accommodation 21, 27–8
accretion learning strategy 53–4, 54–6, 58
action theories of knowledge 86, 161, 162
actions, acts and 158
activity, types of 28–9, 41
aims of science teaching 190–1, 194–202; body of knowledge 198; common sense 197–8; competence 194–7; making people critical of science 202; passing exams 199–200; preparing scientists 200; scientific attitude 200–1
alternative frameworks 45–6, 59, 62–3, 173–4; and learning strategies 56; research frame 1–4, 63–5
amoebae model 48–9, 49, 53–4
analogical transfer 12–13
anthropological perspective 1–2, 63–4
'anthropomorphic' model 158
artificial intelligence 37, 114, 233–4
assimilation 21, 27–8, 36, 97
attitudes: minitheories and 47–8; teaching scientific 200–1
authenticity 144–5, 146
authority 144–5, 146

beliefs 151–2, 158–61
Body in Question, The 136
boundaries, shifting and sharpening 48–9, 53–4
bridging/linking systems 77–80
British Museum (Natural History) 139–42
BUGGY system 117

categorization 211–12, 214–15, 219
causality 33, 34, 42, 177

change, dynamics of 233
children's interests 218
classification game 139–41, 143, 145
clinical method 39
cognitive accommodation 77–8
cognitive psychology: Piaget 11–13, 14, 25; representing representations 80–3, 83
comics 123–4, 132; *see also* common-sense theory of motion
common sense 118, 197–8
common-sense theory of motion 120–32; correctness of theory 130–2; eliciting 123–4; results from pilot study 124–30; sketch 121–3
communication 152–3, 160, 168–9
compensating regulations 28
competence, scientific 194–7
competing representations 74–5
computer analogy 12–13
concentration experiment 81–2
concept mapping 9, 11–12
concept specification 209, 216–27; general criteria 216–18; general strategy 223–4; implementation criteria 218–20
concepts 208–16, 226–7; aquisition of abstract 77–80; changing 213–14; Pask model 110–11; and process skills 209–16; selecting level 214–16
conduit theory 152–3, 160
consensus 88–9, 99
conservation tasks 39
constructivism 14, 41, 63, 232; Piaget 21, 27–32, 40–1
content: concept specification 208, 218–20; emphasis on 62–3, 172–3; localisation of learning 192–3, 201